SIGNALS

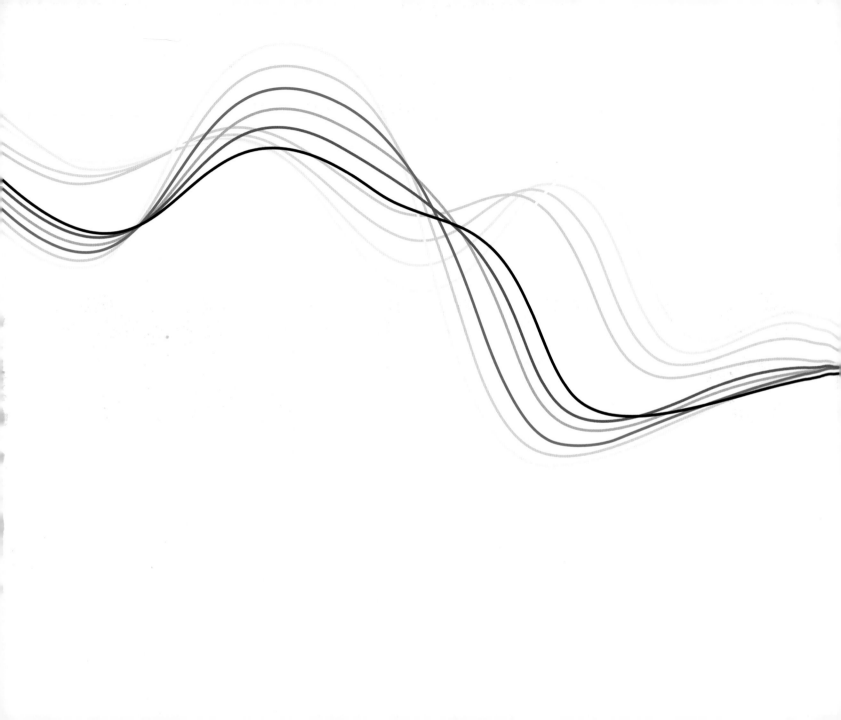

JEFF DESJARDINS

FOUNDER AND EDITOR-IN-CHIEF, VISUAL CAPITALIST

SIGNALS

THE 27 TRENDS DEFINING THE FUTURE OF THE GLOBAL ECONOMY

WILEY

Library of Congress Cataloging-in-Publication Data:
Names: Desjardins, Jeff, author.
Title: Signals : the 27 trends defining the future of the global economy / Jeff Desjardins.
Description: Hoboken, New Jersey : Wiley, [2022] | Includes bibliographical references.
Identifiers: LCCN 2021038139 (print) | LCCN 2021038140 (ebook) | ISBN 9781119853176 (paperback) | ISBN 9781119853183 (adobe pdf) | ISBN 9781119853190 (epub)
Subjects: LCSH: Economic forecasting. | Macrosociology.
Classification: LCC HB3730 .D368 2022 (print) | LCC HB3730 (ebook) | DDC 338.5/44—dc23
LC record available at https://lccn.loc.gov/2021038139
LC ebook record available at https://lccn.loc.gov/2021038140

Cover image: Visual Capitalist
Cover design: Visual Capitalist
SKY119713_110221

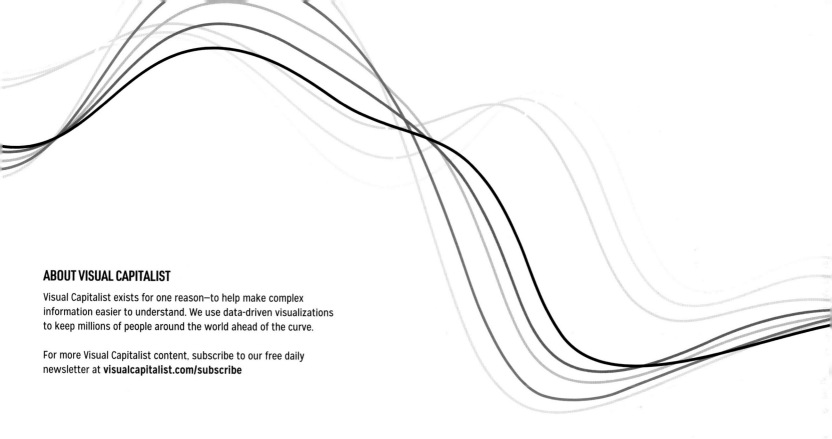

ABOUT VISUAL CAPITALIST

Visual Capitalist exists for one reason—to help make complex information easier to understand. We use data-driven visualizations to keep millions of people around the world ahead of the curve.

For more Visual Capitalist content, subscribe to our free daily newsletter at **visualcapitalist.com/subscribe**

WRITTEN, DESIGNED, & EDITED BY THE VISUAL CAPITALIST TEAM

EDITOR-IN-CHIEF
Jeff Desjardins — Editor-in-Chief

EDITORIAL TEAM
Nick Routley — Managing Editor
Aran Ali — Writer
Carmen Ang — Writer
Dorothy Neufeld — Writer
Govind Bhutada — Writer
Iman Ghosh — Writer
Jenna Ross — Writer
Katie Jones — Writer
Marcus Lu — Writer
Nicholas LePan — Writer
Omri Wallach — Writer
Theras Wood — Writer

CREATIVE TEAM
Melissa Haavisto — Creative Director
Alejandra Dander — Graphic Designer
Amy Kuo — Graphic Designer
Bennett Slater — Graphic Designer
Clayton Wadsworth — Illustrator
Harrison Schell — Graphic Designer
Jennifer West — Graphic Designer
Joyce Ma — Graphic Designer
Miranda Smith — Graphic Designer
Pernia Jamshed — Graphic Designer
Rosey Eason — Graphic Designer
Sabrina Fortin — Graphic Designer
Sabrina Lam — Graphic Designer

WITH ADDITIONAL THANKS TO
Ashley Karol — Editor
Salina Vuong — Editor / Account Director
Aurelia Aritanto — Business Development
Chris Barrett — Business Development
Georgia Tucker — Business Development
Jan Moir — Business Development
Louise Stoddart — Communications Manager
Lydia Adeli — Account Coordinator
Michelle Takenaka — Marketing Coordinator

TABLE OF CONTENTS

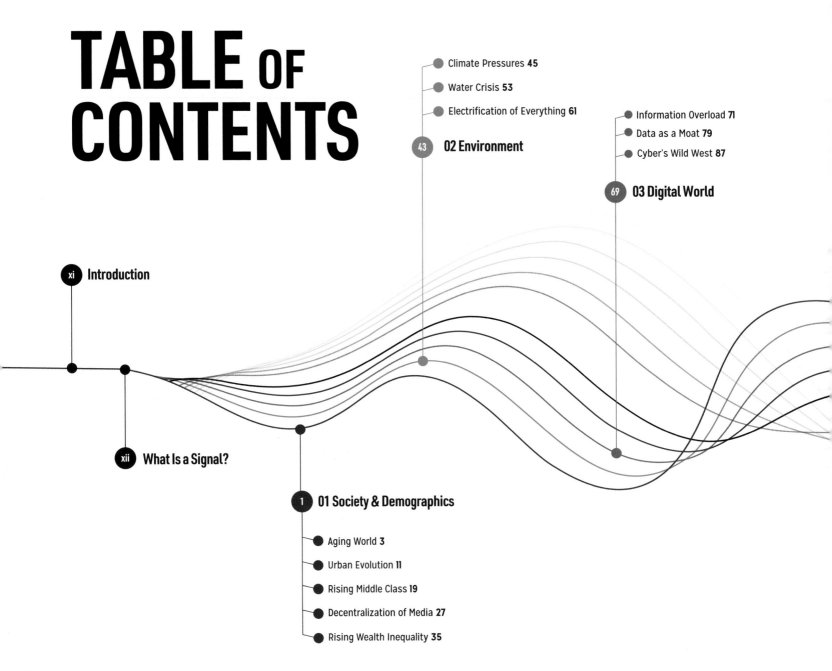

xi **Introduction**

xii **What Is a Signal?**

1 **01 Society & Demographics**

- Aging World **3**
- Urban Evolution **11**
- Rising Middle Class **19**
- Decentralization of Media **27**
- Rising Wealth Inequality **35**

43 **02 Environment**

- Climate Pressures **45**
- Water Crisis **53**
- Electrification of Everything **61**

69 **03 Digital World**

- Information Overload **71**
- Data as a Moat **79**
- Cyber's Wild West **87**

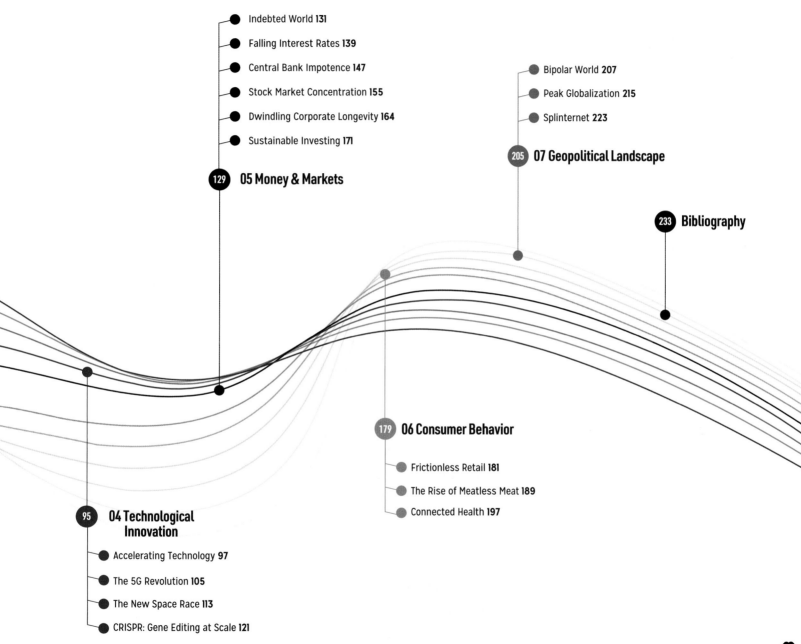

Indebted World **131**

Falling Interest Rates **139**

Central Bank Impotence **147**

Stock Market Concentration **155**

Dwindling Corporate Longevity **164**

Sustainable Investing **171**

129 **05 Money & Markets**

Bipolar World 207

Peak Globalization 215

Splinternet 223

205 **07 Geopolitical Landscape**

233 **Bibliography**

179 **06 Consumer Behavior**

Frictionless Retail **181**

The Rise of Meatless Meat **189**

Connected Health **197**

95 **04 Technological Innovation**

Accelerating Technology **97**

The 5G Revolution **105**

The New Space Race **113**

CRISPR: Gene Editing at Scale **121**

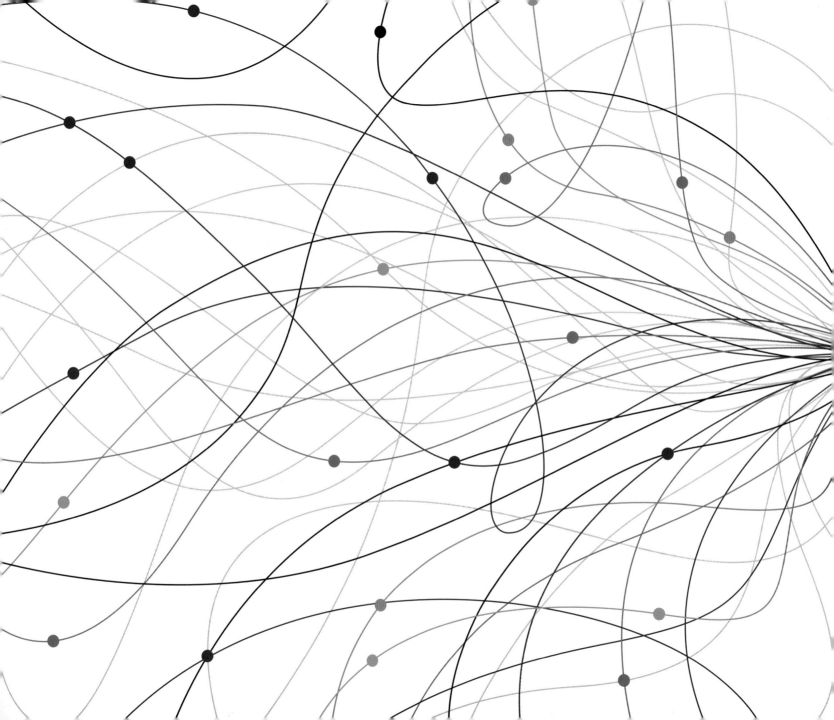

" **We are drowning in information, while starving for wisdom.**

The world henceforth will be run by synthesizers, people able to put together the right information at the right time, think critically about it, and make important choices wisely.

— E. O. WILSON

Did you know that there are

40 TIMES MORE BYTES OF DATA

in existence than there are stars in the known universe?

While it is difficult to wrap our heads around the magnitude of the datasphere, it really is only the beginning.

In fact, over the next three years, our world will create more new data than we have in all the years of preceding human history combined.

Growing Noise

The boom in data is seemingly infinite, but the human brain's ability to process data is not.

For decision-makers, more data is increasingly a double-edged sword. We hope that data can unveil useful insights that help us better understand the world—but more often than not, new data ends up being obtuse, muddy, or even contradictory, helping further complicate our convictions.

More data inevitably means more complexity, and although the world's information is available at our fingertips, it's harder than ever to narrow down the root causes that will lead to future trends.

Searching for Signals

Although our collective view of data is ever more obfuscated with noise, we believe that through the power of visualization there can be clear takeaways—called "signals"—that can be uncovered and understood.

After evaluating thousands of data sets, our team has settled on a framework that highlights 27 signals that can help in piecing together the future direction of the economy, society, and markets.

Some signals are working together in unison to accelerate existing trends; others seem destined to clash in head-on conflicts. And while the ultimate consequences of these signals are often difficult to anticipate, we believe this book can serve as a starting place in navigating a complex and challenging world.

JEFF DESJARDINS
Editor-in-chief, Visual Capitalist

WHAT IS A SIGNAL?

In this book, our sole focus is to show you the simple and clear takeaways on the trends that will define the next decade of the global economy.

Each signal we highlight is a series of data that stands apart from the noise. These are often the root causes—the fundamental shifts—that are already shaping society and markets, and will continue to do so in the coming years.

HOW TO ENJOY SIGNALS ●1 ●2 ●3 ●4

We cover a lot of ground in this book, so to make the topics easier to read through, we gave each signal the same basic structure.

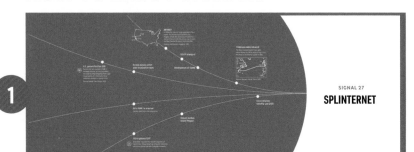

1

SIGNAL 27
SPLINTERNET

ORIGIN STORY

The first spread in each signal explores the sometimes disparate developments that lead up to a signal. These conceptual diagrams aren't just for show—they're infused with useful information.

2

DEFINING THE SIGNAL

On this spread, we introduce the signal and provide clear, data-driven reasons why the signal is worth paying attention to.

NOT ALL SIGNALS ARE CREATED EQUAL

SIGNAL RANGE
Broad (4/5)

▶ ▶ ▶ Signal range is the potential impact on society and the economy

SIGNAL-TO-NOISE RATIO
Moderate (3/5)

▶ ▶ ▶ Signal-to-noise measures the clarity of the signal

Watch out for these information signs along the way. They'll help define complex concepts and explain how visualizations work.

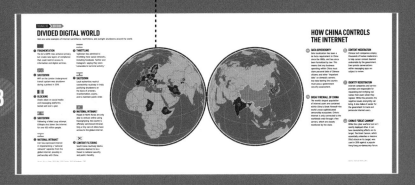

3

DECODING THE SIGNAL

Here, we provide more context on the signal from different angles.

4

ANALYZING THE IMPACT

This spread looks at how the signal is going to affect the world. Occasionally, we explore how different signals intersect.

All data sources are clearly marked, and a full bibliography can be found at the back of the book.

Unless otherwise noted, dollar amounts are in USD.

01

SOCIETY &
DEMOGRAPHICS

NUMBER OF SIGNALS / 05

The state of humanity has always been in flux, but to be able to quantify any of these changes is a much more recent development.

With today's data, there are a multitude of ways we could examine the nearly eight billion people on the planet. However, the clearest signals about society stem from data that is robust and far-reaching:

‣ Where do people live globally, and how is this changing?
‣ Where will tomorrow's consumers come from?
‣ Is wealth growing or shrinking, and is this happening equally?
‣ How does a rapidly aging population factor into all of this?

In this chapter, we take a 10,000-foot view of society to help set the context for the rest of this book. The macro forces you are about to see are perpetually at work in the background, affecting almost every other signal and outcome you can imagine.

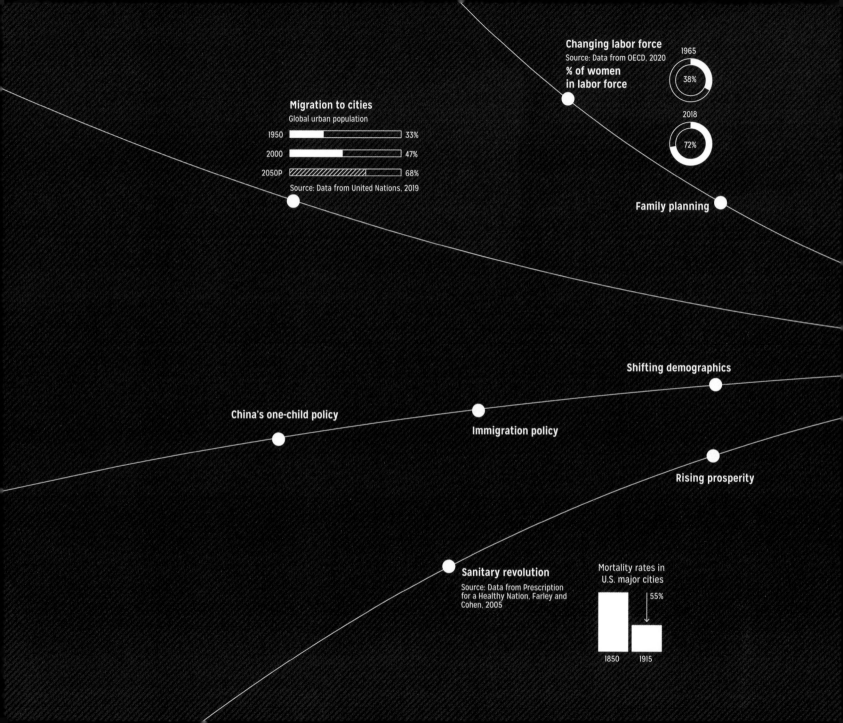

Changing labor force
Source: Data from OECD, 2020

**% of women
in labor force**

1965

38%

2018

72%

Migration to cities
Global urban population

1950		33%
2000		47%
2050P		68%

Source: Data from United Nations, 2019

Family planning

Shifting demographics

China's one-child policy

Immigration policy

Rising prosperity

Sanitary revolution
Source: Data from Prescription
for a Healthy Nation, Farley and
Cohen, 2005

Mortality rates in
U.S. major cities

55%

1850   1915

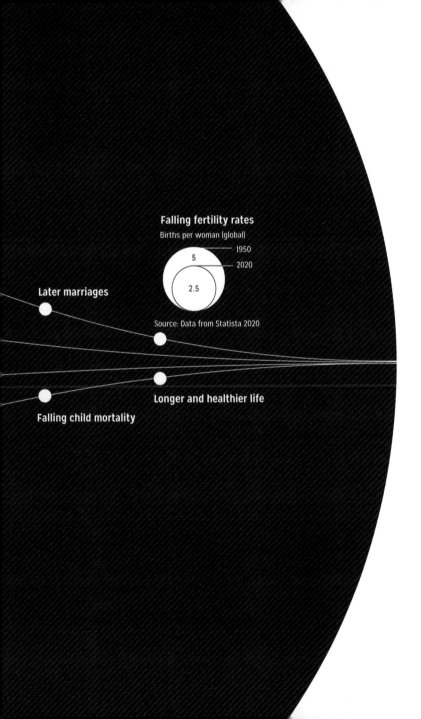

Later marriages

Falling fertility rates

Births per woman (global)

5 —— 1950

2.5 —— 2020

Source: Data from Statista 2020

Longer and healthier life

Falling child mortality

SIGNAL 01

AGING WORLD

AGING WORLD

The average age of the population has increased each year since 1970, and this is predicted to continue until at least the beginning of the 22nd century.

 **SIGNAL RANGE**
Very broad (5/5)

 **SIGNAL-TO-NOISE RATIO**
Very high (5/5)

THE WORLD IS GETTING OLDER

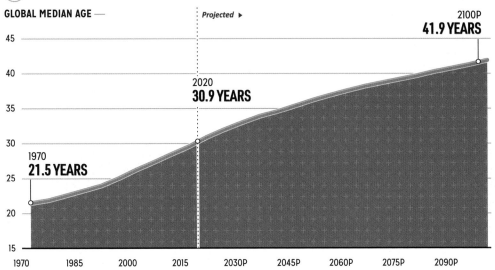

GLOBAL MEDIAN AGE —

Projected ▶

2100P
41.9 YEARS

2020
30.9 YEARS

1970
21.5 YEARS

45 —
40 —
35 —
30 —
25 —
20 —
15 —

1970 1985 2000 2015 2030P 2045P 2060P 2075P 2090P

Source: Data from United Nations, 2019

PRIOR TO THE 19TH CENTURY, the average human did not live a particularly long or prosperous life.

After WWII, this started to shift. New advancements have improved our health, and the world got increasingly wealthy. As a result, it's now normal for people to live well into their senior years.

The challenge? Along with living longer, people are also having fewer babies—and this imbalance changes the demographic make-up of society, creating unique problems and opportunities for governments, businesses, and investors alike.

GLOBAL POPULATION 65 YEARS OR OLDER

2019 **703 MILLION** ⟶ 2050P **1.55 BILLION**

Source: Data from United Nations, 2019

NUMBER OF PEOPLE AGED 65+ BY GEOGRAPHIC REGION, 2019 & 2050

Source: Data from United Nations, 2019

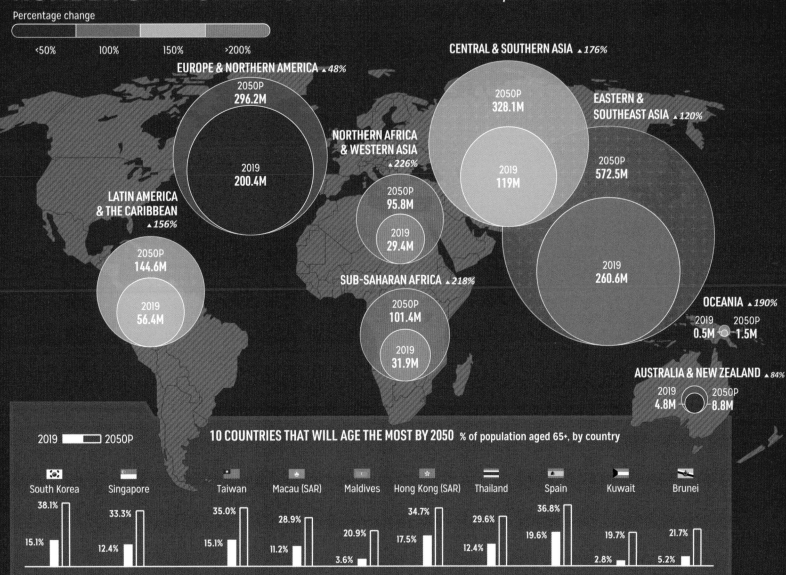

Percentage change

<50% 100% 150% >200%

EUROPE & NORTHERN AMERICA ▲48%
- 2050P 296.2M
- 2019 200.4M

CENTRAL & SOUTHERN ASIA ▲176%
- 2050P 328.1M
- 2019 119M

EASTERN & SOUTHEAST ASIA ▲120%
- 2050P 572.5M
- 2019 260.6M

NORTHERN AFRICA & WESTERN ASIA ▲226%
- 2050P 95.8M
- 2019 29.4M

LATIN AMERICA & THE CARIBBEAN ▲156%
- 2050P 144.6M
- 2019 56.4M

SUB-SAHARAN AFRICA ▲218%
- 2050P 101.4M
- 2019 31.9M

OCEANIA ▲190%
- 2019 0.5M
- 2050P 1.5M

AUSTRALIA & NEW ZEALAND ▲84%
- 2019 4.8M
- 2050P 8.8M

10 COUNTRIES THAT WILL AGE THE MOST BY 2050
% of population aged 65+, by country

2019 ▯ 2050P

Country	2019	2050P
South Korea	15.1%	38.1%
Singapore	12.4%	33.3%
Taiwan	15.1%	35.0%
Macau (SAR)	11.2%	28.9%
Maldives	3.6%	20.9%
Hong Kong (SAR)	17.5%	34.7%
Thailand	12.4%	29.6%
Spain	19.6%	36.8%
Kuwait	2.8%	19.7%
Brunei	5.2%	21.7%

THE GLOBAL POPULATION BY AGE 1950–2100P

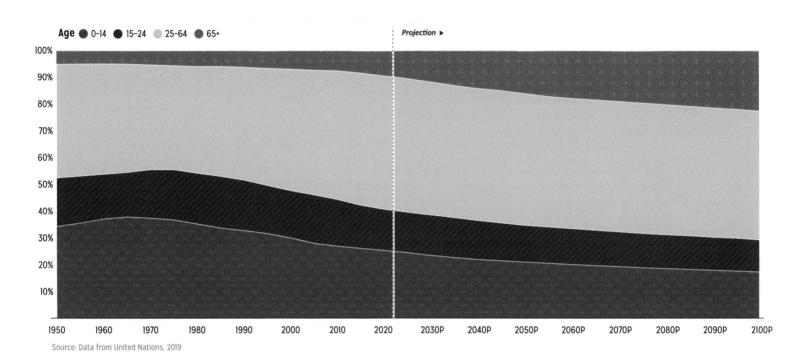

Age ● 0-14 ● 15-24 ● 25-64 ● 65+   *Projection ▶*

Source: Data from United Nations, 2019

GLOBAL POPULATION 65 YEARS OR OLDER ● Male ● Female

Source: Data from United Nations, 2019

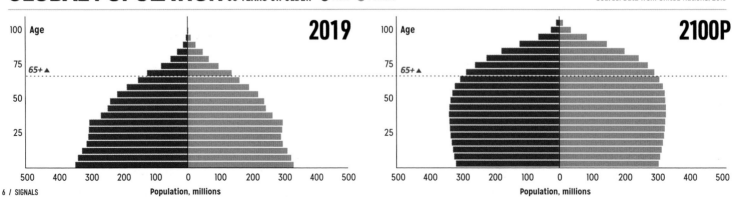

2019

2100P

Population, millions   Population, millions

DEMOGRAPHIC IMPLICATIONS

As the global population grows older on average, some countries will be affected more than others. One way of measuring this is the old-age dependency ratio (OADR), a number that aims to compare the working-age population of a country to the older, less economically active portion.

OLD-AGE DEPENDENCY RATIOS

RATIOS BY REGION, 1990-2050

- ⓘ Europe & North America ——
- ⓘⓘ Eastern & South-Eastern Asia ——
- ⓘⓘⓘ Australia & New Zealand ——
- ⓘⓥ Latin America & the Caribbean ——
- ⓥ World ——
- ⓥⓘ Northern African & Western Asia ——
- ⓥⓘⓘ Central & Southern Asia ——
- ⓥⓘⓘⓘ Oceania ——
- ⓘⓧ Sub-Saharan Africa ——

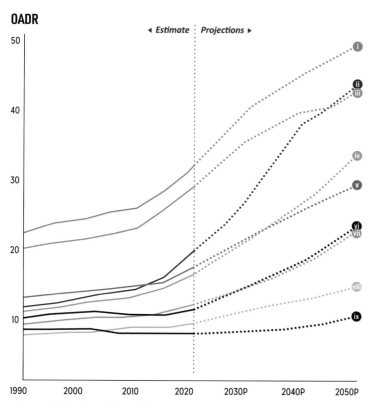

OADR

◄ *Estimate* | *Projections* ►

Source: Data from United Nations, 2019

HIGHEST OLD-AGE DEPENDENCY RATIOS BY COUNTRY

Here are three methods for calculating old-age dependency ratios and the countries projected to have the highest ratios in 2050.

CONVENTIONAL The **number of older individuals** (65+ years) per 100 working age persons (20–64 years).

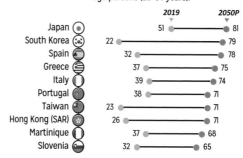

	2019	2050P
Japan	51	81
South Korea	22	79
Spain	32	78
Greece	37	75
Italy	39	74
Portugal	38	71
Taiwan	23	71
Hong Kong (SAR)	26	71
Martinique	37	68
Slovenia	32	65

PROSPECTIVE Measured using **remaining years to live,** instead of age itself.*

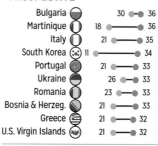

	2019	2050P
Bulgaria	30	36
Martinique	18	36
Italy	21	35
South Korea	11	34
Portugal	21	33
Ukraine	26	33
Romania	23	33
Bosnia & Herzeg.	21	33
Greece	21	32
U.S. Virgin Islands	21	32

*This defines old age based on a remaining life expectancy of 15 years, relative to the number of persons between age 20 and that age. It captures an increase in life expectancy over time.

ECONOMIC **Effective number of consumers aged 65+ years**, divided by the effective number of workers at all ages**

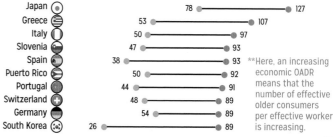

	2019	2050P
Japan	78	127
Greece	53	107
Italy	50	97
Slovenia	47	93
Spain	38	93
Puerto Rico	50	92
Portugal	44	91
Switzerland	48	89
Germany	54	89
South Korea	26	89

**Here, an increasing economic OADR means that the number of effective older consumers per effective worker is increasing.

Source: Data from United Nations, 2019

According to an analysis by the World Economic Forum, the shortfall in pension saving is expected to grow from $67 trillion to $428 trillion by 2050.

SAVINGS SHORTFALL BY COUNTRY

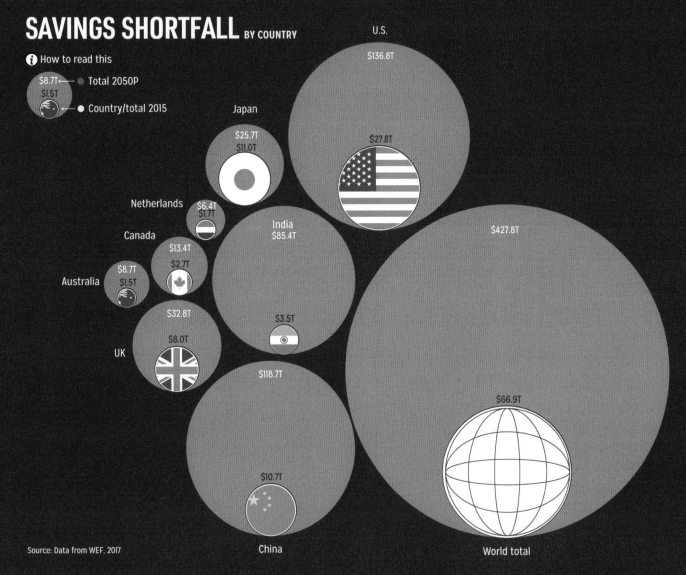

ℹ How to read this

$8.7T ── ● Total 2050P
$1.5T
      ● Country/total 2015

U.S.
$136.8T
$27.8T

Japan
$25.7T
$11.0T

Netherlands
$6.4T
$1.7T

Canada
$13.4T
$2.7T

Australia
$8.7T
$1.5T

UK
$32.8T
$8.0T

India
$85.4T
$3.5T

$427.8T

$66.9T

China
$118.7T
$10.7T

World total

Source: Data from WEF, 2017

SOURCE OF FUNDS FOR THE ELDERLY

BY % OF CONSUMPTION

● Labor income   ○ Public transfers   ◐ Private transfers   ◑ Investment income

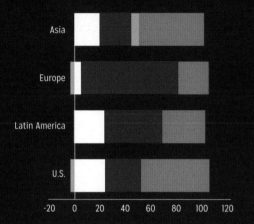

FISCAL OBSTACLES

How will the impact of aging be felt by global economies? It partly depends on how support systems for elderly populations are structured:

FISCAL SUPPORT RATIOS
● 2035P   ◐ 2055P

U.S.	Germany	China	UK
-10%	-16%	-15%	-9%
-12%	-23%	-24%	-14%

Fiscal support ratios measure projected tax revenues relative to public transfers.

In the U.S., for example, it's estimated that tax revenues will need to be 12% higher (or government expenses 12% lower) by 2055 to offset the impact of population aging.

Source: Data from NTA 2016 and IMF 2017

AN AGING POPULATION CHANGES THE STRUCTURE OF OUR SOCIETIES.

Undoubtedly, it creates an array of challenges for decision-makers—but it also opens up new doors of opportunity to entrepreneurs and investors.

This growing cohort of individuals creates a $15 trillion market dubbed the silver economy, which is already being tapped into by ambitious tech innovators and forward-thinking health companies.

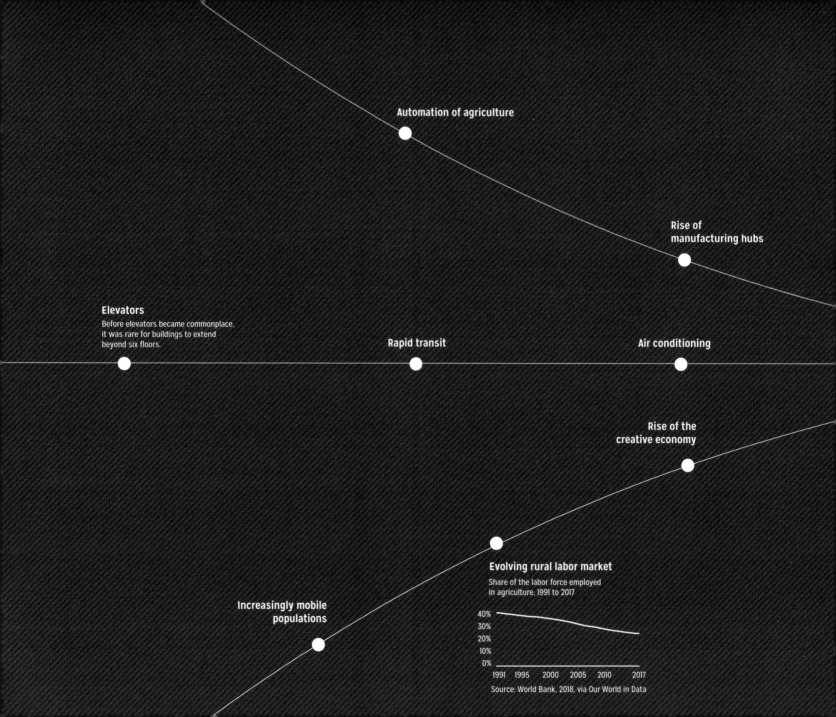

Automation of agriculture

**Rise of
manufacturing hubs**

Elevators
Before elevators became commonplace,
it was rare for buildings to extend
beyond six floors.

Rapid transit

Air conditioning

**Rise of the
creative economy**

**Increasingly mobile
populations**

Evolving rural labor market
Share of the labor force employed
in agriculture, 1991 to 2017

40%
30%
20%
10%
0%
1991 1995 2000 2005 2010 2017

Source: World Bank, 2018, via Our World in Data

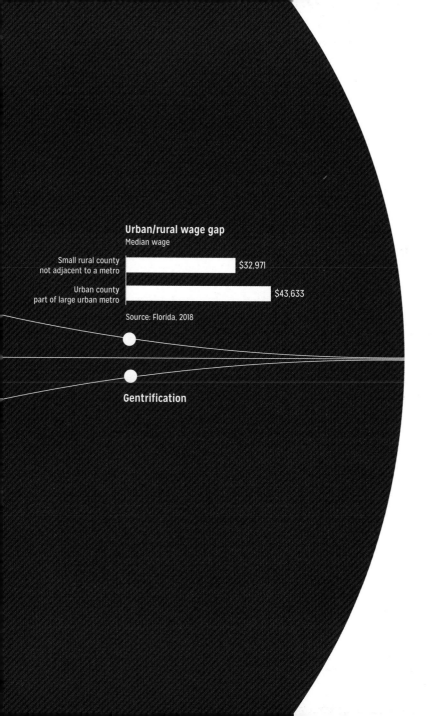

Urban/rural wage gap
Median wage

Small rural county
not adjacent to a metro — $32,971

Urban county
part of large urban metro — $43,633

Source: Florida, 2018

Gentrification

SIGNAL 02

URBAN EVOLUTION

URBAN EVOLUTION

In many parts of the world, the exodus from rural areas to the city will accelerate.

GLOBAL URBAN AND RURAL POPULATION

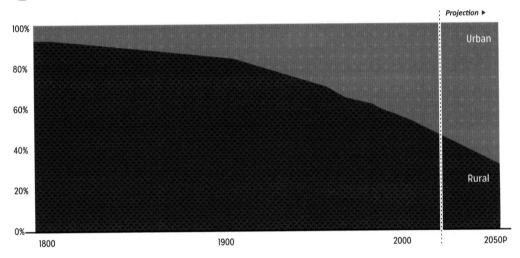

Projection ▶

Urban

Rural

Source: Data from Our World in Data 2019

IT WAS MARK TWAIN who said, "History doesn't repeat itself, but it often rhymes." This is true when it comes to urbanization trends manifesting around the world. The motivations of Nigerian villagers moving to improvised neighborhoods surrounding Lagos are no different than English peasants who moved to growing urban centers in the 1700s. Economic push and pull factors are at work, and many African and Asian countries that still have a high proportion of rural inhabitants will see a big shift over the coming decades.

URBAN CONCENTRATION OF GDP

More than **80%** of global GDP is generated in cities.

Urban

Rural

Source: Data from World Bank. 2020

SIZE OF THE WORLD'S 100 LARGEST CITIES

Not only will the number of cities increase, the scale of urban areas will also continue to grow.

POPULATION

These circles show the median population of the top 100 cities.

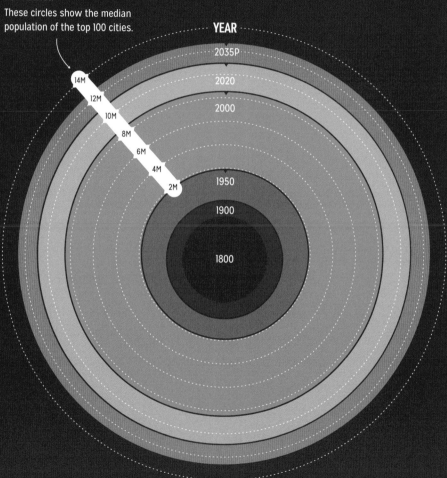

YEAR

2035P
2020
2000
1950
1900
1800

14M
12M
10M
8M
6M
4M
2M

In coming years, an entirely new cities will grow in size and impo global stage. Cities that were pr world's largest will become rela

GLOBAL RANK OF CITIES BY P

	New York	Tokyo	Lon
1950 ►	1	2	3
2050P ►	7	9	
			5

Source: Data from Global Cities Institute

Source: Data from International Institute for Environment and Development 2020

POPULATION DISTRIBUTION

Populations around the world will continue to accumulate around city clusters, or megaregions, following the example of leading economies.

Share of a country's population living in city clusters

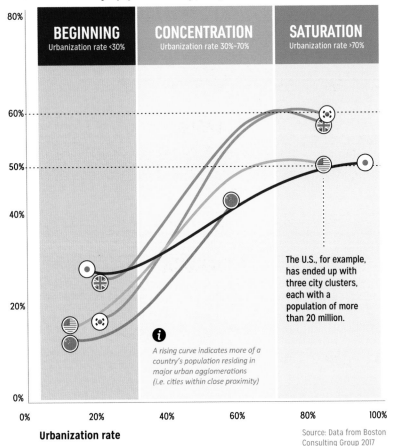

China · U.S. · Japan · UK · South Korea

BEGINNING	CONCENTRATION	SATURATION
Urbanization rate <30%	Urbanization rate 30%–70%	Urbanization rate >70%

The U.S., for example, has ended up with three city clusters, each with a population of more than 20 million.

A rising curve indicates more of a country's population residing in major urban agglomerations (i.e. cities within close proximity)

Urbanization rate

Source: Data from Boston Consulting Group 2017

CLUSTERING EFFECT

Historically, as countries urbanize, more of the population is located within megaregions. These clusters of cities are in close proximity and typically share economic and social links. China is following this path, and it's believed that rapidly urbanizing countries in the developing world will follow a similar trajectory. Here are three examples of city clusters.

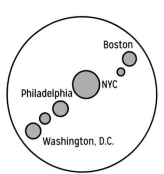

Boston
NYC
Philadelphia
Washington, D.C.

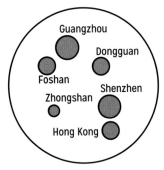

Guangzhou
Dongguan
Foshan
Shenzhen
Zhongshan
Hong Kong

Dallas-Fort Worth
Austin
Houston
San Antonio

In China, city clusters are expected to reach a more mature state of development in the next 20 to 30 years, with five major city clusters making up 50-60% of the country's total population.

The 40 city clusters worldwide account for 20% of the population, but 50% of the world's GDP.

City clusters can span international borders, as is the case with the megaregion spanning from Amsterdam to Brussels in Europe.

URBAN GROWTH IN DEVELOPING COUNTRIES 1995-2035P

Cities in developing countries are on a robust growth trajectory.

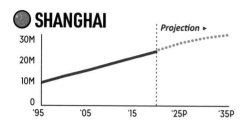

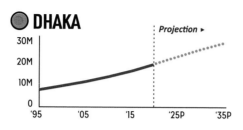

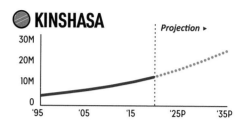

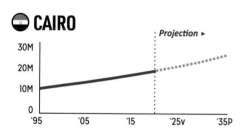

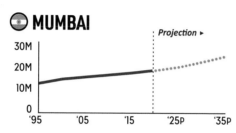

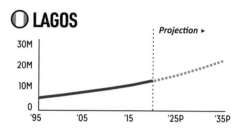

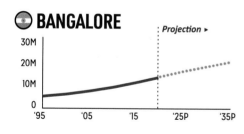

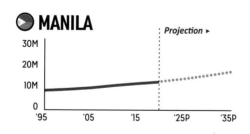

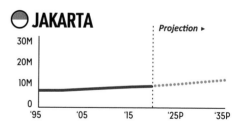

Many mature cities will also continue to grow, albeit at a more modest rate.

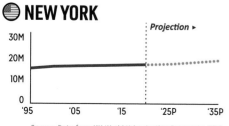

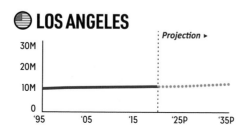

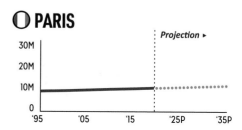

Source: Data from UN World Urbanization Prospects, 2018

CITIES OF THE FUTURE WILL BE:

SMART

Modern urban areas will harness the power of sensor-driven data collection to efficiently run city services. As well, technology will facilitate communication between citizens and government services.

BRAND NEW

The idea of starting a city from scratch is hardly new, but the volume and scale of plans are reaching new heights. Brand new cities are built with the aim of becoming economic engines free from the constraints imposed by existing population centers.

SUPER-SIZED

Tokyo has been the world's largest city since the 1960s, but that crown will likely be passed over to an Indian city within the next decade.

EXAMPLES
- ◎ Songdo / South Korea
- ◎ Xiong'an New Area / China

EXAMPLES
- ◎ Lanzhou New Area / China
- ◎ King Abdullah Economic City / Saudi Arabia

EXAMPLES
- ◎ Delhi / India
- ◎ Jakarta / Indonesia

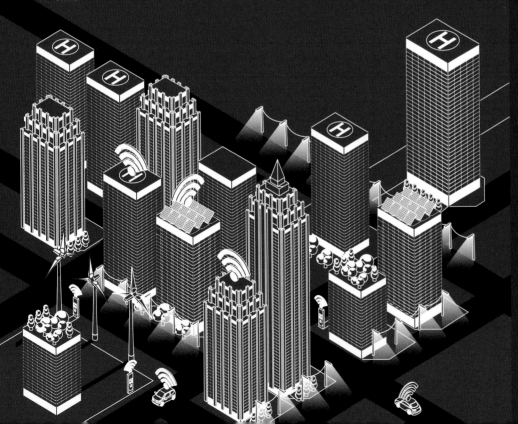

DISSONANCE URBAN EVOLUTION & CLIMATE PRESSURES

Java Sea

35.6%

Jakarta
2050

Sea level rise

JAKARTA

Indonesia's largest city is sinking at a rate of 10 inches per year, and by 2050, one-third of the city could be below sea level.

Source: Data from Phys.org, 2019

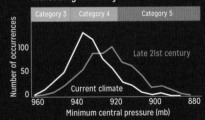

Increasing intensity

| Category 3 | Category 4 | Category 5 |

Late 21st century

Current climate

Number of occurrences: 100, 50, 0

Minimum central pressure (mb): 960, 940, 920, 900, 880

Storm severity

MIAMI

Miami, which is already susceptible to flooding, could see 2.5 million of its residents become climate refugees by 2100 as more severe hurricanes batter the region.

Source: Data from NOAA, 2020

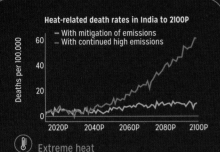

Heat-related death rates in India to 2100P
— With mitigation of emissions
— With continued high emissions

Deaths per 100,000

🌡 Extreme heat

DELHI

Delhi's current summer average temperature of 31.5°C is projected to increase to over 35°C in 2100. India is on a dangerous trajectory, and urban dwellers will be acutely affected by rising temperatures.

Source: Data from CoreLogic, 2019

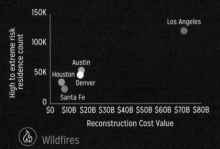

High to extreme risk residence count

Los Angeles

Austin
Houston Denver
Santa Fe

Reconstruction Cost Value

🔥 Wildfires

LOS ANGELES

Broad sections of LA lie within extreme wildfire risk zones. Of the most at-risk cities in the U.S., Los Angeles has by far the highest cost of reconstruction in the event of a devastating wildfire.

Source: Data from UChicago, 2019

FOR THE FIRST TIME IN HUMAN HISTORY, URBAN LIFE HAS BECOME THE NORM.

In Africa and Asia, cities will continue to grow and, in some cases, swell to unprecedented sizes. Much like China's mass migration at the beginning of the 21st century, the scale of urbanization will have wide reaching impacts on society and the global economy.

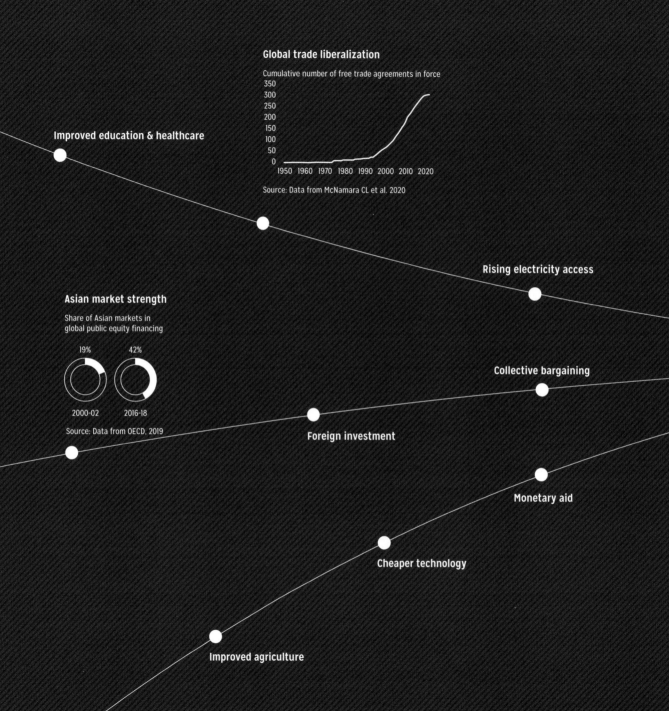

Improved education & healthcare

Global trade liberalization

Cumulative number of free trade agreements in force

350
300
250
200
150
100
50
0

1950 1960 1970 1980 1990 2000 2010 2020

Source: Data from McNamara CL et al. 2020

Rising electricity access

Asian market strength

Share of Asian markets in
global public equity financing

19%   42%

2000-02   2016-18

Source: Data from OECD, 2019

Collective bargaining

Foreign investment

Monetary aid

Cheaper technology

Improved agriculture

Internet proliferation

Every 10% increase in mobile
penetration in India saw a 1.2%
increase in national GDP.

Source: Data from USGLC 2017

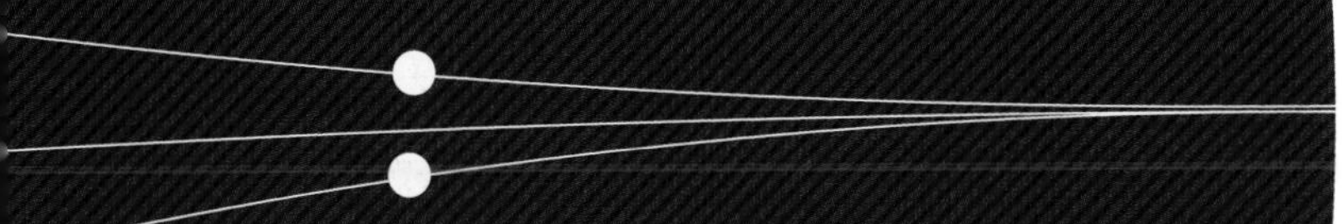

Cheaper financial services

SIGNAL 03

RISING MIDDLE CLASS

RISING MIDDLE CLASS

Fewer people are living in poverty—and more people are living in the middle class—than ever before.

SIGNAL RANGE
Very broad (5/5)

SIGNAL-TO-NOISE RATIO
Very high (5/5)

SIGNAL
GLOBAL NUMBER OF PEOPLE BY INCOME

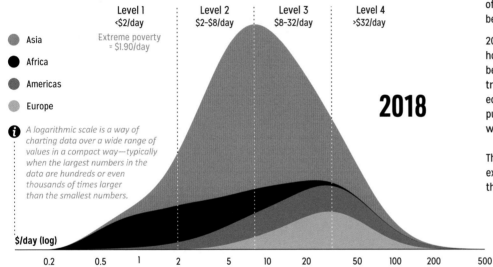

- Asia
- Africa
- Americas
- Europe

ℹ️ *A logarithmic scale is a way of charting data over a wide range of values in a compact way—typically when the largest numbers in the data are hundreds or even thousands of times larger than the smallest numbers.*

Level 1
<$2/day
Extreme poverty
= $1.90/day

Level 2
$2-$8/day

Level 3
$8-32/day

Level 4
>$32/day

2018

$/day (log)

0.2   0.5   1   2   5   10   20   50   100   200   500

FOR THE VAST MAJORITY OF HUMAN HISTORY, wealth has been concentrated in a small segment of the global population. Now, that disparity is slowly being equalized.

2018 marked a global tipping point as half of all households had enough discretionary expenditure to be considered "middle class" or "rich." This ongoing transition will have a dramatic effect on the world economy as patterns of consumption, which include purchases like household appliances and vacations, will continue to increase.

Though poverty is far from being eradicated, and extreme income distributions are still present, the global middle class continues to grow.

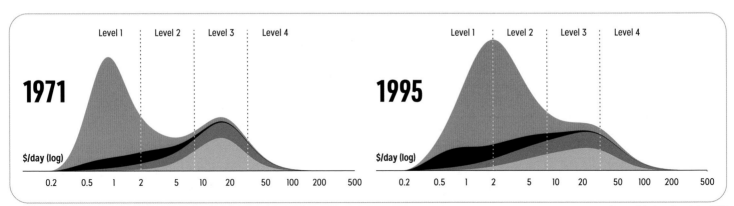

Level 1   Level 2   Level 3   Level 4

1971

$/day (log)

0.2   0.5   1   2   5   10   20   50   100   200   500

Level 1   Level 2   Level 3   Level 4

1995

$/day (log)

0.2   0.5   1   2   5   10   20   50   100   200   500

Source: Data from Gapminder, 2020

FLATTENING GLOBAL INCOME DISTRIBUTION

As people move out of poverty, income has become more evenly distributed among the global population.

% of world population at a given income level

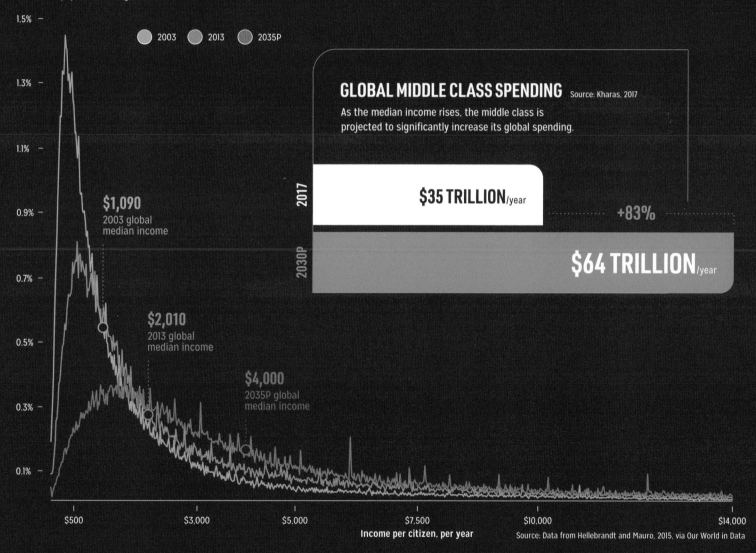

- 2003
- 2013
- 2035P

$1,090
2003 global
median income

$2,010
2013 global
median income

$4,000
2035P global
median income

GLOBAL MIDDLE CLASS SPENDING Source: Kharas, 2017

As the median income rises, the middle class is
projected to significantly increase its global spending.

2017

$35 TRILLION/year

+83%

2030P

$64 TRILLION/year

$500 $3,000 $5,000 $7,500 $10,000 $14,000

Income per citizen, per year   Source: Data from Hellebrandt and Mauro, 2015, via Our World in Data

THE RISE OF THE GLOBAL MIDDLE CLASS

More than half the world is now considered middle class or wealthier.
By 2030, that number will be two-thirds of the global population.

NUMBER OF PEOPLE BY WEALTH CATEGORY

Source: Data from Brookings, 2018

2018

Poor <$1.90/day	630M
Vulnerable $1.90–$11/day	3.2B
Middle class $11–$110/day	3.6B
Upper class >$110/day	200M

2030P

Poor <$1.90/day	450M
Vulnerable $1.90–$11/day	2.3B
Middle class $11–$110/day	5.3B
Upper class >$110/day	300M

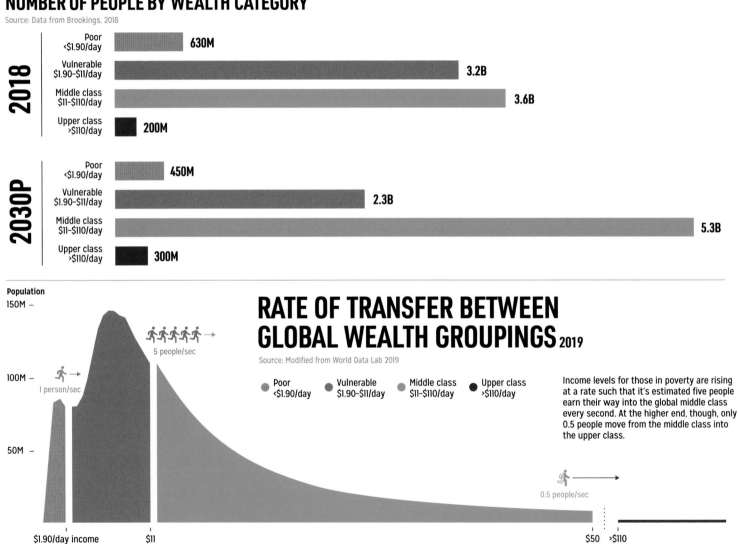

Population
150M –

RATE OF TRANSFER BETWEEN GLOBAL WEALTH GROUPINGS 2019

Source: Modified from World Data Lab 2019

● Poor <$1.90/day ● Vulnerable $1.90–$11/day ● Middle class $11–$110/day ● Upper class >$110/day

Income levels for those in poverty are rising at a rate such that it's estimated five people earn their way into the global middle class every second. At the higher end, though, only 0.5 people move from the middle class into the upper class.

5 people/sec

1 person/sec

100M –

50M –

0.5 people/sec

$1.90/day income $11 $50 >$110

ASIA LEADS THE MIDDLE CLASS RISE

India
380M

China
350M

Rest of Asia
210M

Rest of world
130M

88% of the next billion entrants into the middle class are projected to be in Asia.

MIDDLE CLASS RATE OF GROWTH

U.S., Europe & Japan
0.5%/year

China & India
6.0%/year

Source: Data from Brookings 2017

The rise of the middle class is global, but not equal. China, India, and other emerging countries are driving the majority of middle class growth.

GLOBAL MIDDLE CLASS POPULATION % OF TOTAL POPULATION
Source: Canals, 2019

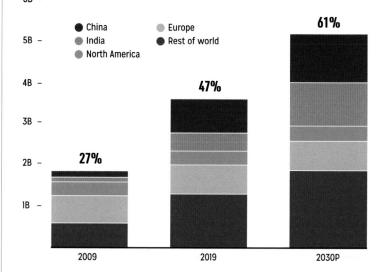

Legend:
- China
- India
- North America
- Europe
- Rest of world

6B
5B
4B
3B
2B
1B

27% — 2009
47% — 2019
61% — 2030P

INCREASING EXPENDITURE OF THE GLOBAL MIDDLE CLASS USD, IN PPP TERMS
Source: Canals, 2019

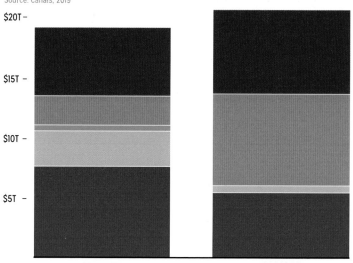

$20T
$15T
$10T
$5T

2009–2019

2019–2030P

INCREASED CONSUMPTION TRENDS

Higher income brings higher consumption of goods and services, from meat to education.
Where will members of the rising middle class spend their money?

MEAT CONSUMPTION VS GDP 2017

As emerging economies grow their wealth, their populations eat more meat.

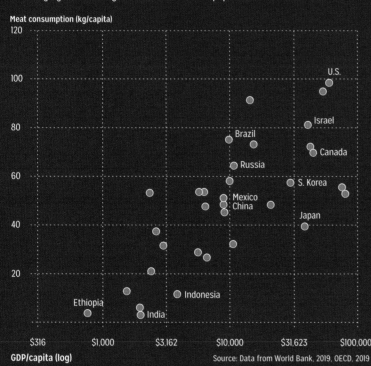

Meat consumption (kg/capita)

Labels visible: U.S., Israel, Brazil, Canada, Russia, S. Korea, Mexico, China, Japan, Indonesia, Ethiopia, India

X-axis: $316, $1,000, $3,162, $10,000, $31,623, $100,000
GDP/capita (log)

Source: Data from World Bank, 2019, OECD, 2019

U.S. HOUSEHOLD CHANGE IN SHARE OF TOTAL EXPENDITURES 1980-2018

The average U.S. consumer is devoting a higher share of their expenditures to health spending, requiring less for other necessities such as food and transportation.

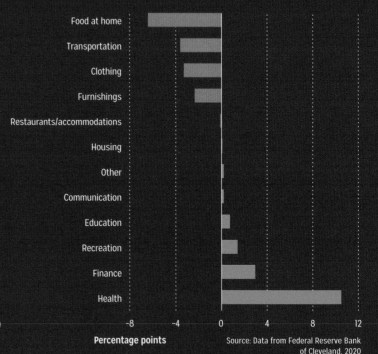

Categories: Food at home, Transportation, Clothing, Furnishings, Restaurants/accommodations, Housing, Other, Communication, Education, Recreation, Finance, Health

X-axis: -8, -4, 0, 4, 8, 12
Percentage points

Source: Data from Federal Reserve Bank of Cleveland, 2020

REGIONAL CONSUMPTION DIFFERENCES BY SHARE OF EXPENDITURE

Source: Modified from World Economic Forum 2015

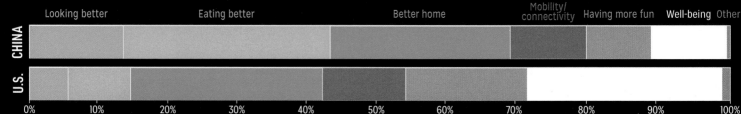

Legend: Looking better | Eating better | Better home | Mobility/connectivity | Having more fun | Well-being | Other

Rows: CHINA, U.S.

X-axis: 0%, 10%, 20%, 30%, 40%, 50%, 60%, 70%, 80%, 90%, 100%

CHANGING GLOBAL CONSUMPTION TRENDS

Growing urban areas, with their younger, working-age populations, will see the biggest increases in consumption — particularly within the education category.

MIDDLE CLASS CONSUMPTION CHANGES
2030P

- Growing cities
- Shrinking cities

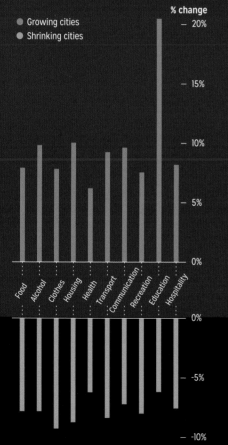

% change
— 20%

— 15%

— 10%

— 5%

— 0%

Food Alcohol Clothes Housing Health Transport Communication Recreation Education Hospitality

— 0%

— -5%

— -10%

Source: Modified from Visa and Oxford Economics 2018

THE RISING MIDDLE CLASS WILL DRIVE CONSUMPTION.

Thanks to rapid growth in emerging countries, this segment of the population will soon vastly outnumber and outspend the rest of the world.

However, the middle class in these areas is often more vulnerable, with a high level of informal employment. As a result, spending will be less stable than that of advanced countries.

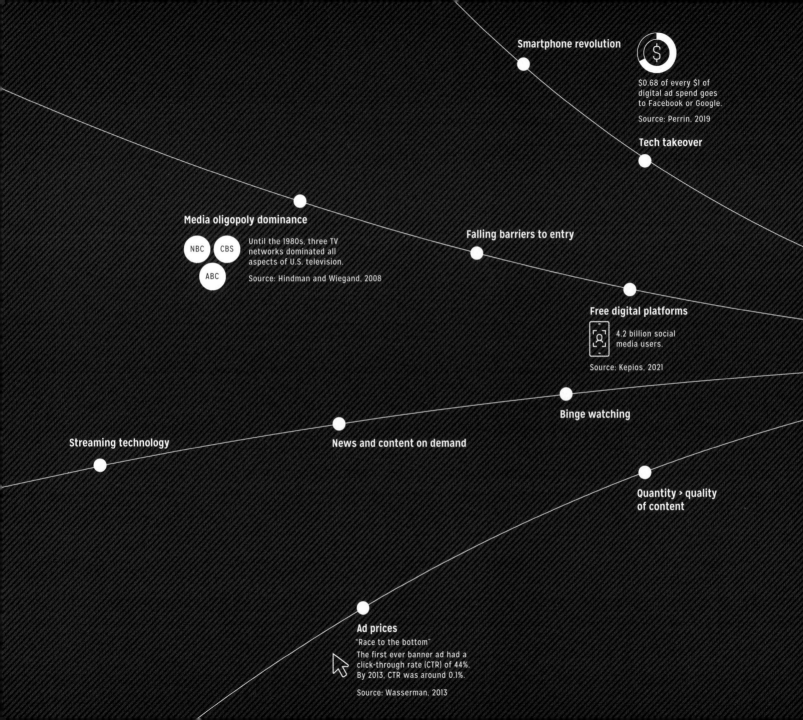

Smartphone revolution

$0.68 of every $1 of digital ad spend goes to Facebook or Google.

Source: Perrin, 2019

Tech takeover

Media oligopoly dominance

NBC CBS
ABC

Until the 1980s, three TV networks dominated all aspects of U.S. television.

Source: Hindman and Wiegand, 2008

Falling barriers to entry

Free digital platforms

4.2 billion social media users.

Source: Kepios, 2021

Binge watching

Streaming technology

News and content on demand

Quantity > quality of content

Ad prices

"Race to the bottom"

The first ever banner ad had a click-through rate (CTR) of 44%. By 2013, CTR was around 0.1%.

Source: Wasserman, 2013

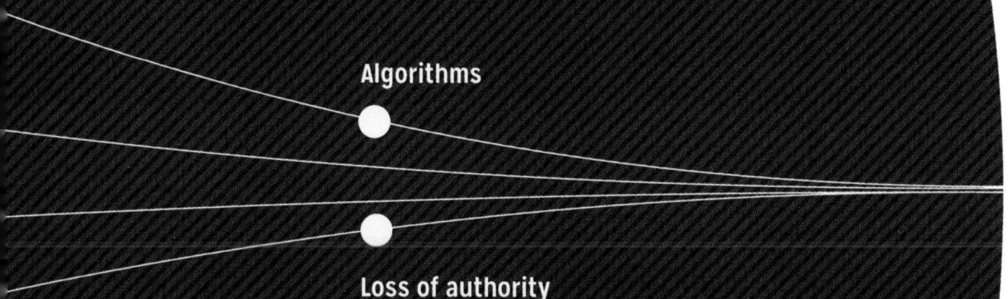

Algorithms

Loss of authority

% of Americans who trust traditional media
2012-2021

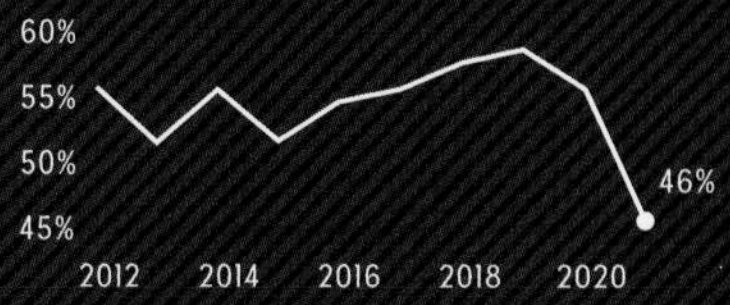

60%
55%
50%
45%
46%

2012　2014　2016　2018　2020

Source: Modified from 2021 Edelman Trust
Barometer via Axios

DECENTRALIZATION OF MEDIA

DECENTRALIZATION OF MEDIA

SIGNAL RANGE
Broad (4/5)

SIGNAL-TO-NOISE RATIO
Medium (3/5)

Technology has increasingly enabled the democratization and proliferation of media, a traditionally oligopolistic market. But falling barriers to entry create new problems as well, including new tech-driven gatekeepers.

MEDIA OPTIONS BY TYPE OVER TIME

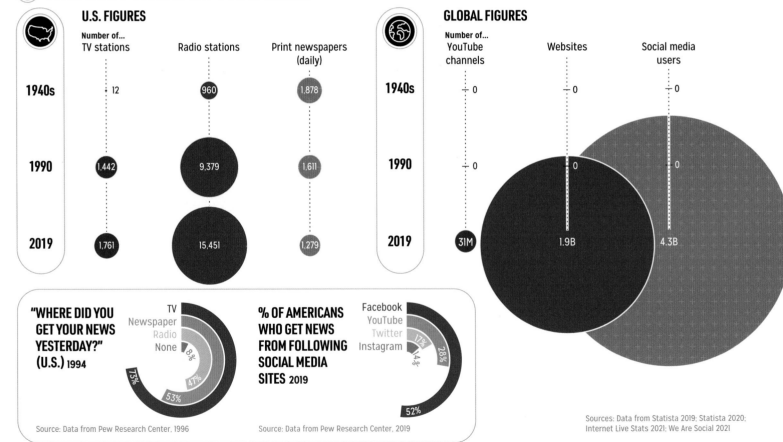

U.S. FIGURES

Number of...
TV stations | Radio stations | Print newspapers (daily)

	TV stations	Radio stations	Print newspapers (daily)
1940s	12	960	1,878
1990	1,442	9,379	1,611
2019	1,761	15,451	1,279

GLOBAL FIGURES

Number of...
YouTube channels | Websites | Social media users

	YouTube channels	Websites	Social media users
1940s	0	0	0
1990	0	0	0
2019	31M	1.9B	4.3B

"WHERE DID YOU GET YOUR NEWS YESTERDAY?" (U.S.) 1994

TV
Newspaper
Radio
None

73%
53%
47%
8%

Source: Data from Pew Research Center, 1996

% OF AMERICANS WHO GET NEWS FROM FOLLOWING SOCIAL MEDIA SITES 2019

Facebook
YouTube
Twitter
Instagram

52%
28%
17%
14%

Source: Data from Pew Research Center, 2019

Sources: Data from Statista 2019; Statista 2020; Internet Live Stats 2021; We Are Social 2021

FALLING BARRIERS TO ENTRY

The media market has historically been oligopolistic due to heavy barriers to entry.

 Traditional media   Modern digital media

Printing presses, equipment, and studios require a substantial initial investment	Hiring on-air personalities, news anchors, journalists, and reporters	Geographic boundaries limited competition, and natural economic moats	Building a reputation in radio, TV, and news took years, but could be destroyed in minutes	Broadcast licenses limited total number of stations and frequencies available	It could take months, or even years, for these factors to come together
CAPITAL COSTS	**TALENT**	**GEOGRAPHY**	**AUTHORITY**	**LEGAL**	**TIME**
Device and an internet connection	Do it yourself or collaborate	Only limited by country firewalls (i.e. China)	Content can "go viral" even without a reputation	Loose and difficult-to-enforce digital media laws	Instant communication worldwide

THE RESULT

With few barriers to entry left, each person and brand is now their own media company— and millions of pieces of content are distributed every minute.

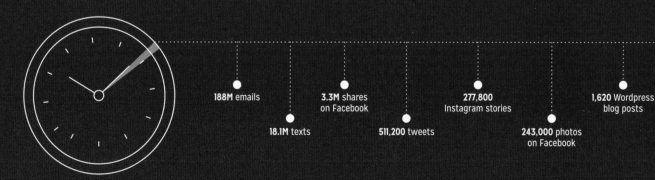

188M emails

18.1M texts

3.3M shares on Facebook

511,200 tweets

277,800 Instagram stories

243,000 photos on Facebook

1,620 Wordpress blog posts

500 hours of YouTube videos

Sources: Adapted from Domo 2019; Wordpress 2020; Statista 2019

SIFTING THROUGH CONTENT CLUTTER

Humans now consume about 5x more information per day than they did in the 1980s—
but compared to the 2.5 quintillion bytes of new data created each day, that only scratches the surface.

While the human brain cannot possibly harness so much information, algorithms can.

ALGORITHMIC 1:1 PERSONALIZATION

Simply put, algorithms are the instructions for computer programs. They're the hidden magic behind everything from Google search results to how content is served on Instagram

Customer experience is optimized using an algorithm based on available data.

Customer creates new interactions and this data is recorded for further optimization.

Historical data is used to create predictive models of customer behavior and outcomes.

Source: Data from Shampnois, 2019

While this algorithmic personalization can predict what you want to see, it does have downsides:

 FILTER BUBBLES
Media consumers become stuck in their "bubble," as algorithms block out information inconsistent with their perception of the world.

 CLICKBAIT
Media companies optimize content for engagement through misleading titles or other tricks, increasing clicks and algorithmic impact.

 OUTRAGE CULTURE
Anger also draws clicks, so users and media are encouraged to use outrage to their advantage.

 "WINNER TAKE ALL" CONTENT
Content views follow a power law dynamic, where the most algorithm-friendly content rises to the top at the expense of all other content.

 MISINFORMATION SPREAD
Content spreads not because of factual validity, but instead because algorithms are trained to push whatever is creating engagement.

 LACK OF ACCOUNTABILITY
Because algorithms did not author the content, a disconnect in accountability emerges.

THE NEW KINGMAKERS

The democratization of content has dramatically altered the media landscape, putting content creation in the hands of digital users—but leaving curation and monetization in the hands of Big Tech and its powerful algorithms.

U.S. ADVERTISING REVENUES AND GROWTH BY MEDIA, 2019

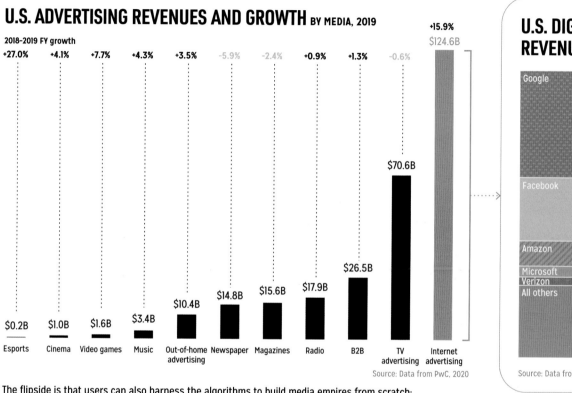

2018-2019 FY growth

Media	Growth	Revenue
Esports	+27.0%	$0.2B
Cinema	+4.1%	$1.0B
Video games	+7.7%	$1.6B
Music	+4.3%	$3.4B
Out-of-home advertising	+3.5%	$10.4B
Newspaper	-5.9%	$14.8B
Magazines	-2.4%	$15.6B
Radio	+0.9%	$17.9B
B2B	+1.3%	$26.5B
TV advertising	-0.6%	$70.6B
Internet advertising	+15.9%	$124.6B

Source: Data from PwC, 2020

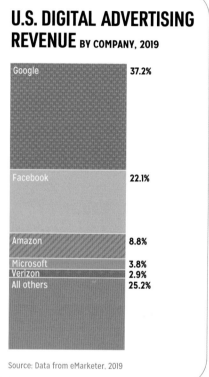

U.S. DIGITAL ADVERTISING REVENUE BY COMPANY, 2019

Company	Share
Google	37.2%
Facebook	22.1%
Amazon	8.8%
Microsoft	3.8%
Verizon	2.9%
All others	25.2%

Source: Data from eMarketer, 2019

The flipside is that users can also harness the algorithms to build media empires from scratch:

BEST PAID YOUTUBE STARS

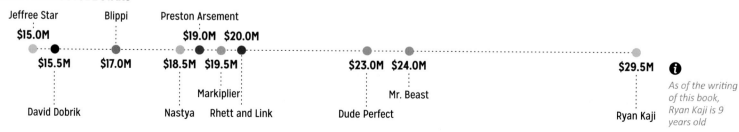

Star	Amount
Jeffree Star	$15.0M
David Dobrik	$15.5M
Blippi	$17.0M
Nastya	$18.5M
Preston Arsement	$19.0M
Rhett and Link	$19.5M
Markiplier	$20.0M
Dude Perfect	$23.0M
Mr. Beast	$24.0M
Ryan Kaji	$29.5M

As of the writing of this book, Ryan Kaji is 9 years old

YouTube data between June 1, 2019 and June 1, 2020. Source: Berg, 2020

RIPPLE EFFECTS: MEDIA AND SOCIETY

TRUST IN MEDIA

Nearly 7 in 10 Americans said they lost trust in the media over 10 years (2008–2018)

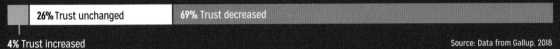

26% Trust unchanged | **69%** Trust decreased

4% Trust increased

Source: Data from Gallup, 2018

DEATH OF LOCAL NEWS
NEWS DESERTS: COUNTIES WITHOUT NEWSPAPERS

In the United States, there has been a net loss of 2,155 newspapers since 2004, a 24% decrease.

Number of newspapers ● 0 ● 1

In the U.S., more than 200 counties do not have a local newspaper.

Nearly half of all counties, 1,540, have only one newspaper, usually a weekly.

Source: UNC Hussman School of Journalism and Media, 2020

DEMOGRAPHIC PROFILES OF COUNTIES WITHOUT NEWSPAPERS

● News deserts ● U.S.

Average poverty rate
18%
12%

Average median income
$45,000
$61,937

Average median age
42
38

Average percent of residents with bachelor's degree or higher
19%
33%

Source: Data from UNC Hussman School of Journalism and Media, 2020

DISRUPTION OF THE TRADITIONAL MEDIA MODEL

To cope with the new media landscape, news media has pivoted to subscriptions, with only 14% of executives now focusing on advertising as a main revenue source.

MOST IMPORTANT REVENUE STREAM GOING FORWARD, ACCORDING TO NEWS MEDIA EXECUTIVES 2020

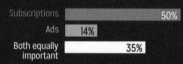

Subscriptions	50%
Ads	14%
Both equally important	35%

Source: Data from Newman, 2020

POLARIZATION

TRUST AND DISTRUST OF TOP 30 NEWS PUBLICATIONS AND NETWORKS

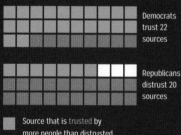

Democrats trust 22 sources

Republicans distrust 20 sources

■ Source that is trusted by more people than distrusted

■ Source that is distrusted by more people than trusted

□ Source that is about equally trusted as distrusted

Source: Pew Research Center, 2020

TRADITIONAL BARRIERS OF ENTRY TO MEDIA HAVE ALL BUT VANISHED.

In one sense, this has opened the door to many more voices and opinions—but it has also enabled a shift in which Big Tech has become the key gatekeeper to both exposure and monetization.

The media landscape has become less trustworthy and more polarizing as a result. If every problem is an opportunity, then the current media landscape is ripe for the picking.

Will it be further decentralized, or will Big Tech continue to consolidate its stranglehold?

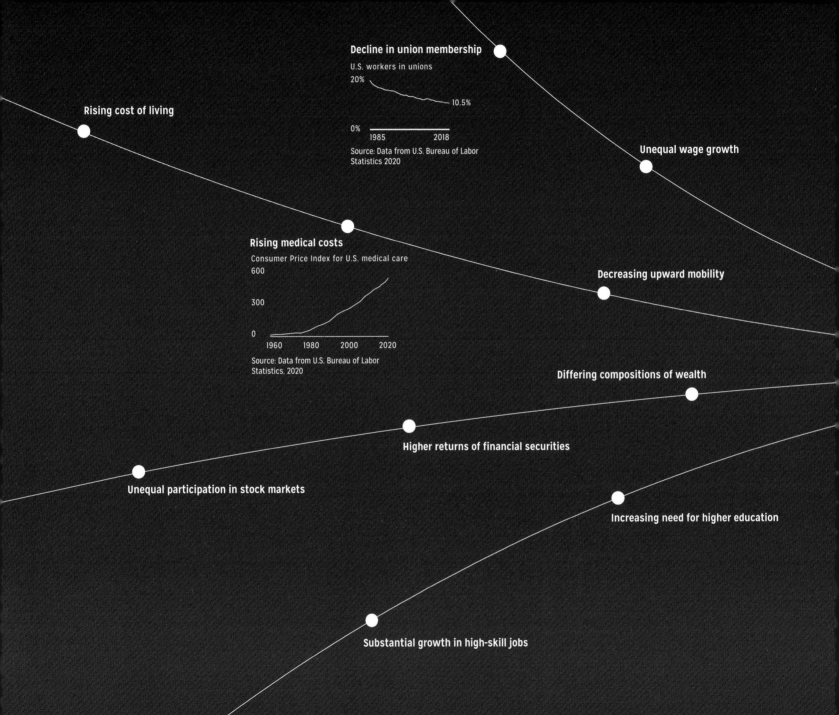

Decline in union membership

U.S. workers in unions

20%

10.5%

0%

1985   2018

Source: Data from U.S. Bureau of Labor
Statistics 2020

Rising cost of living

Unequal wage growth

Rising medical costs

Consumer Price Index for U.S. medical care

600

300

0

1960   1980   2000   2020

Source: Data from U.S. Bureau of Labor
Statistics, 2020

Decreasing upward mobility

Differing compositions of wealth

Higher returns of financial securities

Unequal participation in stock markets

Increasing need for higher education

Substantial growth in high-skill jobs

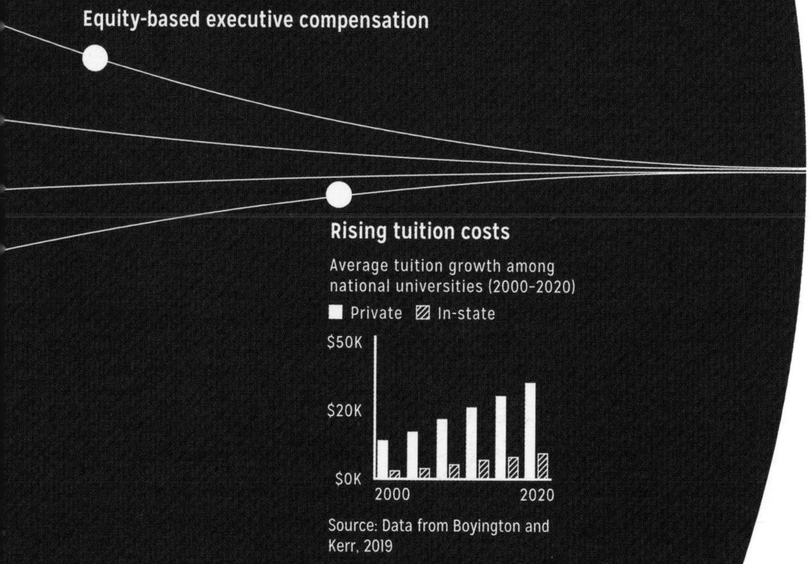

Equity-based executive compensation

Rising tuition costs

Average tuition growth among
national universities (2000-2020)

■ Private ▨ In-state

$50K

$20K

$0K
     2000   2020

Source: Data from Boyington and
Kerr, 2019

RISING WEALTH INEQUALITY

RISING WEALTH INEQUALITY

SIGNAL RANGE
Very broad (5/5)

SIGNAL-TO-NOISE RATIO
Medium (3/5)

The U.S. is home to a vast majority of the world's ultra-high net worth individuals, a visible reminder of growing domestic inequality.

NUMBER OF ADULTS WITH $50+ MILLION IN NET WORTH BY COUNTRY

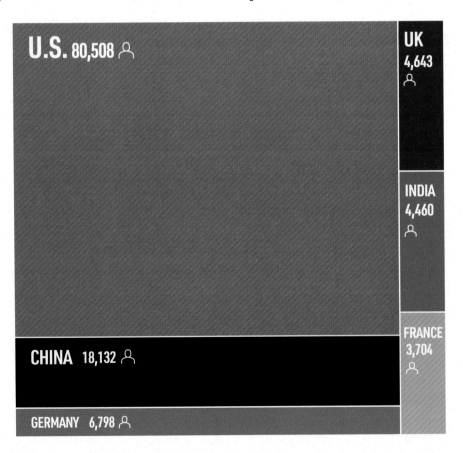

U.S. 80,508

CHINA 18,132

GERMANY 6,798

UK 4,643

INDIA 4,460

FRANCE 3,704

WEALTH INEQUALITY has been a persistent issue throughout human history. Just three decades ago, 36% of the world's population lived in extreme poverty.

While this proportion has fallen to 9% as of 2018, many developed nations are experiencing a new form of economic disparity—one that is exemplified by the boom in ultra-wealthy citizens.

This trend is most prevalent in the U.S., where more than 80,000 individuals have a net worth of $50 million or higher. This figure is larger than the number in the next five countries combined, and equal to 48% of the world's total.

Source: Roser and Ortiz-Ospina 2013

Source: Data from Credit Suisse, 2019

AMERICA'S WEALTH GAP

Although it is the wealthiest country in the world, the U.S. falls behind several other developed nations in terms of median wealth.

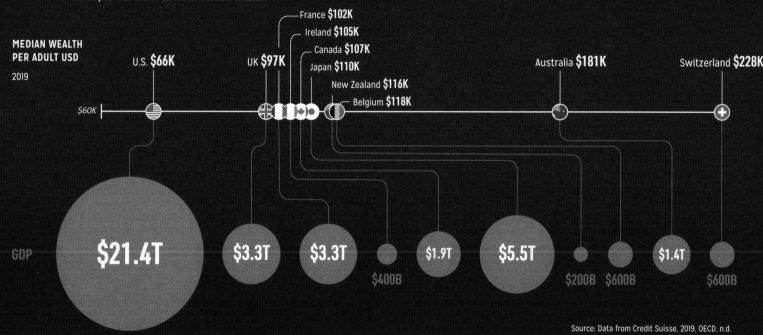

MEDIAN WEALTH PER ADULT USD
2019

$60K

U.S. **$66K**
UK **$97K**
France **$102K**
Ireland **$105K**
Canada **$107K**
Japan **$110K**
New Zealand **$116K**
Belgium **$118K**
Australia **$181K**
Switzerland **$228K**

GDP

$21.4T
$3.3T
$3.3T
$400B
$1.9T
$5.5T
$200B
$600B
$1.4T
$600B

Source: Data from Credit Suisse, 2019, OECD, n.d.

THE TOP 10 BILLIONAIRES' WEALTH VS COUNTRY GDP 2020

The combined wealth of the world's top 10 billionaires has surpassed the GDP of many countries.

◄ *Combined wealth*   GDP ►

Top 10 global billionaires

Of the top ten wealthiest individuals, eight were born in the U.S.

$820B

Colombia — $742B

South Africa — $726B

Switzerland — $614B

Belgium — $598B

Source: Data from Forbes 2019 and OCED 2020

TRENDS IN U.S. WEALTH INEQUALITY

Since 1990, the wealth of America's top 10% has increased by trillions of dollars. The bottom 50%, however, have remained stagnant.

SHARE OF TOTAL WEALTH BY WEALTH GROUP

● Bottom 50%   ● 50% – 90%   ● Top 10%

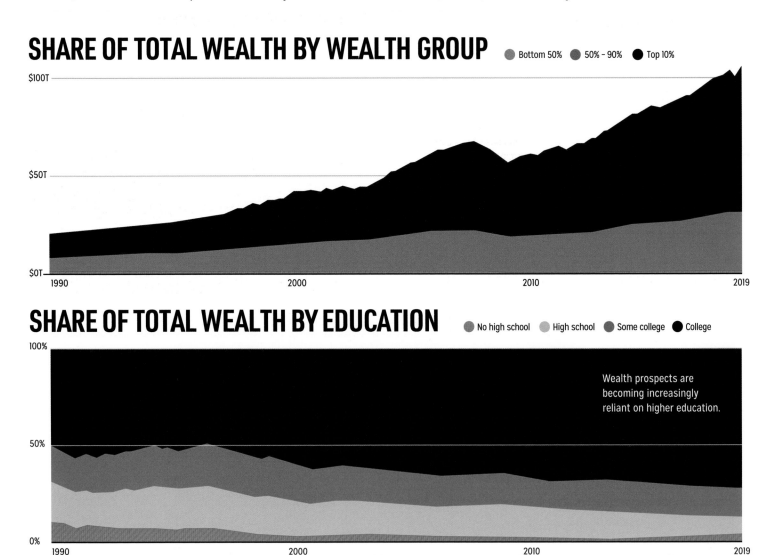

SHARE OF TOTAL WEALTH BY EDUCATION

● No high school   ● High school   ● Some college   ● College

Wealth prospects are becoming increasingly reliant on higher education.

Source: Data from FRED Economic Data, 2019

UNEQUAL SOURCES OF WEALTH

A key driver of the wealth gap is the difference in assets held by America's top 10% and bottom 90%.

SHARE OF U.S. ASSETS OWNED

Percentage share of total

● Top 10% ● Bottom 90%

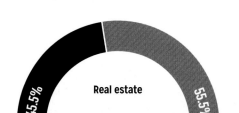

Real estate

45.5%   55.5%

A majority of the bottom 90%'s wealth is derived from their homes.

Stocks and mutual funds

88.1%   11.9%

The top 10% own the vast majority of financial securities.

Source: Data from FRED Economic Data, 2019

EQUITY MARKET PARTICIPATION

Looking at this issue through a different lens tells a similar story, that is, lower-income families have significantly less participation in stock markets.

PERCENTAGE OF FAMILIES WITH INVESTMENTS IN THE STOCK MARKET By family income

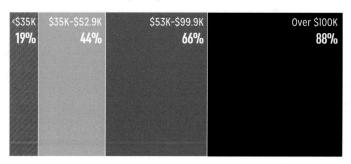

<$35K	$35K-$52.9K	$53K-$99.9K	Over $100K
19%	44%	66%	88%

Source: Data from Parker and Fry, 2020

HISTORICAL PERFORMANCE: EQUITIES VS. REAL ESTATE JAN 1990–JUN 2020

— S&P/Case-Shiller U.S. National Home Price Index   — S&P 500

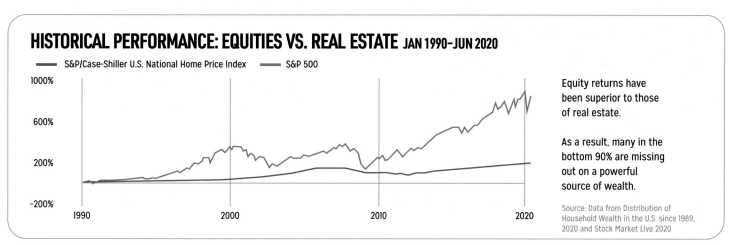

Equity returns have been superior to those of real estate.

As a result, many in the bottom 90% are missing out on a powerful source of wealth.

Source: Data from Distribution of Household Wealth in the U.S. since 1989, 2020 and Stock Market Live 2020

CORPORATE INEQUALITY

In addition to a base salary, executive compensation packages often include equity options and awards, both of which can be significantly more lucrative.

REALIZED CEO COMPENSATION VS S&P 500 INDEX

— CEO realized compensation   — S&P 500 Index (2019 USD)

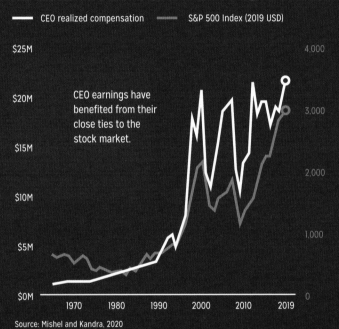

CEO earnings have benefited from their close ties to the stock market.

Source: Mishel and Kandra, 2020

CEO-TO-WORKER COMPENSATION RATIO Ratio values

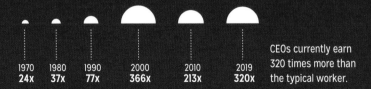

1970	1980	1990	2000	2010	2019
24x	37x	77x	366x	213x	320x

CEOs currently earn 320 times more than the typical worker.

Source: Data from Mishel and Kandra, 2020

THE DECLINE OF COLLECTIVE BARGAINING

Workers who are covered by a union typically earn 13.2% more than those who are not. However, shifting job structures and anti-union efforts contribute to declining participation rates.

UNION MEMBERSHIP RATE

— Canada   — Germany   — United Kingdom   — France

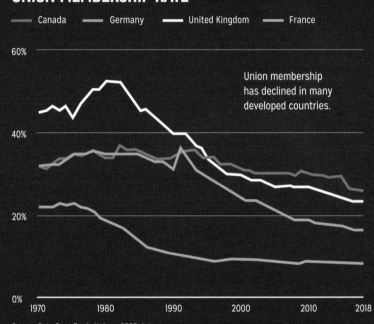

Union membership has declined in many developed countries.

Source: Data from Trade Union - OECD data

HEIGHTENED INEQUALITY IN AMERICA

As union membership declines, America's wealthiest 10% have seen their share of total income increase.

— Share of income going to top 10%

— Union membership

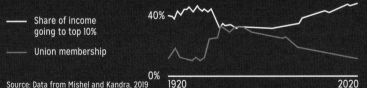

Source: Data from Mishel and Kandra, 2019

A majority of Americans believe there is too much economic inequality—but who should be responsible for reducing it?

VIEWS ON THE LEVEL OF ECONOMIC INEQUALITY IN AMERICA

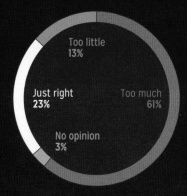

Too little
13%

Just right
23%

Too much
61%

No opinion
3%

OPINIONS ON WHO SHOULD BEAR RESPONSIBILITY FOR REDUCING INEQUALITY

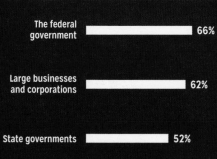

The federal government — 66%

Large businesses and corporations — 62%

State governments — 52%

Wealthy individuals — 46%

Churches and other religious organizations — 13%

Source: Data from Horowitz et al. 2020

AMERICA'S WEALTH GAP SHOWS LITTLE SIGNS OF SHRINKING.

With less exposure to stocks and other financial securities, America's lower-income families will struggle to build wealth at the same rate as those at the top.

This could have long-term implications, as economic inequality in one generation is often linked to unequal opportunities for the next.

02

ENVIRONMENT

NUMBER OF SIGNALS / 03

From a business lens, every problem is an opportunity.

Yes, the world faces big challenges like climate change and water scarcity, and as a society we're going to have to dig deep to solve these issues.

But the upshot is often missed: as consumers and investors demand more out of corporations to help protect the environment, there are massive opportunities to be discovered. Today's ambitious entrepreneurs and investors now have the chance to take part in an exciting transformation to meet the needs of tomorrow.

This chapter examines key environmental signals we see affecting business.

The opening two signals have a direct impact on the sustainability of the planet as a whole. The third shows a partial solution to these problems that is gaining momentum and will affect the infrastructure and everyday lives of people on each continent.

Volcanic eruptions

Naturally occurring greenhouse gases

Fossil fuel consumption
Global primary energy
consumption by fossil fuels

137K
TWh → 2019

41K
TWh → 1965

Source: Data from BP p.l.c. 2020

Agricultural sector growth

Industrial Revolution

Carbon emissions
Atmospheric CO₂ by parts per million
420

0
1960   2020

Source: Data from Earth System Research
Laboratories Global Monitoring Laboratory 2020

Deforestation

Population growth
Population growth and cumulative
deforestation, 1800-2010

—— Deforestation   ⋯⋯ Population
2.2 billion hectares   8B

0.6   0B
1800   2010

Source: Modified from FAO 2012

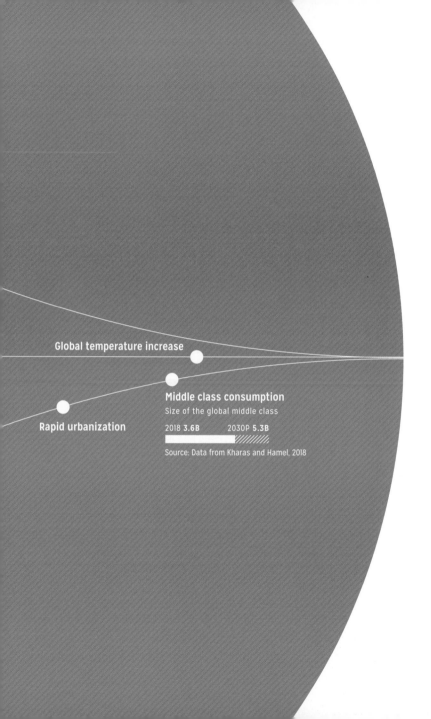

Global temperature increase

Middle class consumption
Size of the global middle class

2018 **3.6B**   2030P **5.3B**

Source: Data from Kharas and Hamel, 2018

Rapid urbanization

CLIMATE PRESSURES

CLIMATE PRESSURES

Global temperatures have been climbing steadily, and pressure is mounting on businesses and governments to solve climate-related challenges.

SIGNAL RANGE
Very broad (5/5)

SIGNAL-TO-NOISE RATIO
High (4/5)

 SIGNAL

GLOBAL SURFACE TEMPERATURES 1850–2020

━━━ Land surface air temperature

━━━ Global land–ocean mean surface temperature (GMST)

Temperature change relative to 1850–1900

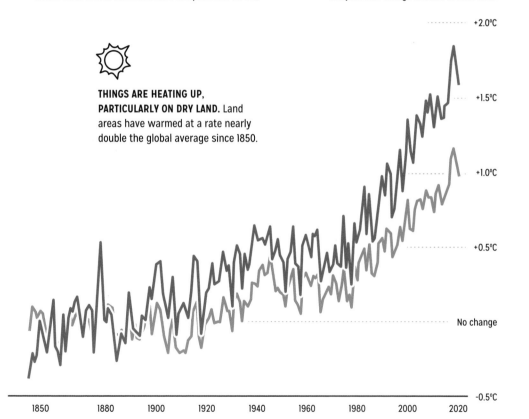

THINGS ARE HEATING UP, PARTICULARLY ON DRY LAND. Land areas have warmed at a rate nearly double the global average since 1850.

+2.0°C

+1.5°C

+1.0°C

+0.5°C

No change

-0.5°C

1850   1880   1900   1920   1940   1960   1980   2000   2020

Source: Data from Jia et al. 2020

SINCE THE INDUSTRIAL REVOLUTION, we've consumed resources at unprecedented rates to support population booms and rapid urbanization. However, we're also feeling the heat. Increased greenhouse gases (GHGs)—chiefly CO_2 emissions—have resulted in rising temperatures.

ATMOSPHERIC CO2 CONCENTRATION

Parts per million

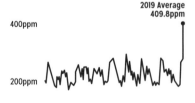

2019 Average
409.8ppm

400ppm

200ppm

0ppm

800,000BCE   2019

Source: Data from Lindsey 2020

WHERE DO GLOBAL EMISSIONS COME FROM?

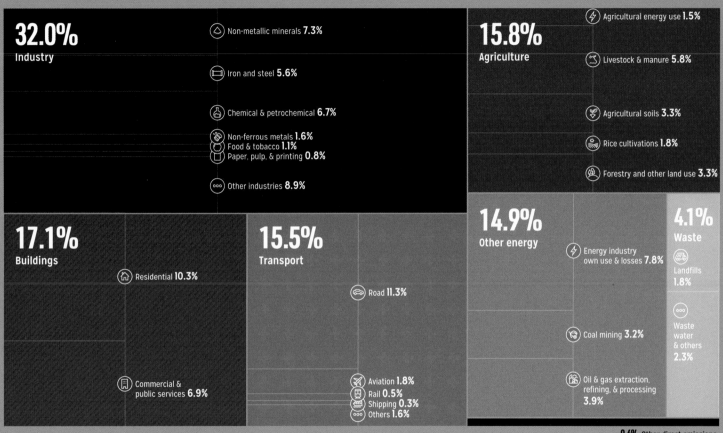

32.0%
Industry

- Non-metallic minerals **7.3%**
- Iron and steel **5.6%**
- Chemical & petrochemical **6.7%**
- Non-ferrous metals **1.6%**
- Food & tobacco **1.1%**
- Paper, pulp, & printing **0.8%**
- Other industries **8.9%**

15.8%
Agriculture

- Agricultural energy use **1.5%**
- Livestock & manure **5.8%**
- Agricultural soils **3.3%**
- Rice cultivations **1.8%**
- Forestry and other land use **3.3%**

17.1%
Buildings

- Residential **10.3%**
- Commercial & public services **6.9%**

15.5%
Transport

- Road **11.3%**
- Aviation **1.8%**
- Rail **0.5%**
- Shipping **0.3%**
- Others **1.6%**

14.9%
Other energy

- Energy industry own use & losses **7.8%**
- Coal mining **3.2%**
- Oil & gas extraction, refining, & processing **3.9%**

4.1%
Waste

- Landfills **1.8%**
- Waste water & others **2.3%**

0.6% Other direct emissions

Sector

EMISSION EXAMPLES

Agriculture	Transport	Residential	Land use
Cows and other livestock emit methane (CH4) by passing gas each day.	CO2 is directly emitted from fossil fuel powered automobiles and aircraft.	Homes use fuel for heating, either directly (i.e., natural gas) or through electricity sources, some of which come from fossil fuels.	Forested areas are cleared to increase agriculture capacity.

Source: Data from Navigant, 2019

GLOBAL CO2 EMISSIONS BY COUNTRY

Percentage of global share (2018, gigatonnes)

- Americas
- Europe & Middle East
- Asia Pacific
- Africa

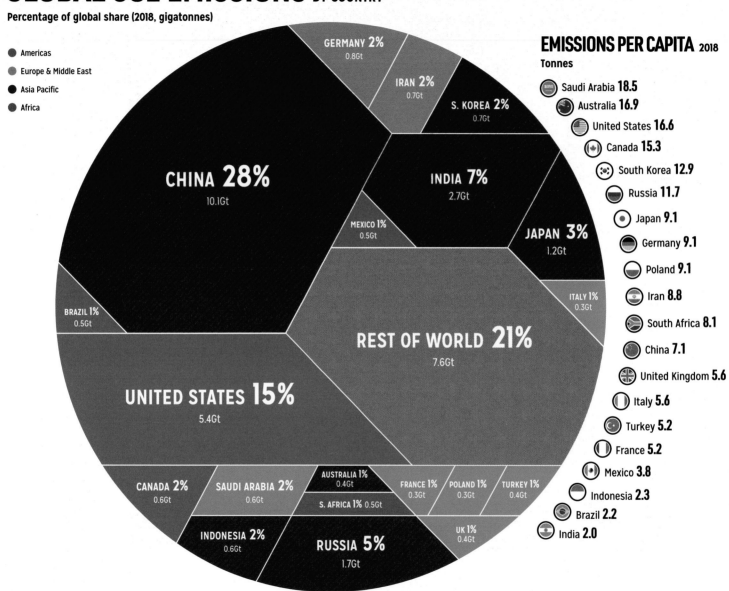

GERMANY 2%
0.8Gt

IRAN 2%
0.7Gt

S. KOREA 2%
0.7Gt

CHINA 28%
10.1Gt

INDIA 7%
2.7Gt

MEXICO 1%
0.5Gt

JAPAN 3%
1.2Gt

BRAZIL 1%
0.5Gt

ITALY 1%
0.3Gt

REST OF WORLD 21%
7.6Gt

UNITED STATES 15%
5.4Gt

CANADA 2%
0.6Gt

SAUDI ARABIA 2%
0.6Gt

AUSTRALIA 1%
0.4Gt

FRANCE 1%
0.3Gt

POLAND 1%
0.3Gt

TURKEY 1%
0.4Gt

S. AFRICA 1% 0.5Gt

INDONESIA 2%
0.6Gt

RUSSIA 5%
1.7Gt

UK 1%
0.4Gt

EMISSIONS PER CAPITA 2018

Tonnes

- Saudi Arabia **18.5**
- Australia **16.9**
- United States **16.6**
- Canada **15.3**
- South Korea **12.9**
- Russia **11.7**
- Japan **9.1**
- Germany **9.1**
- Poland **9.1**
- Iran **8.8**
- South Africa **8.1**
- China **7.1**
- United Kingdom **5.6**
- Italy **5.6**
- Turkey **5.2**
- France **5.2**
- Mexico **3.8**
- Indonesia **2.3**
- Brazil **2.2**
- India **2.0**

Source: Data from Union of Concerned Scientists, 2020

RISKS TO HUMANS AND ECOSYSTEMS

FROM CHANGES IN LAND-BASED PROCESSES AS A RESULT OF CLIMATE CHANGE

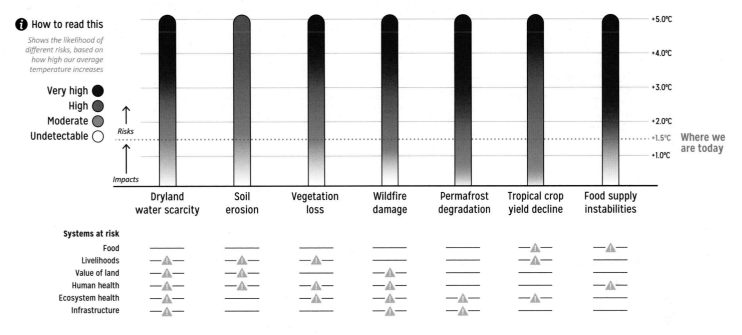

ⓘ How to read this

Shows the likelihood of different risks, based on how high our average temperature increases

Very high ●
High ◗
Moderate ◔
Undetectable ○

Risks ↑

Impacts ↑

+5.0°C
+4.0°C
+3.0°C
+2.0°C
+1.5°C — Where we are today
+1.0°C

Dryland water scarcity | Soil erosion | Vegetation loss | Wildfire damage | Permafrost degradation | Tropical crop yield decline | Food supply instabilities

Systems at risk

	Dryland water scarcity	Soil erosion	Vegetation loss	Wildfire damage	Permafrost degradation	Tropical crop yield decline	Food supply instabilities
Food						⚠	⚠
Livelihoods	⚠	⚠	⚠			⚠	
Value of land	⚠	⚠		⚠			
Human health	⚠	⚠	⚠				⚠
Ecosystem health	⚠	⚠	⚠	⚠	⚠	⚠	
Infrastructure	⚠		⚠	⚠	⚠		

Source: Data from Intergovernmental Panel on Climate Change 2020

CONNECTION BETWEEN CLIMATE CHANGE AND EXTREME WEATHER EVENTS

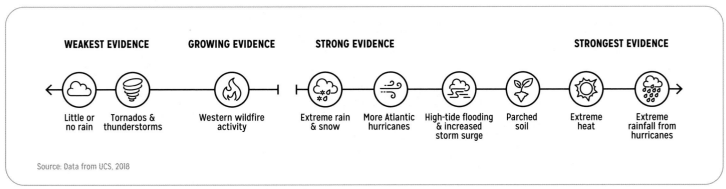

WEAKEST EVIDENCE

Little or no rain | Tornados & thunderstorms

GROWING EVIDENCE

Western wildfire activity

STRONG EVIDENCE

Extreme rain & snow | More Atlantic hurricanes | High-tide flooding & increased storm surge | Parched soil

STRONGEST EVIDENCE

Extreme heat | Extreme rainfall from hurricanes

Source: Data from UCS, 2018

CLIMATE PRESSURES: COMING TO A STEAM

CLIMATE CHANGE PROJECTIONS BY POLICY MIX 2000–2100P

AVERAGE GLOBAL GHG EMISSIONS IN GT OF CO2 EQUIVALENTS

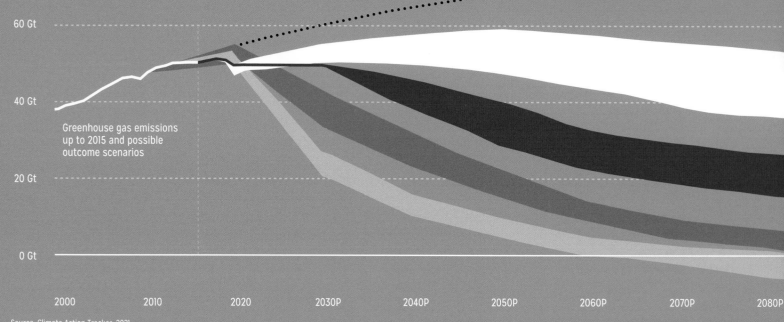

Greenhouse gas emissions up to 2015 and possible outcome scenarios

60 Gt

40 Gt

20 Gt

0 Gt

2000   2010   2020   2030P   2040P   2050P   2060P   2070P   2080P

Source: Climate Action Tracker, 2021

PROJECTED ECONOMIC IMPACTS OF CLIMATE CHANGE BY 2050

AVERAGE REAL GDP LOSS BY 2050

1.1%	1.7%	2.6%	3.0%	3.7%	3.8%	4.7%
North America	Western Europe	Asia Pacific	Eastern Europe	Middle East	Latin America	Africa

Source: Data from Economist Intelligence Unit, 2019

4.1-4.8°C NO CLIMATE POLICIES

Rise in emissions expected if countries do not implement climate reduction policies

2.7-3.1°C CURRENT POLICIES

Expected emissions with current policies in place

2.0-2.4°C PLEDGES & TARGETS

Reduction in emissions expected if countries achieve varying targets to contain global temperature rise

1.6-1.7°C

1.3-1.5°C

90P   2100P

A SHIFT IN PUBLIC PERCEPTION ● 2013 ● 2020

% of people viewing climate change as a "major" threat to their country

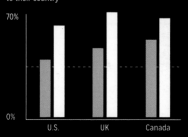

70%

0%

U.S.   UK   Canada

Source: Data from Fagan and Huang, 2020

CLIMATE CHANGE IS BECOMING AN INCREASINGLY IMPORTANT ISSUE.

It concerns not only scientists but also business leaders and the general public as well.

It's a complex problem that poses a long-term threat, but such threats can also double as opportunities for strategic investors, entrepreneurs, and decision-makers.

As climate pressure mounts, how will the world react?

Limited freshwater

Growing water consumption
Global freshwater use, trillion m³

4

2

0

1901   2014

Source: Ritchie and Roser, 2014

Population growth
in arid climates

Water conflict

Growth of urban slums

■ ■ ■ ■ ▪ ▪ ▪ ▪ ▪ ▪

3 in 10 people lack access to
drinking water that is safe and
instantly accessible.

Source: Data from WHO, 2019

Hydroelectric dams

Pollution of rivers and lakes

Irrigated agriculture

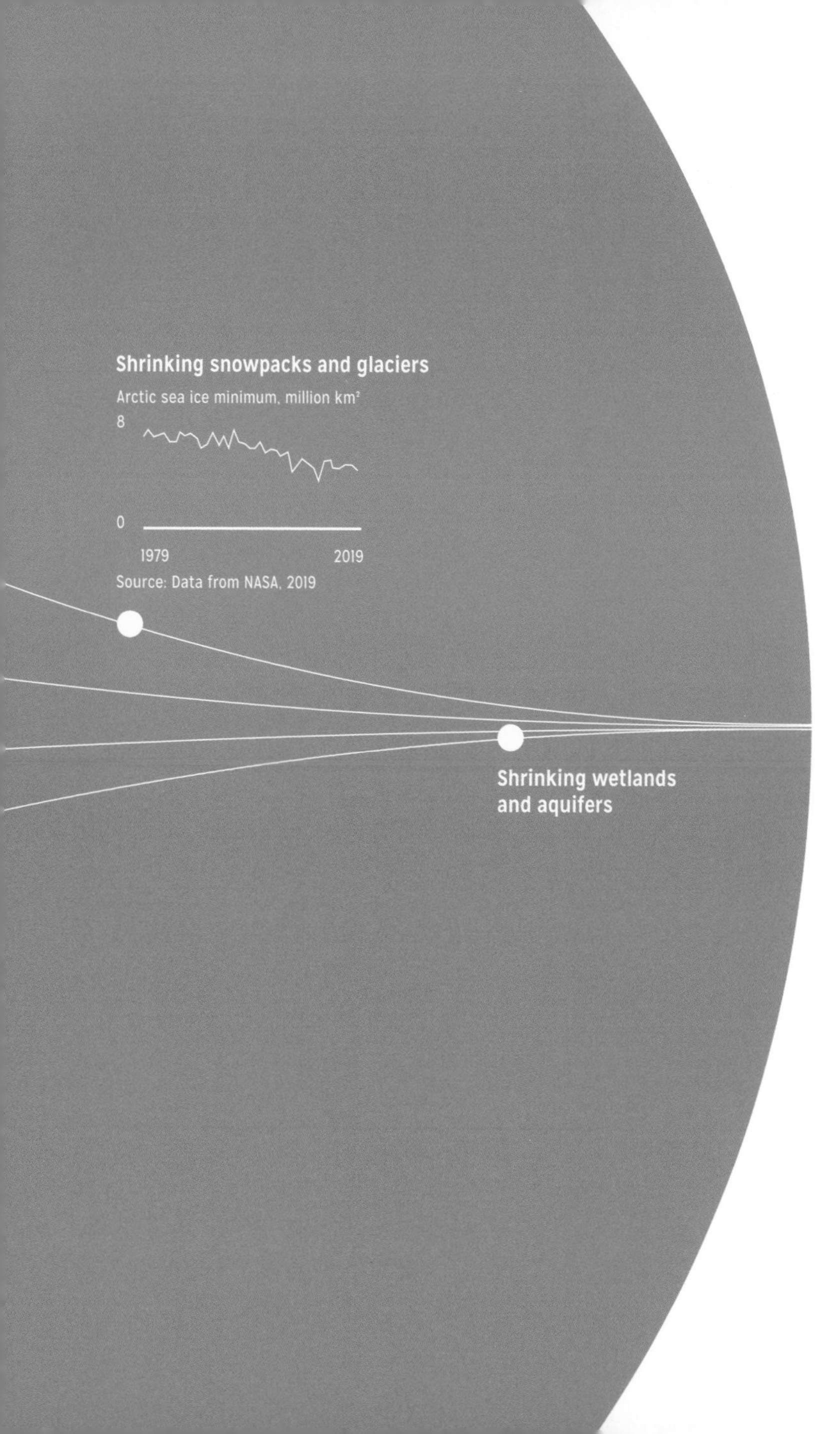

Shrinking snowpacks and glaciers

Arctic sea ice minimum, million km²

8

0

1979   2019

Source: Data from NASA, 2019

Shrinking wetlands and aquifers

WATER CRISIS

WATER CRISIS

The demand for water has increased alongside the global population, placing an incredible amount of stress on an already limited supply.

SIGNAL RANGE Very broad (5/5)	**SIGNAL-TO-NOISE RATIO** Very high (5/5)

SIGNAL

COUNTRY-LEVEL WATER STRESS 2040P

Ratio of water withdrawal to available water

Low ← | | | | | → Extremely high

<10%   10–20%   20–40%   40–80%   >80%

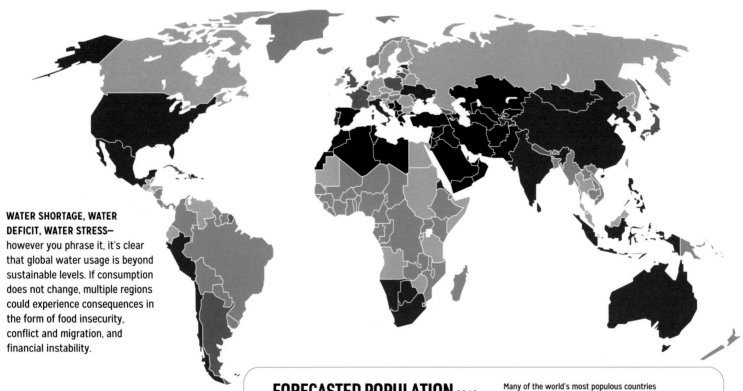

WATER SHORTAGE, WATER DEFICIT, WATER STRESS—

however you phrase it, it's clear that global water usage is beyond sustainable levels. If consumption does not change, multiple regions could experience consequences in the form of food insecurity, conflict and migration, and financial instability.

FORECASTED POPULATION 2040

Many of the world's most populous countries could face a high level of water stress by 2040

 China **1,407,803,754**   India **1,610,413,933**   U.S. **359,173,981**

Source: Data from Luo, 2015, UN Water, 2019

WATER INEQUALITY

A country's supply of fresh water can vary greatly depending on its geographic location. Other factors, such as wealth and demographics, can lead to further inequalities.

NUMBER OF PEOPLE LIVING UNDER WATER STRESS

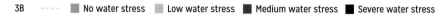

3B · · · · · ■ No water stress ■ Low water stress ■ Medium water stress ■ Severe water stress

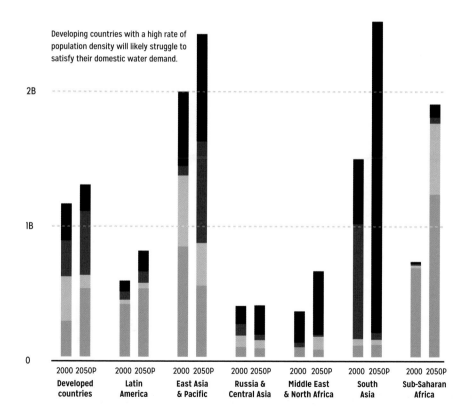

Developing countries with a high rate of population density will likely struggle to satisfy their domestic water demand.

Assumes no new policies are introduced.
Source: Data from UN Water, 2020

THE GLOBAL DISTRIBUTION OF WATER

The world's supply of water, and, more importantly, fresh water, is incredibly scarce.

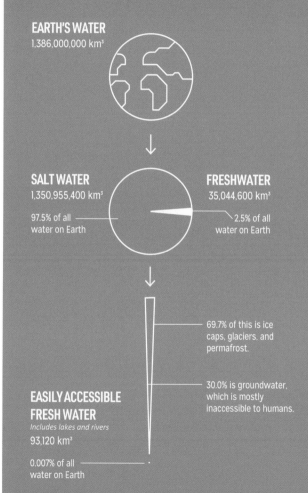

EARTH'S WATER
1,386,000,000 km³

SALT WATER
1,350,955,400 km³
97.5% of all water on Earth

FRESHWATER
35,044,600 km³
2.5% of all water on Earth

69.7% of this is ice caps, glaciers, and permafrost.

30.0% is groundwater, which is mostly inaccessible to humans.

EASILY ACCESSIBLE FRESH WATER
Includes lakes and rivers
93,120 km³

0.007% of all water on Earth

Source: Data from Perlman et al. via U.S. Geological Survey 2019

TRENDS IN GLOBAL WATER USAGE

Household water use has increased by over 600% since 1960, greatly outpacing growth in the agricultural and industrial sectors.

GROWTH IN GLOBAL WATER DEMAND BY SECTOR

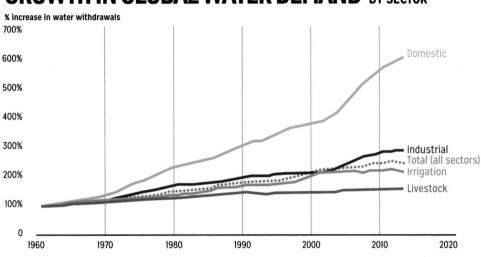

% increase in water withdrawals

- Domestic
- Industrial
- Total (all sectors)
- Irrigation
- Livestock

Source: Data from Otto & Schleifer 2020, World Bank Group 2020

Rising domestic demand can be attributed to the growth of the urban population, which often has better access to water and sanitation.

Urban population as % of total population

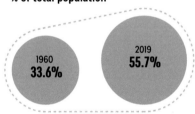

1960
33.6%

2019
55.7%

 While not growing as rapidly as other sectors, agriculture has a higher demand for water withdrawals than any other sector, and is likely to remain the top water consumer (by volume) for the foreseeable future.

GLOBAL WATER USAGE BY SECTOR

● Primary energy production ● Power generation ● Industry ● Domestic ● Agriculture

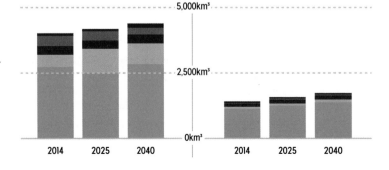

WATER WITHDRAWAL

The total amount of water withdrawn. A portion of withdrawals are typically returned to their original source.

WATER CONSUMPTION

The portion of withdrawn water that is permanently lost.

5,000km³

2,500km³

0km³

2014 2025 2040   2014 2025 2040

Source: Data from UN Water, 2019

AGRICULTURE'S RISING WATER FOOTPRINT

Shifting dietary preferences are likely to increase the agriculture sector's water usage even further.

WATER FOOTPRINT OF FOODS

Liters per kilogram of food

Animal-based food production often has a much larger water use footprint than plant-based crops.

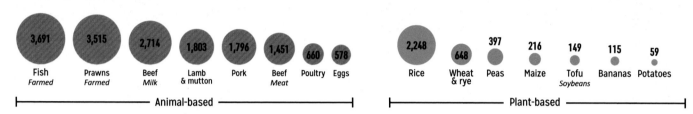

3,691	**3,515**	**2,714**	**1,803**	**1,796**	**1,451**	**660**	**578**	**2,248**	**648**	**397**	**216**	**149**	**115**	**59**
Fish *Farmed*	Prawns *Farmed*	Beef *Milk*	Lamb & mutton	Pork	Beef *Meat*	Poultry	Eggs	Rice	Wheat & rye	Peas	Maize	Tofu *Soybeans*	Bananas	Potatoes

—————— Animal-based ——————   —————— Plant-based ——————

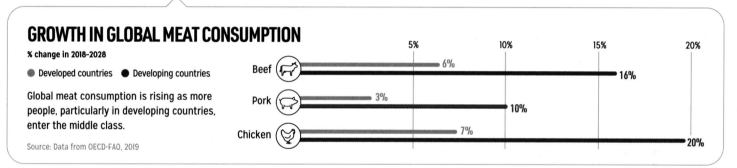

GROWTH IN GLOBAL MEAT CONSUMPTION

% change in 2018-2028

● Developed countries   ● Developing countries

Global meat consumption is rising as more people, particularly in developing countries, enter the middle class.

Source: Data from OECD-FAO, 2019

	Developed	Developing
Beef	6%	16%
Pork	3%	10%
Chicken	7%	20%

CONTAMINATION CHALLENGES

Expanding food production is also leading to higher levels of pesticide usage, increasing the risk of water contamination.

GLOBAL PESTICIDE USE 1990–2017

Tonnes consumption per year

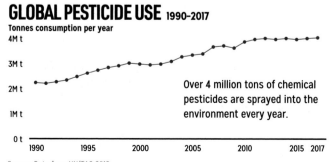

Over 4 million tons of chemical pesticides are sprayed into the environment every year.

Source: Data from UN/FAO 2019

PESTICIDE CONSUMPTION BY REGION 1990–2017

% growth

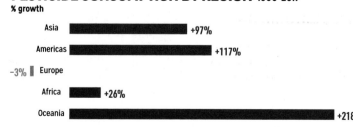

Region	% growth
Asia	+97%
Americas	+117%
Europe	–3%
Africa	+26%
Oceania	+218%

RIPPLE EFFECTS

In recent decades, the number of water-related conflicts has increased dramatically.

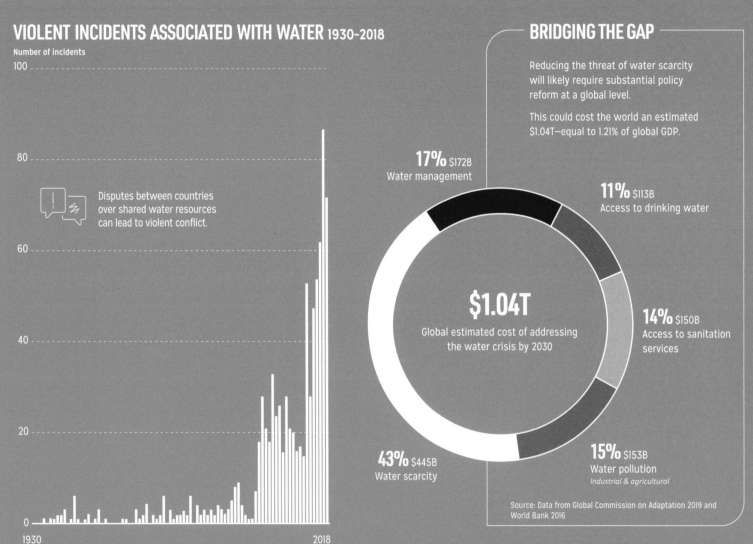

VIOLENT INCIDENTS ASSOCIATED WITH WATER 1930-2018

Number of incidents

Disputes between countries over shared water resources can lead to violent conflict.

1930 — 2018

Source: Data from Gleick et al. 2018 and World Bank 2016

BRIDGING THE GAP

Reducing the threat of water scarcity will likely require substantial policy reform at a global level.

This could cost the world an estimated $1.04T—equal to 1.21% of global GDP.

$1.04T
Global estimated cost of addressing the water crisis by 2030

17% $172B
Water management

11% $113B
Access to drinking water

14% $150B
Access to sanitation services

15% $153B
Water pollution
Industrial & agricultural

43% $445B
Water scarcity

Source: Data from Global Commission on Adaptation 2019 and World Bank 2016

A DROP IN THE OCEAN

While it may cost $1.04T to manage the global water crisis, the alternative is bleak.

Failure to implement efficient water policies, that is, continuing "business as usual," could result in up to 10% drop in GDP for hard-hit regions.

PROJECTED CHANGE IN GDP 2050

Change in GDP

○ -10%　○ -6%　● -2%　● 0%　● +1%　○ +2%　○ +6%

NO CHANGE
IN WATER
POLICIES

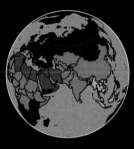

EFFICIENT
WATER
POLICIES
IMPLEMENTED

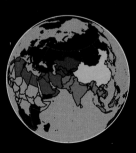

Source: Data from Global Commission on Adaptation 2019;
World Bank, 2016

WATER IS A VITAL RESOURCE FOR ALL ASPECTS OF LIFE.

However, it also happens to be in short supply. As demand continues to rise, many countries are predicted to face droughts and other water-related issues in the future.

Devising a solution for water scarcity on a global scale will be an expensive and complicated challenge, but it's one that the world will ultimately need to solve.

Decarbonization

Renewable energy

Increasing battery capacity

Motor strength

Load flexibility

Flexible building systems can shift electricity demand
for devices like heaters and washing machines,
resulting in significant yearly savings.

-24% | Annual peak net load (MW)

-40% | Annual curtailment (MWh)

-23% | Annual CO2 emissions (Tons)

Source: Goldenberg, 2018

Electric vehicle incentives

Grid strength and connectivity

In 2019, 10% of the world's
population still didn't have
access to electricity.

Source: The World Bank, 2019

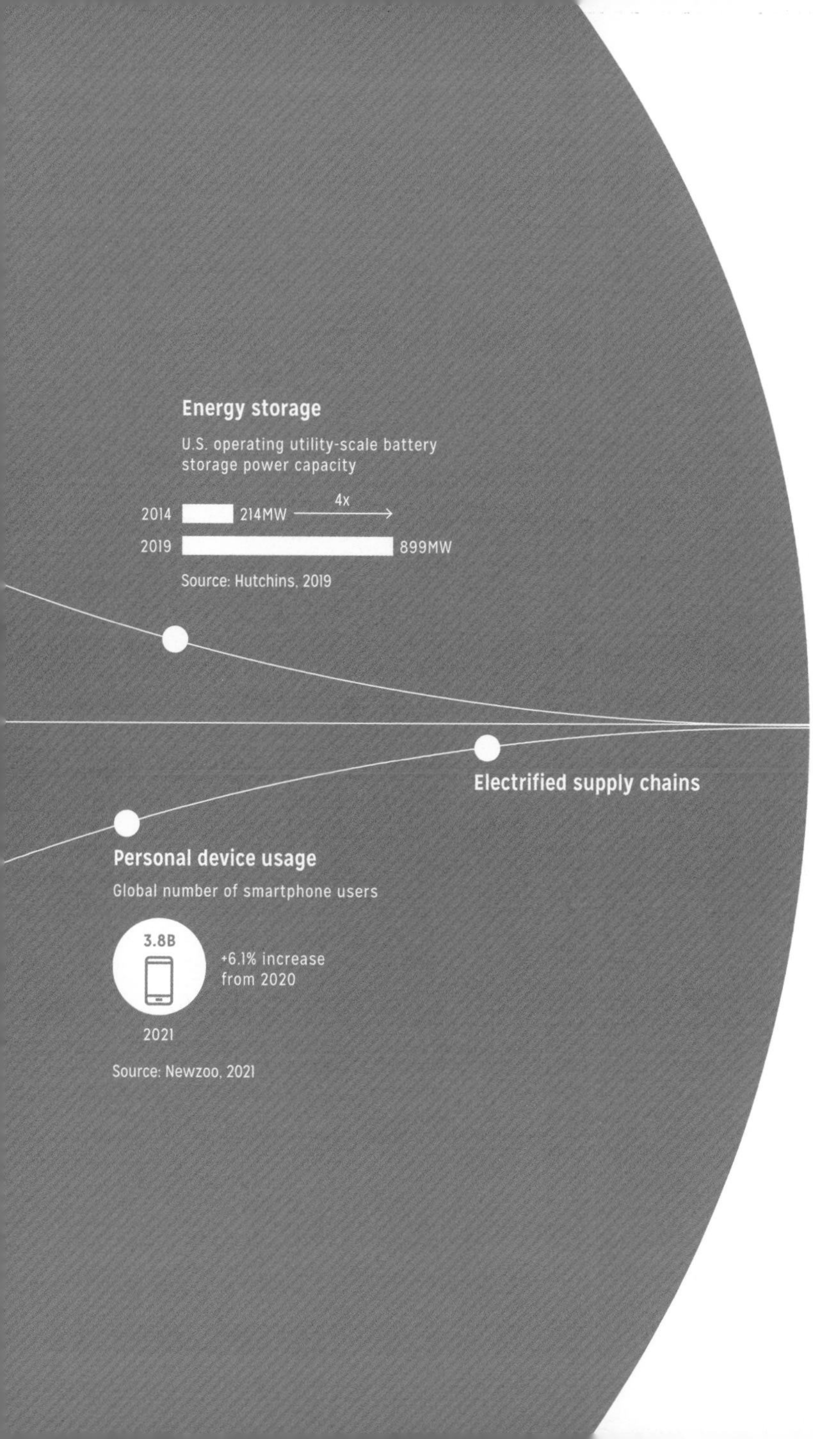

Energy storage

U.S. operating utility-scale battery storage power capacity

2014	▭ 214MW	4x →
2019	▬ 899MW	

Source: Hutchins, 2019

Electrified supply chains

Personal device usage

Global number of smartphone users

3.8B +6.1% increase from 2020

2021

Source: Newzoo, 2021

ELECTRIFICATION OF EVERYTHING

ELECTRIFICATION OF EVERYTHING

SIGNAL RANGE
Broad (4/5)

SIGNAL-TO-NOISE RATIO
Medium (3/5)

Electricity consumption is projected to increase over the next few decades with the general desire to reduce dependence on fossil fuels. However, the magnitude of the increase will largely depend on the rate at which various industries and technologies can evolve.

U.S. PROJECTED ELECTRICITY CONSUMPTION 1950-2050

By electrification scenario

◄ *Historical* ⋮ *Modeled* ► Electricity consumption, TWh

- Transportation
- Commercial
- Residential
- Industrial

The shift for electrification can impact the demand side of the U.S. energy system.

◄ *Higher demand potential from electrification*

◄ *Regular demand*

7.0K

3.5K

0.0

1950 1960 1970 1980 1990 2000 2010 2020P 2030P 2040P 2050P

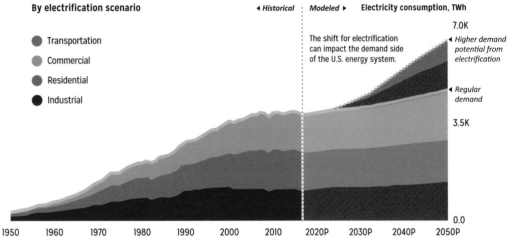

Source: Data from National Renewable Energy Laboratory, 2018

COMPLETE ELECTRIFICATION is one of the strongest and most transformative methods of dealing with climate change.

It's not just in terms of access or an increased use of electric devices. It's a revolution that will make most products and services reliant on electricity.

Combined with a global push for renewable sources of electricity and ballooning energy demand, electrification is both well on the way, yet also just getting started.

ELECTRICITY GENERATION BY FUEL GLOBAL, 2018-2040

● Coal ● Gas ● Oil ● Nuclear ● Hydro ● Wind ● Solar ● Other

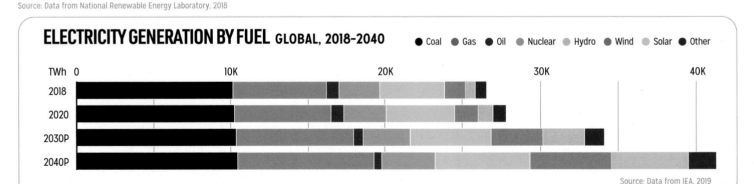

TWh 0   10K   20K   30K   40K

2018
2020
2030P
2040P

Source: Data from IEA, 2019

WHAT DOES ELECTRIFICATION LOOK LIKE?

The transportation and industrial sectors have huge potential for electrification.

% OF TOTAL ENERGY CONSUMPTION BY SECTOR 2015

☐ Non-electricity   ■ Electricity

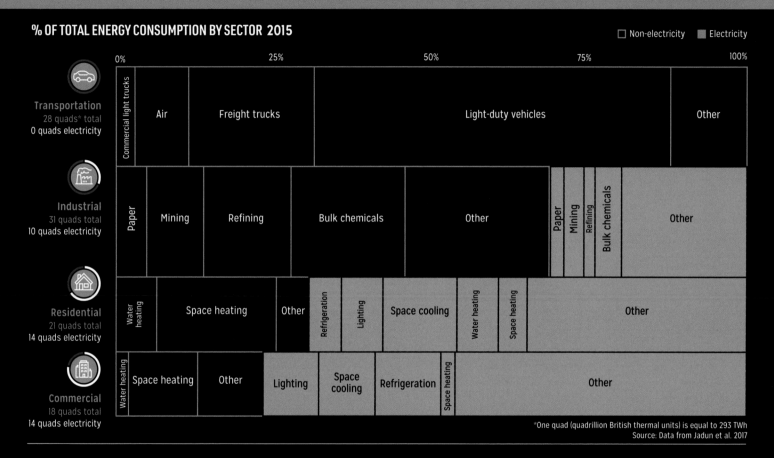

0%   25%   50%   75%   100%

Transportation
28 quads* total
0 quads electricity

Commercial light trucks | Air | Freight trucks | Light-duty vehicles | Other

Industrial
31 quads total
10 quads electricity

Paper | Mining | Refining | Bulk chemicals | Other | Paper | Mining | Refining | Bulk chemicals | Other

Residential
21 quads total
14 quads electricity

Water heating | Space heating | Other | Refrigeration | Lighting | Space cooling | Water heating | Space heating | Other

Commercial
18 quads total
14 quads electricity

Water heating | Space heating | Other | Lighting | Space cooling | Refrigeration | Space heating | Other

*One quad (quadrillion British thermal units) is equal to 293 TWh
Source: Data from Jadun et al. 2017

RISING GLOBAL ELECTRICITY DEMAND
2000–2040

The promise of electrification would further increase the already growing demand for electricity worldwide, significantly.

Source: Data from IEA, 2019

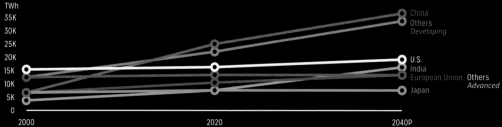

TWh

35K
30K
25K
20K
15K
10K
5K
0

2000   2020   2040P

China
Others *Developing*
U.S.
India
European Union **Others** *Advanced*
Japan

ELECTRIFICATION IN ACTION

Electrification will largely affect industrial sectors, but noticeable effects will also be seen in transportation, buildings, and many other aspects of our everyday lives.

ELECTRICITY DEMAND
GROWTH BY END-USE 2018-2040
By terawatt-hour, TWh

● Advanced economies ● Developing economies

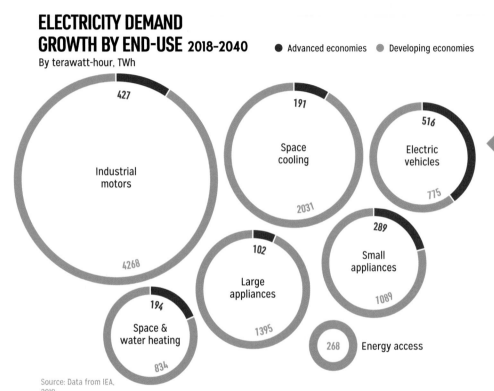

Industrial motors
427
4268

Space cooling
191
2031

Electric vehicles
516
775

Large appliances
102
1395

Small appliances
289
1089

Space & water heating
194
834

Energy access
268

Source: Data from IEA, 2019

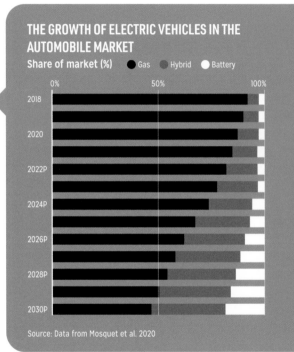

THE GROWTH OF ELECTRIC VEHICLES IN THE AUTOMOBILE MARKET
Share of market (%) ● Gas ● Hybrid ○ Battery

0%   50%   100%

2018
2020
2022P
2024P
2026P
2028P
2030P

Source: Data from Mosquet et al. 2020

HEAT PUMP ECONOMICS AND EMISSION REDUCTIONS
● Natural gas ● Heat pump (electricity)

One application of electrification is utilizing heat pumps in buildings, which can run both on and off the energy grid and provide significant costs and emissions savings.

	OAKLAND	HOUSTON	PROVIDENCE	CHICAGO
15-year net present cost *Thousand USD*	$13.70 / $11.50	$15.10 / $11.50	$16.60 / $14.30	$14.60 / $9.60
Annual emissions *Thousand /b. CO₂*	3.2 / 2.5	8 / 7	6.8 / 4.5	9.6 / 14.1

Current heat pumps are less efficient than natural gas in cold climates, but can run on renewable sources of electricity.

Source: Data from Billimoria et al 2018

WHERE ELECTRICITY WILL COME FROM

In order to properly tap into the power of electrification to reduce greenhouse gas emissions, renewable energy sources are a must. Renewable power generation is already exceeding expectations and improving faster than expected.

GLOBAL POWER GENERATION CAPACITY BY TECHNOLOGY

Gigawatt

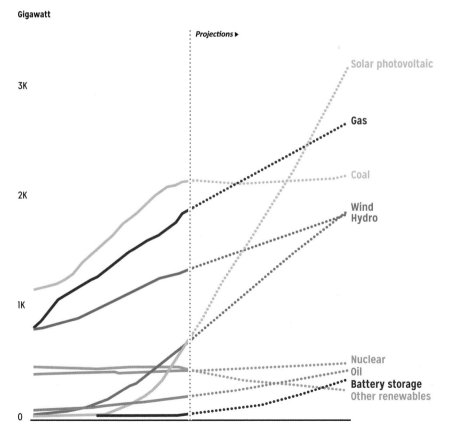

Projections ▶

- Solar photovoltaic
- **Gas**
- Coal
- Wind
- Hydro
- Nuclear
- Oil
- **Battery storage**
- Other renewables

3K
2K
1K
0

2000 2005 2010 2015 2020 2025P 2030P 2035P 2040P

Source: Data from IEA, 2020

PROJECTED COST OF ELECTRICITY BY TYPE GERMANY

$ per megawatt-hour, full cost

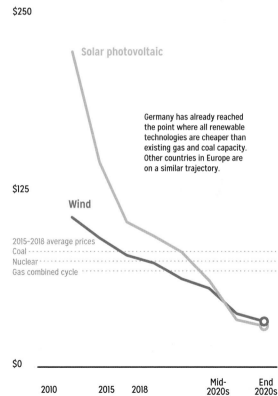

$250

Solar photovoltaic

Germany has already reached the point where all renewable technologies are cheaper than existing gas and coal capacity. Other countries in Europe are on a similar trajectory.

$125

Wind

2015–2018 average prices
Coal
Nuclear
Gas combined cycle

$0

2010   2015   2018   Mid-2020s   End 2020s

Source: Data from Heiligtag via McKinsey & Company 2019

ELECTRICITY ISN'T ALL GREEN (YET)

New electrified products bring heightened demand for necessary metals, and with many different scenarios left to play out, the final impact of electrification is hard to pinpoint.

FORECAST FOR RENEWABLES BECOMING CHEAPER THAN FOSSIL FUELS

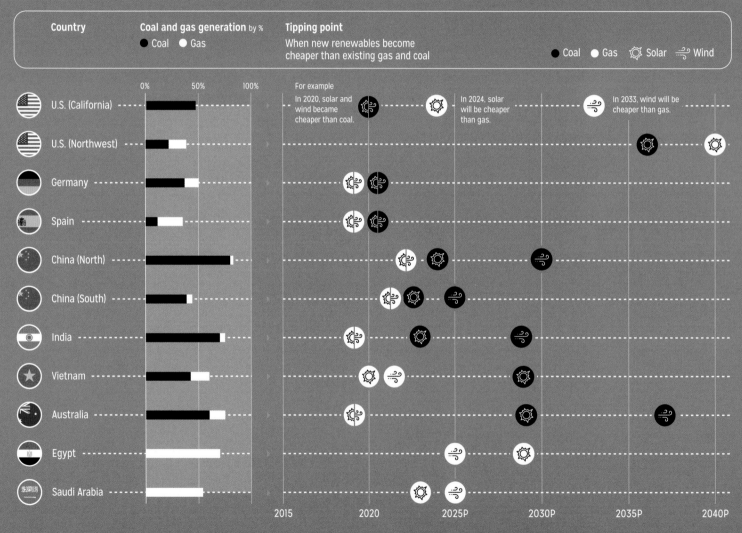

Source: Data from Heiligtag via McKinsey & Company 2019

INCREASED DEMAND FOR BATTERY METALS 2018-2028

- ⬜ Lithium
- ⬛ Graphite anode
- ⬜ Cobalt
- ⬛ Nickel

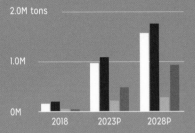

2.0M tons

1.0M

0M

2018   2023P   2028P

Source: Benchmark Mineral Intelligence, 2019

BATTERY COST REDUCTION SCENARIOS 2018-2030

Battery pack cost ($/kWh)

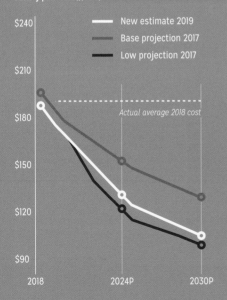

— New estimate 2019
— Base projection 2017
— Low projection 2017

$240

$210

$180 ····· Actual average 2018 cost

$150

$120

$90

2018   2024P   2030P

Source: Data from Mosquet et al 2020

ELECTRIFICATION WILL CREATE UNIMAGINABLE PRODUCTS AND TRANSFORM ENTIRE INDUSTRIES.

As a tool to combat climate change, it paves the way for more advanced electric vehicles, power systems, and storage capabilities.

Factor in the rapid technological advances being made in other areas like automation and renewable energy, and electrification is set to be as revolutionary as it promises.

03

DIGITAL WORLD

NUMBER OF SIGNALS / 03

In the intangible realm of bits and bytes, there is no shortage of data to be analyzed and exploited.

And while the dizzying growth in information can be troublesome to the human brain, harnessing it is becoming a key competitive advantage for the biggest tech firms in the world.

In this chapter we look at this unique contrast. We show you the coping mechanisms that human beings are developing to manage information overload—and also the tech giants on the opposite end that are amassing this data in complex databases and extracting new value from it.

On the frontiers of this new dichotomy exists the growing "Wild West" of cybercrime, where nefarious actors use digital tools to exploit value for themselves, even if it's against the rules.

Our relationship to the digital world is becoming integral to work and life, and as we spend more of our time immersed in bits and bytes, these signals will continue to define the future of how we interface with technology.

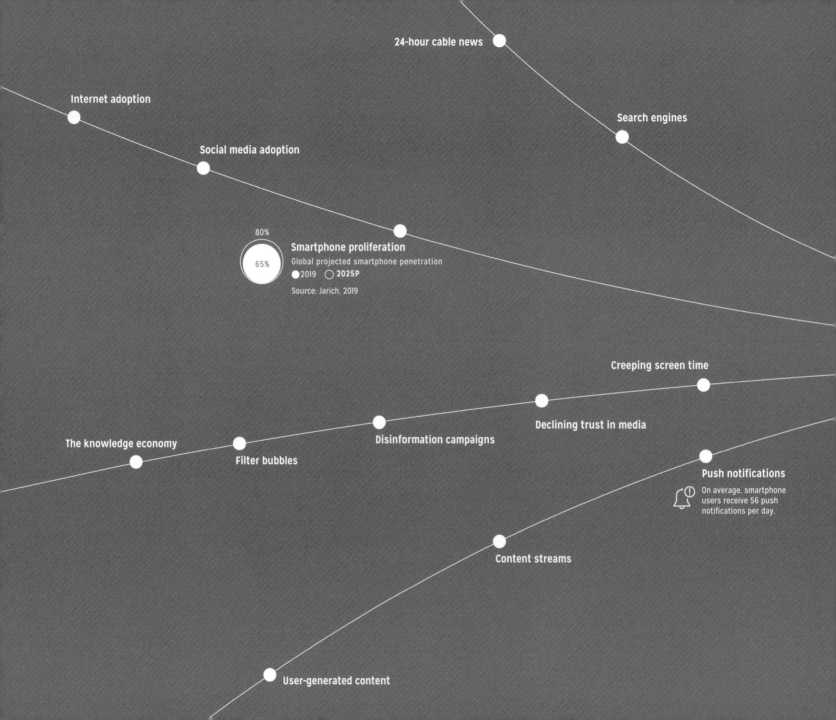

24-hour cable news

Internet adoption

Search engines

Social media adoption

80%

65%

Smartphone proliferation
Global projected smartphone penetration
● 2019 ○ **2025P**
Source: Jarich, 2019

Creeping screen time

Declining trust in media

The knowledge economy

Disinformation campaigns

Filter bubbles

Push notifications

On average, smartphone
users receive 56 push
notifications per day.

Content streams

User-generated content

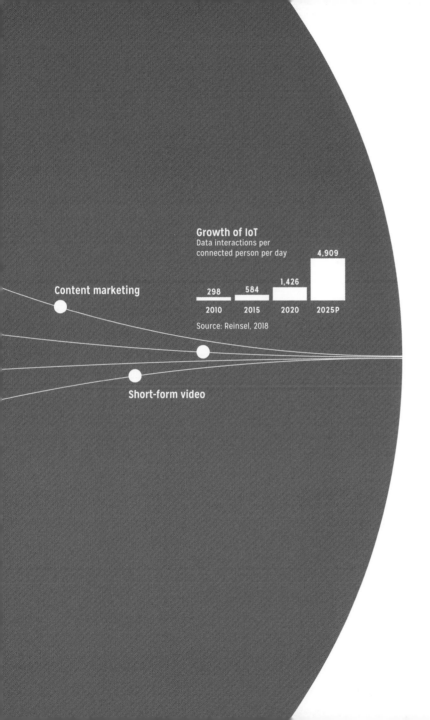

Content marketing

Growth of IoT
Data interactions per
connected person per day

298	584	1,426	4,909
2010	2015	2020	2025P

Source: Reinsel, 2018

Short-form video

INFORMATION OVERLOAD

INFORMATION OVERLOAD

Humanity is creating, analyzing, and consuming more data than ever before. Can we cope with this rising tide of information?

WORLDWIDE DATA CAPTURED, CREATED, AND REPLICATED

ZETTABYTES*

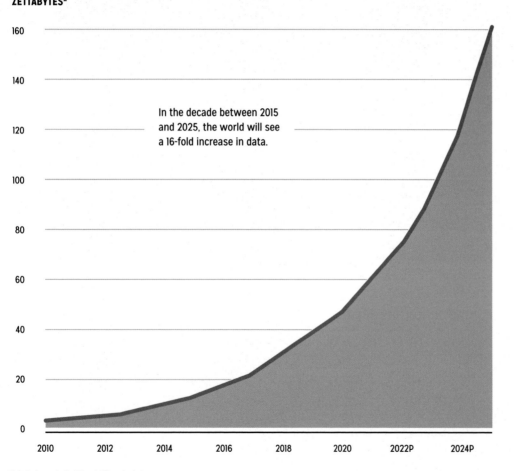

In the decade between 2015 and 2025, the world will see a 16-fold increase in data.

CREATING, PUBLISHING, AND SHARING CONTENT HAS NEVER BEEN EASIER. As well, the proliferation of connected devices is resulting in a staggering increase in the amount of data being created. This sea of information is easy to access, but hard to glean insight from.

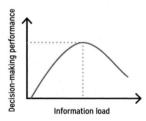

Information overload occurs when the amount of input to a system exceeds its processing capacity. Decision-makers have fairly limited cognitive processing capacity. Consequently, when information overload occurs, it is likely that a reduction in decision quality will occur.

–ALVIN TOFFLER

*One zettabyte is equivalent to a trillion gigabytes.
Source: Data from Reinsel et al. via IDC 2018

SCREEN LIFE TAKES HOLD

Screen time has gone up dramatically in recent years, and people now consume more than twice as much digital media than in 2008.

DAILY HOURS SPENT WITH DIGITAL MEDIA
U.S. ADULTS

2018

3.6 HOURS
Mobile

2008

0.3 HOURS
Mobile

2.0 HOURS
Computer

2.7 HOURS
Computer

0.7 HOURS
Other connected devices

0.2 HOURS

Other connected devices

Source: Data from Trends 2019

TRENDING UP

Livestreaming ···· Hours watched on Twitch, Facebook Gaming, YouTube, and Mixer
Especially gaming

	2017	2018	2019	2020
3B				
1.5B				
0B				

Podcasts ········· Monthly podcast listeners in the U.S.

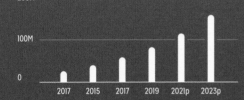

	2017	2015	2017	2019	2021p	2023p
200M						
100M						
0						

TRENDING DOWN

Books ············· Reading for personal interest (average minutes per day, U.S. adults)
Thank you for reading this book though

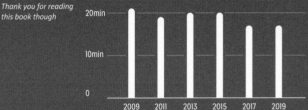

	2009	2011	2013	2015	2017	2019
20min						
10min						
0						

Television ········ Daily hours watched by age group / Q2, 2020
Especially live

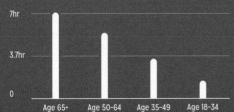

	Age 65+	Age 50-64	Age 35-49	Age 18-34
7hr				
3.7hr				
0				

OUR SEARCH FOR MEANING

As technology evolves, our human drive to consume information and understand the world hasn't changed.
In fact, the way we evaluate the quality of information can be summed up by this equation from
Doug Clinton (Managing Partner, Loup Ventures):

UTILITY
The value of meaning
divided by time

$=$

$$\text{UTILITY} = \frac{\text{MEANING}}{\text{TIME}}$$

MEANING How the individual interprets
the information

TIME The amount of time it takes an
individual to consume the information

Source: Modified from Clinton via Loup Ventures 2018

Faced with this overwhelming tsunami of information, we've adopted certain
behaviors and created frameworks that help us quickly evaluate content.

COMPRESSION

Packing more information and meaning into consumable units.

Memes, GIFs,
& emojis

Dashboards

Explainer
videos

FILTERING

Leveraging algorithms, aggregators, and crowd wisdom to help us
eliminate information we aren't interested in.

Twitter
influencers

Newsfeeds

Upvotes
& likes

THE INCREASING DENSITY OF INFORMATION

As we become more comfortable with information intake, our methods of content consumption become denser. Consider the following practical examples.

TWITTER

ON THE COUCH

VIDEO

2010

Text, 140 characters

Low resolution, low shareability

DVR, Blackberry (3G)

2020

280 characters, gifs, video, images, geotagging, tagging, hashtags, emojis, livestreaming, threading, quote tweet

High resolution, stickers, filters, gifs, text overlays, tagging, geotagging, hashtags, music

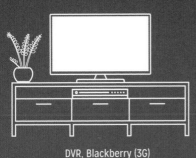

Smartphone (LTE or 5G), Netflix, smartspeaker, Nintendo Switch, Apple Watch

OUR DATA-DRIVEN FUTURE

Our rapidly expanding universe of information is permeating every facet of our lives. Here are a few less obvious ways our future will be shaped by data.

REAL-TIME EVERYTHING

By 2025, it's estimated that one-third of all information will be "real time." These are data collected from sensors and billions of connected devices.

Source: Reinsel et al., 2018

AR
THE HIDDEN REAL WORLD

Pokémon Go offered millions of people a first glimpse of how the real world can be infused with layers of digital information. Using a smartphone as a tool to interact with this "digital overlay" is just the beginning.

QUANTIFIED SELF

As we surround ourselves with connected technology, our daily lives will increasingly spin off large amounts of data. With further advancements in tech, that data can be harnessed to augment our lives and even improve our health.

DISINFORMATION

Our unprecedented access to information and content creation tools are a blessing in many ways, but they can also be a curse. This is the malicious side of information overload.

RINSE, REPEAT: THE FAKE NEWS CYCLE

In recent years, the internet has seen a flood of misleading, hyperbolic, and outright false content. Not surprisingly, there are economic incentives at play.

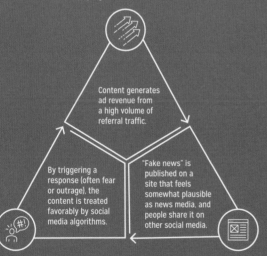

Content generates ad revenue from a high volume of referral traffic.

"Fake news" is published on a site that feels somewhat plausible as news media, and people share it on other social media.

By triggering a response (often fear or outrage), the content is treated favorably by social media algorithms.

The proliferation of fake and hyperpartisan content is largely distributed by bots. Research on Twitter found that:

 66%
of all tweeted links were shared by suspected bots.

 89%
of tweeted links to popular news aggregation sites were posted by bots.

Source: Data from Pew Research Center 2018

SUCCESS IN THE DATA-DRIVEN FUTURE MEANS GETTING COMFORTABLE WITH COMPLEXITY.

We've progressed from TV to TikTok in a single generation, so growing pains are an expected and natural part of our progression into a fully-integrated digital era. The ability to identify credible information and harness the automated tools that deliver content will be key to thriving in this strange, exciting future. Finding the signal in the noise has never been more valuable.

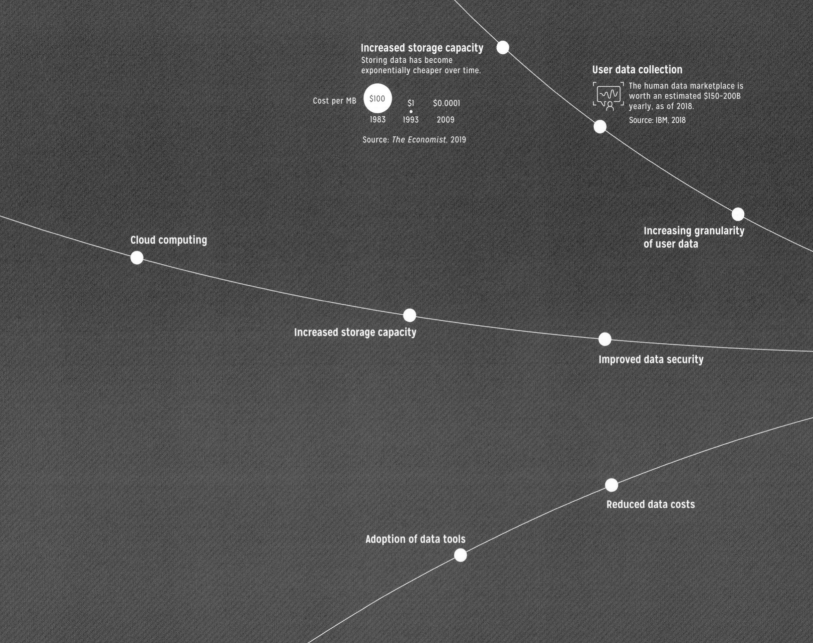

Increased storage capacity
Storing data has become
exponentially cheaper over time.

Cost per MB $100 $1 $0.0001

1983   1993   2009

Source: *The Economist*, 2019

User data collection

The human data marketplace is
worth an estimated $150–200B
yearly, as of 2018.

Source: IBM, 2018

Cloud computing

**Increasing granularity
of user data**

Increased storage capacity

Improved data security

Reduced data costs

Adoption of data tools

IT modernization

Operational data collection

Improved data analysis

In 2019, nearly 60% of chief information officers surveyed indicated that their CEO depended on them to achieve the organization's top 3 business priorities.

2019 ▐▬▬▬▬▬////////▌

60%

Source: Elumalai and Roberts, 2019

DATA AS A MOAT

DATA AS A MOAT

SIGNAL RANGE	SIGNAL-TO-NOISE RATIO
Moderate (3/5)	Moderate (3/5)

From data moats emerge business giants. Protected by their massive user bases and resultant data—big and unique data—tech giants are experiencing unfettered economic growth.

BIG TECH'S REVENUE GROWTH SINCE 2005

a. Amazon   Apple   G Alphabet   Microsoft   f Facebook

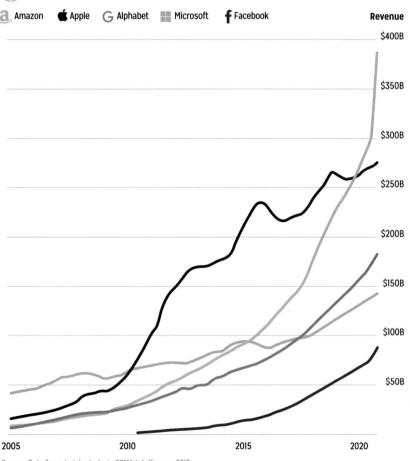

Source: Data from Jarich et al. via GSMA Intelligence 2019

AS CRITICAL BARRIERS TO ENTRY to would-be competitors, data moats have enabled Big Tech's runaway progress, leading to the burgeoning AI revolution. Composed of both user data and operational data, Big Tech's data moats are a potent form of an "economic moat."

ⓘ *Popularized by Warren Buffett in 1995, economic moats block potential market entrants from challenging a company for market share*

USER BASES THAT GIVE RISE TO DATA MOATS

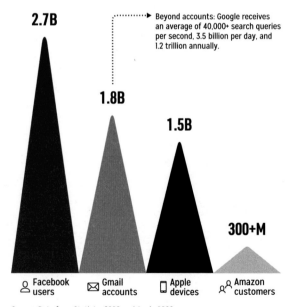

Beyond accounts: Google receives an average of 40,000+ search queries per second, 3.5 billion per day, and 1.2 trillion annually.

2.7B — Facebook users
1.8B — Gmail accounts
1.5B — Apple devices
300+M — Amazon customers

Source: Data from Statista. 2020 and Apple 2020

DATA MOATS BREED BIG TECH

The more data there are, the more Big Tech can harness the power of AI.

This is why companies like Apple and Alphabet have been gobbling up AI startups and talent at an increasingly rapid pace over the last decade.

CUMULATIVE NUMBER OF AI ACQUISITIONS
MADE BY LEADING TECH COMPANIES

Amazon · Apple · Alphabet · Microsoft · Facebook

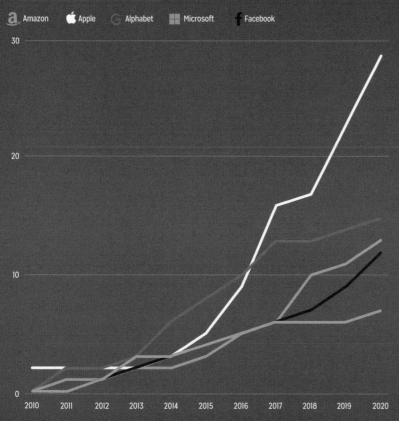

Source: CB Insights, 2019

DATA MOATS CONVERGE WITH AI APPLICATIONS

Concentration of AI acquisitions by category, 2011–Sept. 2019

>1   >20   >100

INDUSTRIES

Aerospace & defense ▶
Agriculture ▶
Consumer electronics ▶
Education ▶
Finance & insurance ▶
Government ▶
Healthcare ▶
Manufacturing ▶
Legal & compliance ▶
Media & entertainment ▶
Real estate ▶
Retail & CPG ▶
Semiconductor ▶
Transportation & logistics ▶
Travel & hospitality ▶
Utility & energy ▶
Other industries ▶

APPLICATIONS

Data management & analytics ▶
Cybersecurity ▶
Software development ▶
IT & devops ▶
Speech, NLP(G), computer vision ▶
BI & operational intelligence ▶
Process automation ▶
Sales & CRM ▶
Ad & marketing ▶
Productivity & project mgmt ▶
HR tech ▶
Other research & consultancies ▶

Sources: CB Insights, 2019

DATA MOAT FOUNDATIONS

Companies collect massive amounts of user and account holder data—from personal details like name and home address, to search terms, GPS locations, and shopping behavior. Paired with analytics, AI, and operational insights, human data provide a staggering competitive advantage for businesses.

	Google	Amazon	Apple	Facebook
Name	✓	✓	✓	✓
Phone number	✓	✓	✓	✓
Location	✓	✓	✓	✓
Physical address	✓	✓	✓	✓
Email address	✓	✓	✓	✓
Documents & spreadsheets	✓	✗	✓	✗
Calendar events	✓	✗	✓	✓
Interests	✗	✗	✓	✓
Religious & political views	✗	✗	✗	✓
Payment information	✓	✓	✓	✓
Credit card information	✗	✓	✗	✓
Purchase history	✓	✓	✗	✓
Chat and messages	✓	✗	✗	✓
Websites visited	✓	✓	✓	✓
Browsing history	✓	✓	✗	✓
Search history	✓	✓	✗	✓
Videos watched	✓	✓	✗	✓
Photos uploaded	✓	✓	✓	✓
Usage data	✗	✓	✗	✓
Interaction between apps, browsers, and devices	✓	✓	✓	✓

Source: Data from Vigderman and Turner 2020

MANAGING MOATS & AI: MIGRATION TO CLOUD STORAGE

Continued cloud adoption and IT modernization are critical to the success of the AI revolution. In tandem, they are crucial to data management and the proliferation of AI and associated benefits.

WORKLOAD CLOUD DISTRIBUTION 2019 VS 2022

Public cloud   Private cloud   On premise

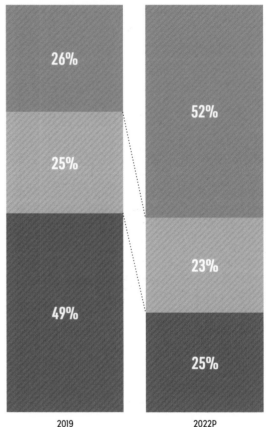

Percent of cloud-based workload

2019: 26%, 25%, 49%
2022P: 52%, 23%, 25%

Source: Elumalai and Roberts, 2019

REVENUE GENERATED FROM DATA MOATS & AI

Directly and indirectly, the bulk of Big Tech's revenue is thanks to the leveraging of its user data, analytics, and AI application. Even in the case of ecommerce juggernaut Amazon, much of its retail revenue can be attributed to its proprietary user data, where analytics and AI tap into consumer spending patterns.

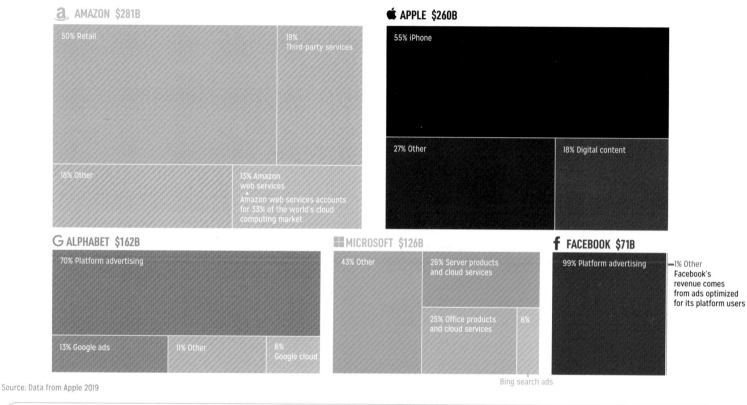

a AMAZON $281B

- 50% Retail
- 19% Third-party services
- 18% Other
- 13% Amazon web services
  - Amazon web services accounts for 33% of the world's cloud computing market

🍎 APPLE $260B

- 55% iPhone
- 27% Other
- 18% Digital content

G ALPHABET $162B

- 70% Platform advertising
- 13% Google ads
- 11% Other
- 6% Google cloud

⊞ MICROSOFT $126B

- 43% Other
- 26% Server products and cloud services
- 25% Office products and cloud services
- 6% Bing search ads

f FACEBOOK $71B

- 99% Platform advertising
- 1% Other

Facebook's revenue comes from ads optimized for its platform users

Source: Data from Apple 2019

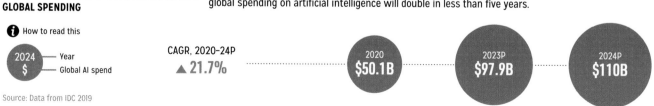

CONTINUED AI INVESTMENT
GLOBAL SPENDING

While Big Tech improves its business with user data and AI, it is far from alone. It's estimated that global spending on artificial intelligence will double in less than five years.

ℹ How to read this

2024 $ — Year
— Global AI spend

CAGR, 2020–24P
▲ 21.7%

- 2020 $50.1B
- 2023P $97.9B
- 2024P $110B

Source: Data from IDC 2019

GLOBAL IMPACT OF DATA AND AI INVESTMENT

While the entire globe stands to gain from investment in and adoption of AI, North America and China are the expected economic winners. Developing nations will see fewer gains due to lower rates of technological adoption.

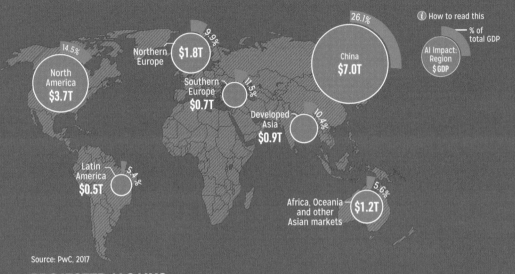

26.1%

China
$7.0T

14.5%
North America
$3.7T

9.9%
Northern Europe
$1.8T

11.5%
Southern Europe
$0.7T

10.4%
Developed Asia
$0.9T

5.4%
Latin America
$0.5T

5.6%
Africa, Oceania and other Asian markets
$1.2T

ⓘ How to read this
— % of total GDP
AI Impact: Region $ GDP

Source: PwC, 2017

PROJECTED AI GAINS PERSONALIZED SERVICE AND QUALITY

From high-quality personalized experiences to improved productivity, AI is expected to impact industries at both the operational and service level.

Global GDP impact of AI

ⓘ The AI market is expected to reach $733.7 billion by 2027
Source: Grand View Research, 2020

- ◯ Labor productivity
- ⬤ Personalization
- ◯ Time saved
- ◯ Quality

By 2030, AI's global economic contribution is estimated to reach $15.7T

Global GDP expected to rise 14% due to AI

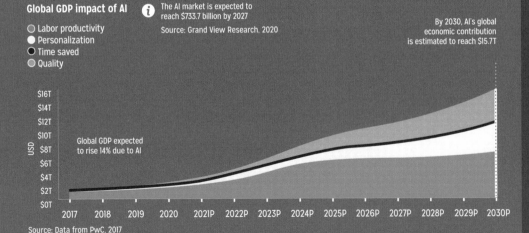

Source: Data from PwC, 2017

DATA AND AI ACROSS INDUSTRIES

With decreasing costs associated with cloud storage and data analysis, companies large and small will be able to better harness data moats and AI integrations. Sectors like healthcare and the automotive industry are likely to be affected the most.

POTENTIAL AI CONSUMPTION IMPACT*

◖ Impact scale: 1–5

SECTOR	SUBSECTOR
Healthcare **3.7**	Providers/health services Pharma/life sciences Insurance Consumer health
Automotive **3.7**	OEM Aftermarket and repair Component suppliers Personal mobility as a service Financing
Financial services **3.3**	Asset wealth management Banking and capital Insurance
Transportation and logistics **3.2**	Transportation Logistics
Technology, communications, **3.1** and entertainment	Technology Entertainment, media, and communication
Retail **3.0**	Consumer products Retail
Energy **2.2**	Oil and gas Power and utilities
Manufacturing **2.2**	Industrial manufacturing Industrial products/raw materials

*Based on PwC's AI impact index evaluation. Scale of 1–5, with 5 being the highest potential impact due to AI.

Source: Data from PwC, 2017

AI ADOPTION MATURITY

The quickest AI adoption is likely to be led by retailers, which is already evidenced by ecommerce leader Amazon.

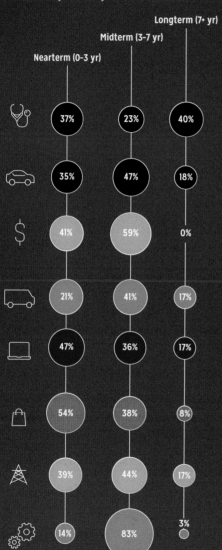

Nearterm (0–3 yr)	Midterm (3–7 yr)	Longterm (7+ yr)
37%	23%	40%
35%	47%	18%
41%	59%	0%
21%	41%	17%
47%	36%	17%
54%	38%	8%
39%	44%	17%
14%	83%	3%

Source: Data from PwC, 2017

"I LOOK FOR ECONOMIC CASTLES PROTECTED BY UNBREACHABLE MOATS."

—Warren Buffett, chairman and CEO, Berkshire Hathaway

There's much to be learned from tech giants. Their economic dominance is largely attributable to their creation of wide and deep data moats. Initially built on user data, those moats have compounded in power over time.

With improvements in cloud technology, analytics tools, and the emergence of AI, data moats gain strength. And the possibility for new data-based empires grows.

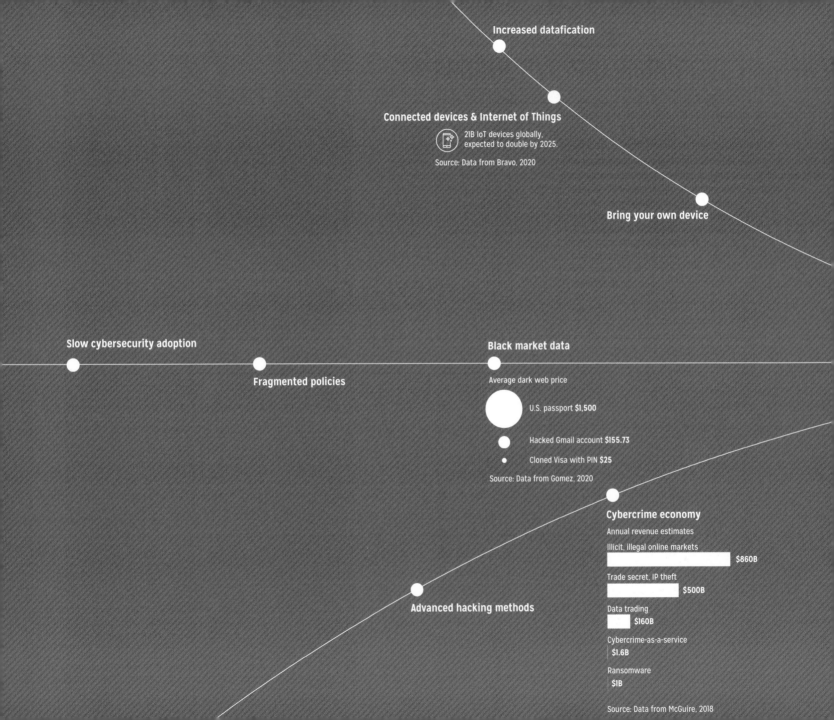

Increased datafication

Connected devices & Internet of Things

21B IoT devices globally,
expected to double by 2025.

Source: Data from Bravo, 2020

Bring your own device

Slow cybersecurity adoption

Black market data

Fragmented policies

Average dark web price

U.S. passport **$1,500**

Hacked Gmail account **$155.73**

Cloned Visa with PIN **$25**

Source: Data from Gomez, 2020

Cybercrime economy

Annual revenue estimates

Illicit, illegal online markets

$860B

Trade secret, IP theft

$500B

Advanced hacking methods

Data trading

$160B

Cybercrime-as-a-service

$1.6B

Ransomware

$1B

Source: Data from McGuire, 2018

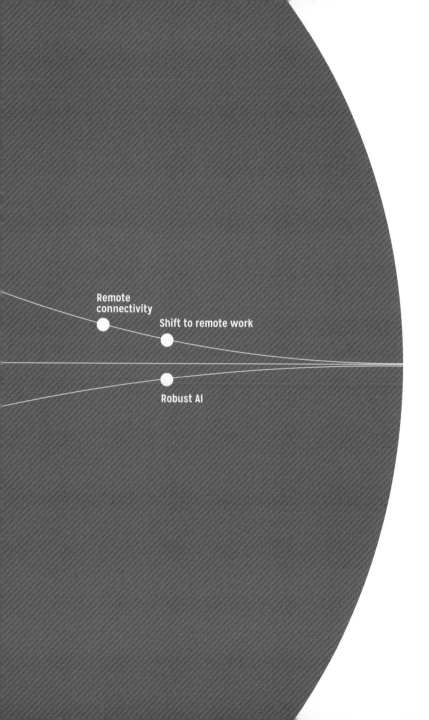

Remote
connectivity

Shift to remote work

Robust AI

CYBER'S WILD WEST

CYBER'S WILD WEST

SIGNAL RANGE
Broad (4/5)

SIGNAL-TO-NOISE RATIO
Moderate (3/5)

The digital frontier has introduced new vulnerabilities across industries, with rapid exploitation by cyber criminals over the past 15 years. Cyber resilience will be increasingly crucial for the future.

SIGNAL
DATA BREACHES U.S. 2005-2019

DATA BREACHES AND RECORDS EXPOSED ━ Data breaches ━ Millions of records exposed

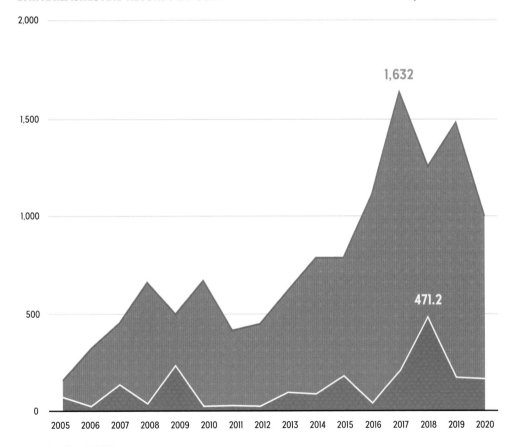

Source: Data from ITRC, 2021

CYBER WEAPONRY is reshaping the way we think about crime and warfare. It strikes with invisible force, in 0s and 1s, compromising hundreds of thousands of machines at once.

Nation state cyber warfare is also becoming increasingly costly. Disinformation campaigns, malware injections, and phishing attacks are common occurrences, and the average cost of a data breach is now $3.9 million. The implications are steep, with future elections and critical national infrastructure at stake.

ONLY 3-IN-1,000 CYBER INCIDENTS EVER SEE AN ARREST

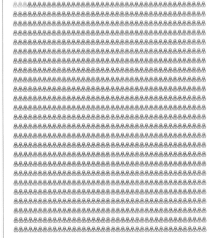

Source: Data from Eoyang et al., 2018

NATION STATE ATTACKS

Backed by sizable government budgets, nation state attacks were the most financially damaging, but least frequent across threat actors.

Costliest threat actors   ● Share of malicious breaches per threat actor type

Average total cost   Malicious breach share, %

Source: IBM, 2020

MOST TARGETED INDUSTRIES

Cyber criminals target the financial services industry to access online banking accounts and transfer credentials, among a mountain of other sensitive data.

Share of attacks on the top 10 most targeted industries

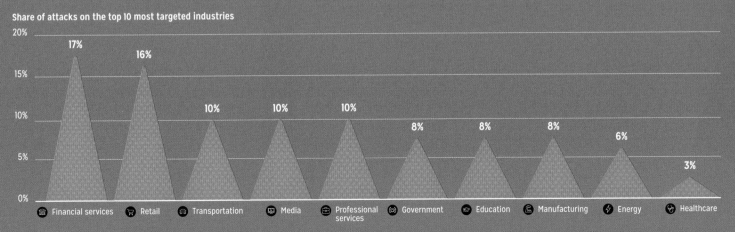

Source: IBM 2020, F-Secure, 2019

WHAT'S AT STAKE?

When troves of personal data are leaked, the range of consequences can vary widely from nuisance spam calls to devastating financial losses.

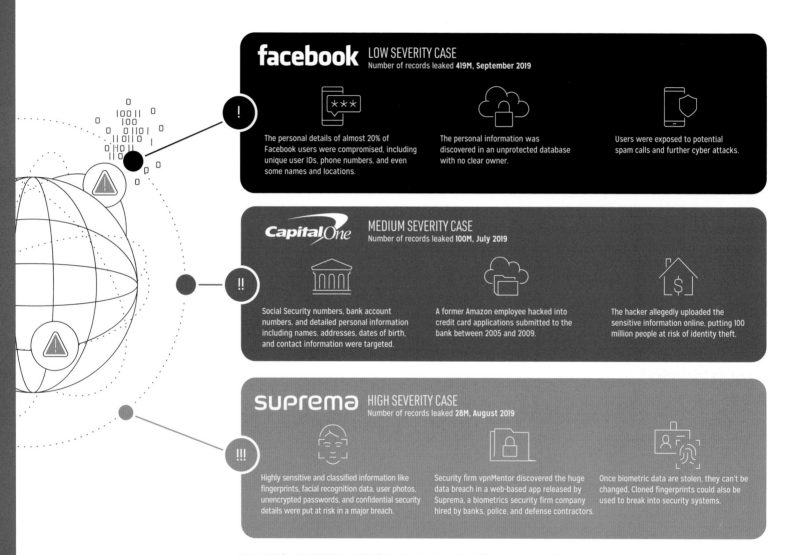

facebook — LOW SEVERITY CASE
Number of records leaked **419M, September 2019**

The personal details of almost 20% of Facebook users were compromised, including unique user IDs, phone numbers, and even some names and locations.

The personal information was discovered in an unprotected database with no clear owner.

Users were exposed to potential spam calls and further cyber attacks.

CapitalOne — MEDIUM SEVERITY CASE
Number of records leaked **100M, July 2019**

Social Security numbers, bank account numbers, and detailed personal information including names, addresses, dates of birth, and contact information were targeted.

A former Amazon employee hacked into credit card applications submitted to the bank between 2005 and 2009.

The hacker allegedly uploaded the sensitive information online, putting 100 million people at risk of identity theft.

SUPREMA — HIGH SEVERITY CASE
Number of records leaked **28M, August 2019**

Highly sensitive and classified information like fingerprints, facial recognition data, user photos, unencrypted passwords, and confidential security details were put at risk in a major breach.

Security firm vpnMentor discovered the huge data breach in a web-based app released by Suprema, a biometrics security firm company hired by banks, police, and defense contractors.

Once biometric data are stolen, they can't be changed. Cloned fingerprints could also be used to break into security systems.

Source: Data from databreaches.net, IDTheftCentre and media reports via McCandless, D. et al. 2020

GLOBAL BREACHES

No country is immune to online security breaches; however, the U.S. faces by far the highest potential in financial damage.

AVERAGE COST A BREACH BY REGION ● 2019 ● 2020

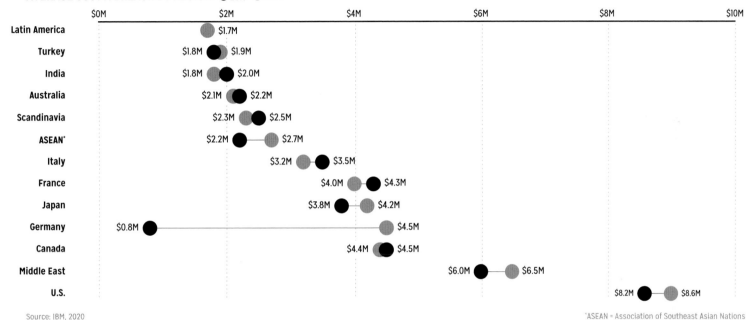

Region	2019	2020
Latin America		$1.7M
Turkey	$1.8M	$1.9M
India	$1.8M	$2.0M
Australia	$2.1M	$2.2M
Scandinavia	$2.3M	$2.5M
ASEAN*	$2.2M	$2.7M
Italy	$3.2M	$3.5M
France	$4.0M	$4.3M
Japan	$3.8M	$4.2M
Germany	$0.8M	$4.5M
Canada	$4.4M	$4.5M
Middle East	$6.0M	$6.5M
U.S.	$8.2M	$8.6M

Source: IBM, 2020

*ASEAN = Association of Southeast Asian Nations

MILLIONS IN DAMAGES

Average cost of a breach
2020 **$3.86M**

Average time to identify and contain
2020 **280 days**

Companies using AI-enabled security automations
2020 **59% of organizations**

Source: IBM, 2020

CATCHING UP TO CYBERCRIMINALS

As cyber weaponry rapidly advances, the pressure is on for cybersecurity tactics to stay ahead of the game.

EMERGING CYBER DEFENSE TRENDS

⊙ IT governance, risk, and compliance   ⊕ Network security   ⊘ Data security   Source: Modified from CBInsights 2019

TRANSITORY
Adoption has begun, but market opportunity remains uncertain

NECESSARY
Widespread implementation is already underway

High

Industry adoption

⊙ **Container security**

⊙ **Identity-as-a-service (IDAAS)**
▲
IDAAS is projected to become a $23B market by 2025, grounded on simplifying online authentifications

⊕ **Behavioral analytics**

Automates security operations against growing automated attacks. Protects containers which allow software to run virtually, typically on the cloud
▼

⊕ **Software defined networking**

⊙ **Data provenance**

Quantum encryption secures communications through photons of light
▼

⊕ **Autonomous SOC**

⊘ **Quantum encryption**

⊙ **Cyber insurance**

⊙ **Edge intelligence**

⊙ **Disinformation defense**
▲
Large-scale tech designed to counter "deepfakes" and information attacks

⊙ **Open source security**

⊙ **Firmware security**

⊘ **Zero-knowledge proofs**

⊘ **Homomorphic encryption**

⊙ **Blockchain security**

Low ————————————— Market strength ————————————— High

EXPERIMENTAL
Few products are functional, but media interest has grown

THREATENING
Security tactic is on the edge of widespread adoption; early adopters already embracing trend

BIGGEST IMPACTS OF CYBER ATTACKS

Cyber attacks can render businesses and operations useless, affecting workforce productivity, reputation, and revenue. In addition, lack of cybersecurity can result in regulatory fines.

21%
Loss of revenue due to operational disruption

21%
Loss of customer trust

17%
Change in leadership

16%
Reputational loss

14%
Regulatory fines

12%
Drop in share price

Source: Modified from Deloitte 2019

CYBER SECURITY MARKET FORECAST

Rising attack incidents and cyber regulation are key forces behind the global cybersecurity market. By 2026, it is predicted to reach $270 billion—an 86% leap from 2018.

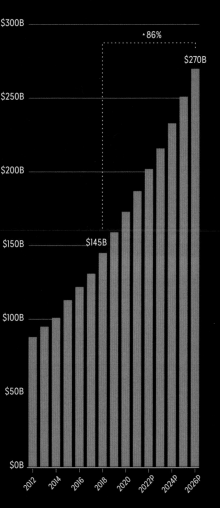

$300B

•86%

$270B

$250B

$200B

$150B · · · · · · · $145B

$100B

$50B

$0B

2012 2014 2016 2018 2020 2022P 2024P 2026P

Source: Australian Cyber Security Growth Network, 2019
USD B per annum, 2018 = latest actual data (constant exchange rates)

ANYONE CAN BE A VICTIM OF CYBER CRIME.

Even businesses and entire governments. As the world becomes ever more connected and reliant on technology, it opens the door for online hackers to exploit critical security flaws in our systems.

To combat this growing threat, our cybersecurity capabilities must match—and better yet, surpass—the sophistication of cybercriminals.

04

TECHNOLOGICAL INNOVATION

NUMBER OF SIGNALS / 04

The digital world is moving forward at a breakneck pace, but physical innovation in the realm of atoms and molecules can be just as captivating.

All over the world, scientists and technologists are making breakthroughs in a number of fields that will pave the way toward a new future. Likely the most familiar area of innovation is in semiconductors themselves, where Moore's Law continues to hold true.

But there are other groundbreaking fields where signals emerge as well. The cost of sequencing a human genome has fallen even faster than Moore's Law could have predicted. Meanwhile, the space business is about to blast off, although it's moving in a completely different direction than the media might lead you to believe.

Finally, in the more established field of telecommunications, we're also about to see the results of billions of dollars of global investment in 5G infrastructure. To break it down, we look at who will be the winners from this macro current that is expected to propel technology forward for years to come.

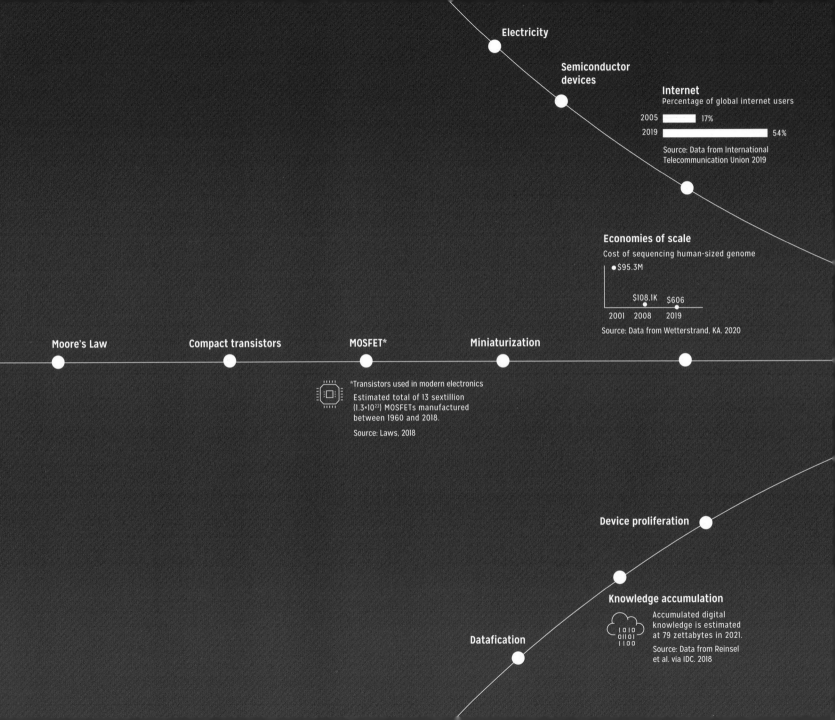

Electricity

Semiconductor devices

Internet
Percentage of global internet users

2005 ▮▮▮ 17%
2019 ▮▮▮▮▮▮▮▮ 54%

Source: Data from International
Telecommunication Union 2019

Economies of scale
Cost of sequencing human-sized genome

● $95.3M

$108.1K $606

2001   2008   2019

Source: Data from Wetterstrand, KA. 2020

Moore's Law   **Compact transistors**   **MOSFET***   **Miniaturization**

*Transistors used in modern electronics
Estimated total of 13 sextillion
(1.3•10²²) MOSFETs manufactured
between 1960 and 2018.

Source: Laws, 2018

Device proliferation

Knowledge accumulation
Accumulated digital
knowledge is estimated
at 79 zettabytes in 2021.

Source: Data from Reinsel
et al. via IDC. 2018

Datafication

"Enabling" technology

 Satellites

 Data farms

 WiFi

 Robotics

Machine learning

 DeepMind's MuZero computer program learned and mastered chess, Go, and Shogi without being taught the rules.

Source: Schrittweiser et al., 2019

SIGNAL 12

ACCELERATING TECHNOLOGY

ACCELERATING TECHNOLOGY

Advances in technology are happening exponentially, building on each other and rapidly changing the world.

 SIGNAL RANGE
Very broad (5/5)

 SIGNAL-TO-NOISE RATIO
High (4/5)

MOORE'S LAW OVER TIME
INCREASING PROCESSING POWER

Moore's Law: The number of transistors on a microchip doubles every two years, though the cost of computers is halved.

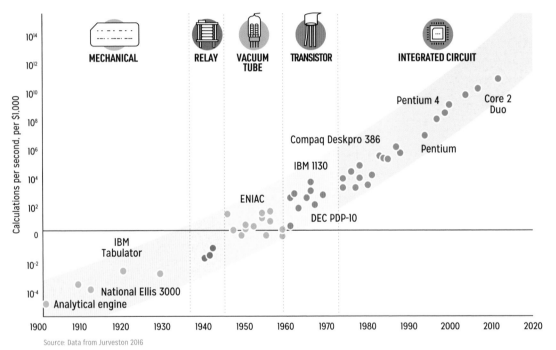

FROM THE LIGHTBULB TO AI-DRIVEN CARS, the rate of technological innovation has continued to increase. At first, Moore's Law of exponentially increasing processing power referred only to circuits. Now, we understand that rapid technological advancements started long ago, and are set to continue—bringing societal change with them.

Source: Data from Jurveston 2016

VISUALIZING TECHNOLOGY EQUIVALENTS

14,000+
Books

 = 1 Kindle

213,000
5.25" floppy disks

= 1 256GB MicroSD card

100
Kodak Box Camera No.1 (100 exposures)

 = 1 Smartphone ~10,000 photos

Source: Data from Experts Exchange 2015 via Routley, N. 2017

THE SHRINKING TIMELINE OF TECHNOLOGICAL BREAKTHROUGHS

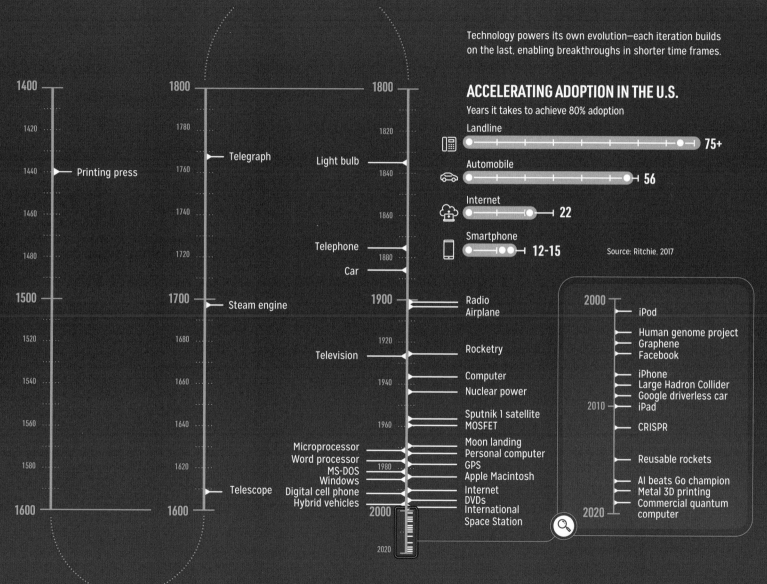

Technology powers its own evolution—each iteration builds on the last, enabling breakthroughs in shorter time frames.

ACCELERATING ADOPTION IN THE U.S.
Years it takes to achieve 80% adoption

Landline — 75+
Automobile — 56
Internet — 22
Smartphone — 12-15

Source: Ritchie, 2017

Timeline 1 (1400–1600):
- 1440 — Printing press

Timeline 2 (1800–1600):
- Telegraph
- Steam engine
- Telescope

Timeline 3 (1800–2020):
- Light bulb
- Telephone
- Car
- Radio
- Airplane
- Rocketry
- Computer
- Nuclear power
- Sputnik 1 satellite
- MOSFET
- Moon landing
- Personal computer
- GPS
- Apple Macintosh
- Internet
- DVDs
- International Space Station
- Television
- Microprocessor
- Word processor
- MS-DOS
- Windows
- Digital cell phone
- Hybrid vehicles

Timeline 4 (2000–2020):
- iPod
- Human genome project
- Graphene
- Facebook
- iPhone
- Large Hadron Collider
- Google driverless car
- iPad
- CRISPR
- Reusable rockets
- AI beats Go champion
- Metal 3D printing
- Commercial quantum computer

RAPID GROWTH ACROSS TECHNOLOGICAL FIELDS

It's not just semiconductor devices (such as circuits) that are improving exponentially. We can see evidence of Moore's Law type growth in multiple different sectors.

PERFORMANCE OF THE
500 MOST POWERFUL SUPERCOMPUTERS LOGARITHMIC

Supercomputer performance is measured in floating-point operations per second (FLOPS), the number of complex arithmetic calculations the system can complete in one second.

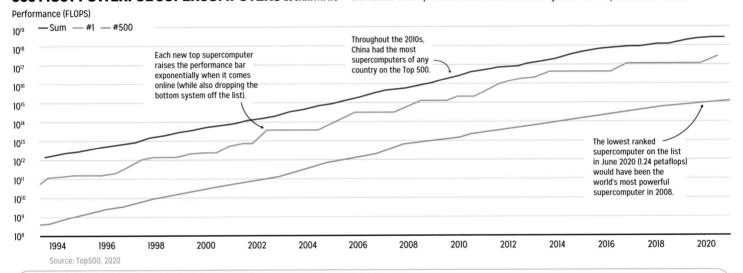

Each new top supercomputer raises the performance bar exponentially when it comes online (while also dropping the bottom system off the list).

Throughout the 2010s, China had the most supercomputers of any country on the Top 500.

The lowest ranked supercomputer on the list in June 2020 (1.24 petaflops) would have been the world's most powerful supercomputer in 2008.

Source: Top500, 2020

MACHINE-TO-MACHINE CONNECTIONS

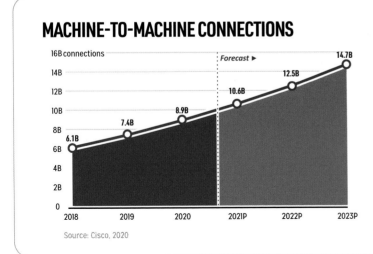

Source: Cisco, 2020

ACCUMULATED GLOBAL DATA

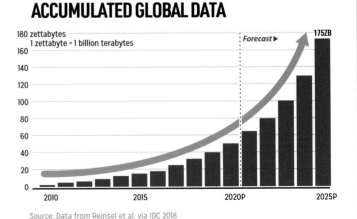

Source: Data from Reinsel et al. via IDC 2018

MORE ADVANCEMENTS (AND INVESTMENTS) ON THE HORIZON

As technology has advanced, so too has the market share of the sector and the amount of money being invested in further inventions.

SECTOR SHARE OF THE U.S. STOCK MARKET OVER TIME

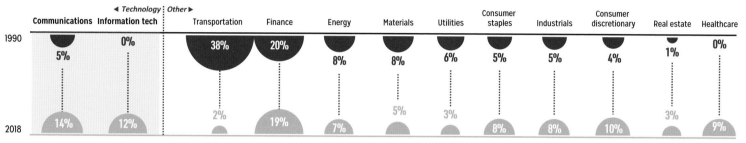

◄ Technology : Other ►

	Communications	Information tech	Transportation	Finance	Energy	Materials	Utilities	Consumer staples	Industrials	Consumer discretionary	Real estate	Healthcare
1990	5%	0%	38%	20%	8%	8%	6%	5%	5%	4%	1%	0%
2018	14%	12%	2%	19%	7%	5%	3%	8%	8%	10%	3%	9%

Source: Taylor, 2018

TOTAL R&D EXPENDITURE BY COUNTRY
BY PURCHASING POWER PARITY (PPP) AND PERCENTAGE OF GDP, USD

PPP$ % of GDP

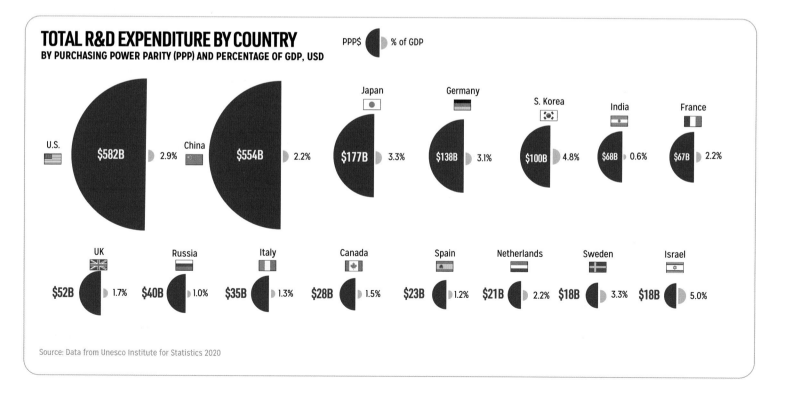

Country	PPP$	% of GDP
U.S.	$582B	2.9%
China	$554B	2.2%
Japan	$177B	3.3%
Germany	$138B	3.1%
S. Korea	$100B	4.8%
India	$68B	0.6%
France	$67B	2.2%
UK	$52B	1.7%
Russia	$40B	1.0%
Italy	$35B	1.3%
Canada	$28B	1.5%
Spain	$23B	1.2%
Netherlands	$21B	2.2%
Sweden	$18B	3.3%
Israel	$18B	5.0%

Source: Data from Unesco Institute for Statistics 2020

INCREASINGLY CONSEQUENTIAL ADVANCEMENT

Technology's momentum shows no signs of slowing down, and investors are focused on new opportunities. However, unchecked advancement may have negative consequences.

PERCEIVED BENEFITS AND CONSEQUENCES OF EMERGING TECHNOLOGIES*

Respondents answered two questions on a scale of 1-7. "How likely is this emerging technology to bring significant benefits within the next 10 years?" and "How likely is this emerging technology to bring severe negative consequences within the next 10 years?"

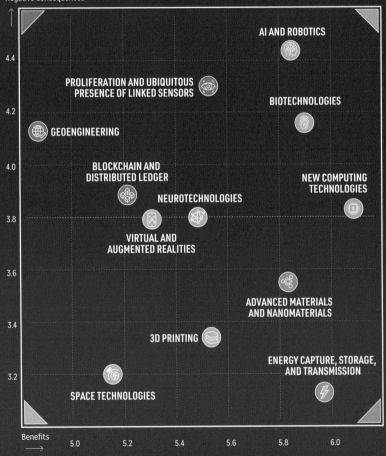

Negative consequences

- AI AND ROBOTICS
- PROLIFERATION AND UBIQUITOUS PRESENCE OF LINKED SENSORS
- BIOTECHNOLOGIES
- GEOENGINEERING
- BLOCKCHAIN AND DISTRIBUTED LEDGER
- NEW COMPUTING TECHNOLOGIES
- NEUROTECHNOLOGIES
- VIRTUAL AND AUGMENTED REALITIES
- ADVANCED MATERIALS AND NANOMATERIALS
- 3D PRINTING
- ENERGY CAPTURE, STORAGE, AND TRANSMISSION
- SPACE TECHNOLOGIES

Benefits

PERCENTAGE OF LEADERS WHO SAY TECHNOLOGY NEEDS BETTER GOVERNANCE*

Respondents selected three emerging technologies they believe most need better governance.

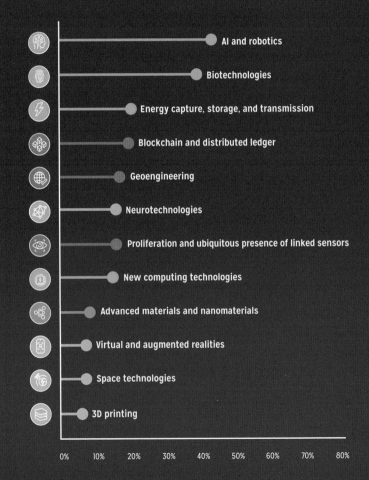

- AI and robotics
- Biotechnologies
- Energy capture, storage, and transmission
- Blockchain and distributed ledger
- Geoengineering
- Neurotechnologies
- Proliferation and ubiquitous presence of linked sensors
- New computing technologies
- Advanced materials and nanomaterials
- Virtual and augmented realities
- Space technologies
- 3D printing

Source: World Economic Forum, 2016

*Based on a survey of 745 leaders in business, government, academia, and nongovernmental organizations.

TECH IPOs AND PROCEEDS IN THE U.S.

Innovation and investor interest are thriving in the tech sector.

▪▪▪▪▪ Number of IPOs   ◖ IPO proceeds in billion USD

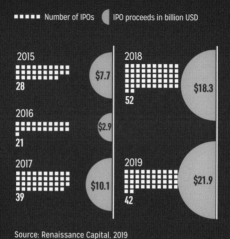

2015
28    $7.7

2016
21    $2.9

2017
39    $10.1

2018
52    $18.3

2019
42    $21.9

Source: Renaissance Capital, 2019

SEMICONDUCTORS AS A PERCENTAGE OF TOTAL VEHICLE COST

All automotive electronics:

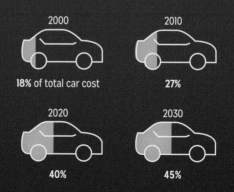

2000
18% of total car cost

2010
27%

2020
40%

2030
45%

Source: Data from IDC 2020

TECHNOLOGY IS ADVANCING AT LIGHTNING SPEED.

It has become entrenched in nearly every industry, with an almost endless array of applications. While technological innovation creates promising opportunities for investors and consumers alike, the resulting disruption can cause challenges as well.

In some cases, technology is so successful it outstrips our ability to properly manage it. The global semiconductor supply crunch and content moderation problems on social media are two examples of this in action. Properly managing the quickening pace of innovation will be a key challenge for decision-makers and business leaders as the 21st century progresses.

Demand for high speed

Increased data consumption

Aging 4G infrastructure

```
3G              WLAN
2000            2004
    |————•————————•————|
        LTE                |
        2008               |
    |————•——————————|
                5G
                2019
            •————————•
```

Rollout of 5G standard

3GPP is the global mobile technology
standards organization.

Source: 3GPP, 2020

Backing infrastructure

Network installation race

5G node installations

Global 5G infrastructure market size, USD

$50.6B   ⟶ 2026P
                CAGR: 76.3%

$0.7B
   ○   ⟶ 2018

Source: Data from Business Insights 2019

Vehicles & machinery

Connected cars are estimated
to make up 39% of the global
5G IoT endpoint market by 2023.

28%↑

11%   39%
2020   2023P

Source: Gartner, 2019

Next-gen smartphones

New AI functionality

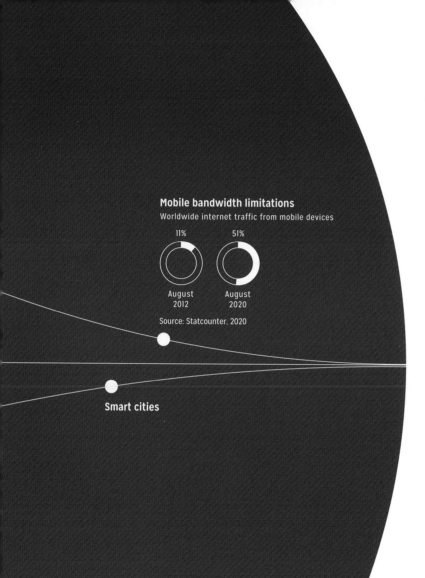

Mobile bandwidth limitations
Worldwide internet traffic from mobile devices

11%

51%

August
2012

August
2020

Source: Statcounter, 2020

Smart cities

THE 5G REVOLUTION

THE 5G REVOLUTION

The adoption and potential of 5G networks will transform life and business over the next decade.

SIGNAL RANGE	SIGNAL-TO-NOISE RATIO
Very broad (5/5)	High (4/5)

FORECAST 5G IoT UNIT SALES
BY APPLICATION

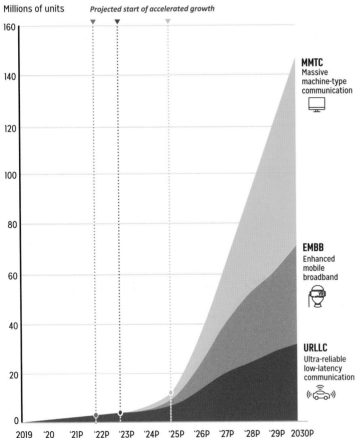

Millions of units   *Projected start of accelerated growth*

MMTC
Massive machine-type communication

EMBB
Enhanced mobile broadband

URLLC
Ultra-reliable low-latency communication

2019 '20 '21P '22P '23P '24P '25P '26P '27P '28P '29P 2030P

Source: McKinsey & Company, 2020

THE NEXT GENERATION OF MOBILE NETWORKS has been heralded for a long time, but 5G is already here and making an impact.

Across cities, industries, and many aspects of life, that impact will be transformational. Not only does 5G offer exponential improvements over current wireless standards, it will also unlock a new wave of AI and Internet of Things (IoT) capabilities.

The race to capitalize—and control—this enabling technology is on.

HOW 5G COMPARES TO WIRELESS STANDARDS

— 5G   — 4G   — Wi-Fi 6   — Narrowband IoT

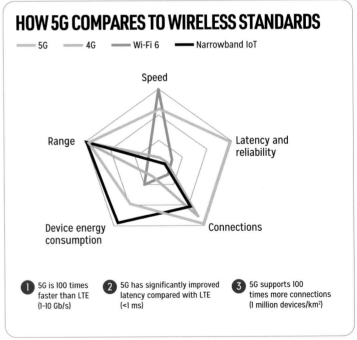

1. 5G is 100 times faster than LTE (1–10 Gb/s)
2. 5G has significantly improved latency compared with LTE (<1 ms)
3. 5G supports 100 times more connections (1 million devices/km²)

THE GLOBAL ROLLOUT OF 5G NETWORKS

5G is on track to surpass 4G and other network standards in terms of connections and usage.

USE CASES OF 5G BY EXPECTED NETWORK MATURITY

Single network launched — Multiple networks launched — Fully launched

SWEDEN
NORWAY
UNITED KINGDOM
FINLAND
IRELAND
GERMANY
LATVIA
POLAND
NETHERLANDS
HUNGARY
BELGIUM
SWITZERLAND
ROMANIA
AUSTRIA
SPAIN
ITALY

CANADA
U.S.

KUWAIT
BAHRAIN
QATAR
UNITED ARAB EMIRATES
OMAN
SAUDI ARABIA

SOUTH KOREA
JAPAN
CHINA

THAILAND
PHILIPPINES
MALDIVES

TRINIDAD AND TOBAGO

AUSTRALIA
SOUTH AFRICA
NEW ZEALAND

Source: GSMA, 2020

PROJECTED GLOBAL 5G ADOPTION, 2025
BY % OF COUNTRY'S MOBILE NETWORK

%	Region
50%	China, Japan, South Korea
48%	North America
34%	Europe
22%	Rest of Asia
21%	GCC Arab States
20%	Global average
12%	Russia & CIS
7%	Latin America
4%	Rest of MENA
3%	Sub-Saharan Africa

Source: GSMA, 2020

USE CASES OF 5G BY EXPECTED NETWORK MATURITY

2019 — Enhanced mobile broadband / Fixed wireless access

2020 — Public safety comms. / Smart home

2021 — Consumer AR/VR (retail)

2022 — Smart factory (real-time remote control)

2023 — Fleet and inventory managment and tracking / AR/VR in healthcare

2024 — Energy and utility / Autonomous cars / Real-time banking

2025 — Widespread IoT smart cities and agriculture

5G NETWORK CAPACITY

Speed: 1-5 Gbps
Latency: <20 ms

Speed: 10 Gbps
Latency: <10 ms

Reliability: 99.99%
Latency: <5 ms

Reliability: 99.99%
Latency: <1 ms

Reliability: >10 year battery
Devices: up to 1 m/km²

Source: Data from Pwc 2020

5G BUSINESS TRANSFORMATION

5G will enable $13.2 trillion in global sales activity in 2035.

IMPACT OF 5G BY INDUSTRY AND CASE CATEGORY

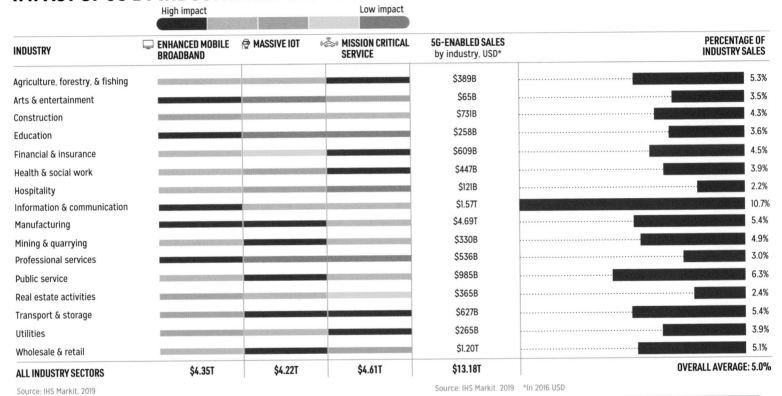

High impact — Low impact

INDUSTRY	ENHANCED MOBILE BROADBAND	MASSIVE IOT	MISSION CRITICAL SERVICE	5G-ENABLED SALES by industry, USD*	PERCENTAGE OF INDUSTRY SALES
Agriculture, forestry, & fishing				$389B	5.3%
Arts & entertainment				$65B	3.5%
Construction				$731B	4.3%
Education				$258B	3.6%
Financial & insurance				$609B	4.5%
Health & social work				$447B	3.9%
Hospitality				$121B	2.2%
Information & communication				$1.57T	10.7%
Manufacturing				$4.69T	5.4%
Mining & quarrying				$330B	4.9%
Professional services				$536B	3.0%
Public service				$985B	6.3%
Real estate activities				$365B	2.4%
Transport & storage				$627B	5.4%
Utilities				$265B	3.9%
Wholesale & retail				$1.20T	5.1%
ALL INDUSTRY SECTORS	**$4.35T**	**$4.22T**	**$4.61T**	**$13.18T**	**OVERALL AVERAGE: 5.0%**

Source: IHS Markit, 2019

Source: IHS Markit, 2019   *In 2016 USD

FORECAST B2B UNIT SALES OF 5G IoT DEVICES IN MILLIONS

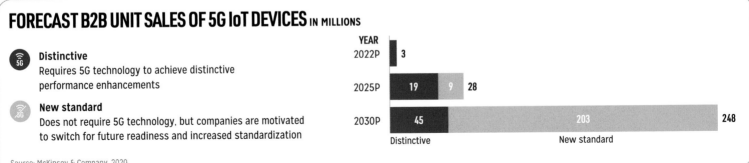

Distinctive
Requires 5G technology to achieve distinctive performance enhancements

New standard
Does not require 5G technology, but companies are motivated to switch for future readiness and increased standardization

YEAR		
2022P	3	
2025P	19 / 9	28
2030P	45 / 203	248

Distinctive   New standard

Source: McKinsey & Company, 2020

MAKING THE 5G TRANSFORMATION HAPPEN

Private and public sector anticipation around the economic benefits of 5G are fueling its rapid growth.

5G B2B UNIT SALES BY SEGMENT 2030 FORECAST

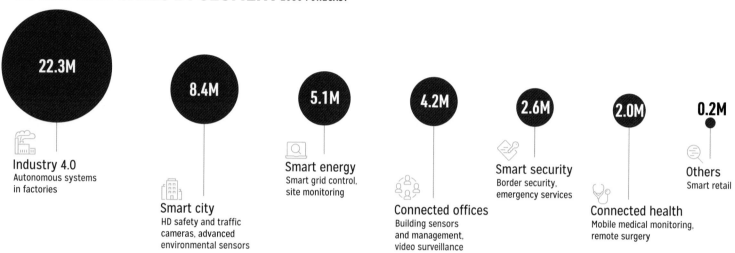

22.3M
Industry 4.0
Autonomous systems
in factories

8.4M
Smart city
HD safety and traffic
cameras, advanced
environmental sensors

5.1M
Smart energy
Smart grid control,
site monitoring

4.2M
Connected offices
Building sensors
and management,
video surveillance

2.6M
Smart security
Border security,
emergency services

2.0M
Connected health
Mobile medical monitoring,
remote surgery

0.2M
Others
Smart retail

Source: McKinsey & Company, 2020

GLOBAL ECONOMIC IMPACT OF 5G SECTOR 2035 FORECAST

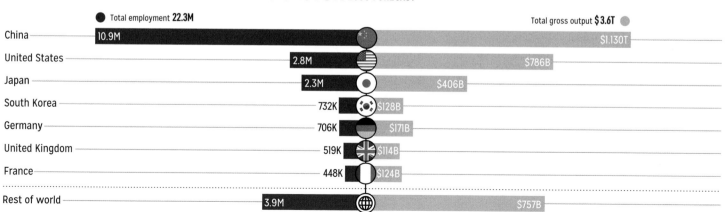

● Total employment **22.3M**   Total gross output **$3.6T** ●

Country	Total employment	Total gross output
China	10.9M	$1.130T
United States	2.8M	$786B
Japan	2.3M	$406B
South Korea	732K	$128B
Germany	706K	$171B
United Kingdom	519K	$114B
France	448K	$124B
Rest of world	3.9M	$757B

Source: IHS Markit, 2019

PRODUCTIVE AND DISRUPTIVE TRANSFORMATION

The 5G transformation is expected to significantly affect productivity. At the same time, it will also bring about disruption and widen the gap between those with 5G and those without.

EXPECTED SECTORS FOR LARGEST 5G DISRUPTION BY COMMUNICATION SERVICE PROVIDERS

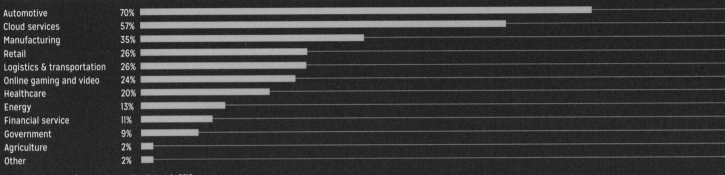

Sector	Percent
Automotive	70%
Cloud services	57%
Manufacturing	35%
Retail	26%
Logistics & transportation	26%
Online gaming and video	24%
Healthcare	20%
Energy	13%
Financial service	11%
Government	9%
Agriculture	2%
Other	2%

Source: Business Performance Innovation Network, 2019

THE POLITICAL RACE TO 5G

The disruptive nature of 5G is leading many countries to protect their domestic industries from foreign competition.

LIMITS ON HUAWEI
5G EQUIPMENT BY COUNTRY AUGUST 2020

- Allowed
- On the fence
- Unlikely to use
- Restrictions
- Ban in effect
- No position yet

Source: Data from Kennedy via Center for Strategic & International Studies 2020

Excluding licensed IoT

● 2G   ● 3G   ● 4G   ● 5G

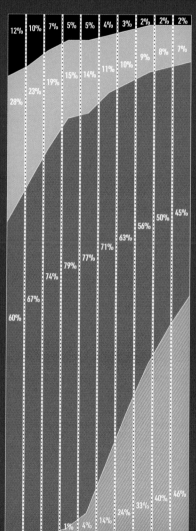

	2016	2017	2018	2019	2020	2021P	2022P	2023P	2024P	2025P
2G	12%	10%	7%	5%	5%	4%	3%	2%	2%	2%
3G	28%	23%	19%	15%	14%	11%	10%	9%	8%	7%
4G	60%	67%	74%	79%	77%	71%	63%	56%	50%	45%
5G				1%	4%	14%	24%	33%	40%	46%

Source: GSMA, 2020

THE IMPACT OF 5G IS NOT A MATTER OF "IF" BUT "WHEN."

Over the next decade, it is expected to transform a broad range of human experiences, from education to transportation.

As an enabling technology, that transformation will be largely positive. But being ready ahead of time, and taking advantage, will be vital.

Data demands

Need for connectivity

35% of all satellites launched in
2019 provide telecommunications,
the largest associated application.

Source: Euroconsult, 2019

Satellite technology shifts

**Smallsat, nanosat,
and cubesat proliferation**

**Cheaper manufacturing
for smaller satellites**

Global smallsat market projections

2020	▮▮▮▮	$2.8B	▲ CAGR of 20.5%
2025P	▮▮▮▮▮▮▮▮	$7.1B

Source: Markets and Markets, 2020

**NASA warms up to
commercial partners**

**Launch technology
and frequency**

**Land monitoring
and tracking needs**

More than 27% of all
commercial satellites provide
Earth Observation services.

Source: UCS, 2020

Increased launch options

In 2018, SpaceX broke the record
for the most commercial rocket
launches in a single year.

Source: Mosher, 2018

SIGNAL 14

THE NEW SPACE RACE

THE NEW SPACE RACE

Space business has been heating up, sparked by a demand for data and connection.

SIGNAL RANGE
Moderate (3/5)

SIGNAL-TO-NOISE RATIO
High (4/5)

SIGNAL
ⒶⒶ SKYROCKETING SATELLITE LAUNCHES

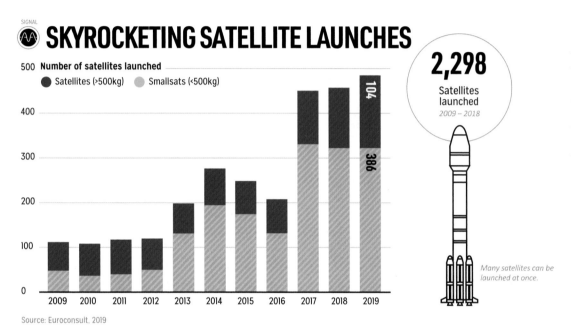

Number of satellites launched
● Satellites (>500kg)   ● Smallsats (<500kg)

500
400
300
200
100
0

2009 2010 2011 2012 2013 2014 2015 2016 2017 2018 2019

104
386

2,298
Satellites launched
2009 – 2018

Many satellites can be launched at once.

Source: Euroconsult, 2019

THE SATELLITE MARKET'S PAST AND FUTURE 2019 FORECAST

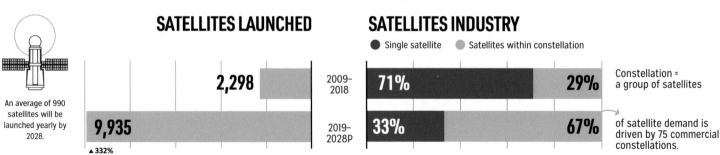

An average of 990 satellites will be launched yearly by 2028.

SATELLITES LAUNCHED

2009-2018	2,298
2019-2028P	9,935 ▲332%

SATELLITES INDUSTRY

● Single satellite   ● Satellites within constellation

	Single satellite	Satellites within constellation
2009-2018	71%	29%
2019-2028P	33%	67%

Constellation = a group of satellites

→ of satellite demand is driven by 75 commercial constellations.

THE NEW SPACE RACE isn't to the moon—it's a race toward a connected world of data and analytics. From startup visions to satellite constellations built by tech giants like Amazon, the surge in satellite missions highlights the widespread demand for data and connectivity. It also reveals the need for commercial launch capacity.

Source: Euroconsult, 2019

COUNTRIES WITH THE MOST OPERATIONAL SATELLITES

The countries leading the new space race don't look much different than they did in the 1950s. Today, the U.S. tops the world with almost half of the planet's operational satellites, followed most closely by China, then Russia.

● = 10 SATELLITES

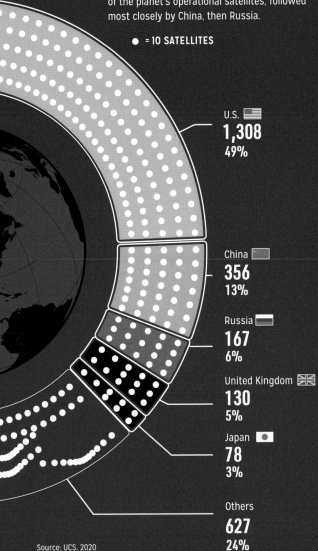

U.S. 🇺🇸
1,308
49%

China 🇨🇳
356
13%

Russia 🇷🇺
167
6%

United Kingdom 🇬🇧
130
5%

Japan 🇯🇵
78
3%

Others
627
24%

Source: UCS, 2020

OPERATIONAL SATELLITES BY PURPOSE

Of the thousands of operational satellites orbiting the globe, most have been launched for commercial purposes.

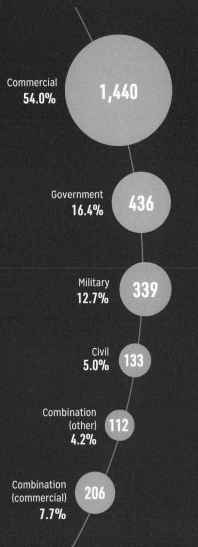

Commercial
54.0% — **1,440**

Government
16.4% — **436**

Military
12.7% — **339**

Civil
5.0% — **133**

Combination (other)
4.2% — **112**

Combination (commercial)
7.7% — **206**

Source: UCS, 2020

MAJOR COMMERCIAL PLAYERS

The U.S.'s SpaceX and Planet Labs lead commercial operators with constellations that serve applications like GPS and environmental monitoring.

Satellites as of April 2020

% OF COMMERICAL SATELLITES

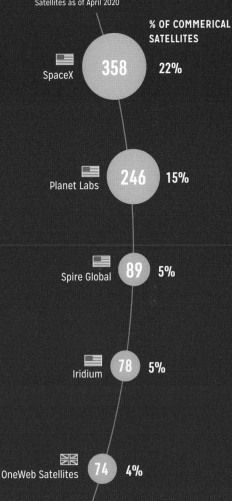

SpaceX 🇺🇸 — **358** — 22%

Planet Labs 🇺🇸 — **246** — 15%

Spire Global 🇺🇸 — **89** — 5%

Iridium 🇺🇸 — **78** — 5%

OneWeb Satellites 🇬🇧 — **74** — 4%

Source: UCS, 2020

A NEW FRONTIER

20 YEARS OF ORBITAL LAUNCHES
BY COUNTRY

China continues to lead the world in the number of orbital rocket launches performed, while in the U.S., SpaceX broke the record for the most commercial rocket launches in a single year in 2018.

CAPACITY OF MAJOR ROCKETS

Thanks to its advanced launch technology and reusable rockets, SpaceX is quickly becoming a go-to launcher for satellite payloads. Payload space is incredibly expensive, but with more frequent launches available, the costs become less astronomical.

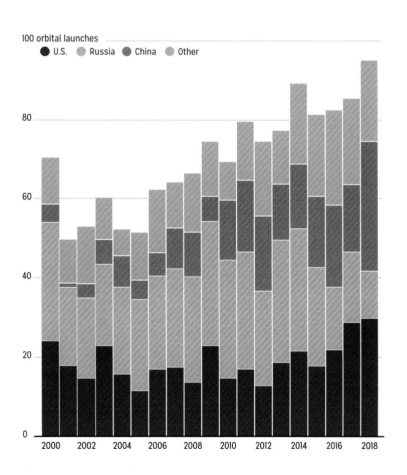

100 orbital launches
● U.S. ● Russia ● China ○ Other

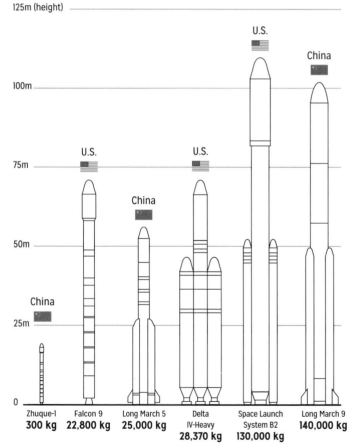

125m (height)

Zhuque-1	Falcon 9	Long March 5	Delta IV-Heavy	Space Launch System B2	Long March 9
300 kg	22,800 kg	25,000 kg	28,370 kg	130,000 kg	140,000 kg

Source: Johnson-Freese, 2018

Source: Johnson-Freese, 2018

TRIANGULATING NEW OPPORTUNITIES

Telecommunications continue to be the leading purpose of operational satellites, both commercial satellites and otherwise. Connectivity uses are followed by earth observation—for environmental monitoring, precision agriculture, etc.—and security, which includes border monitoring. GPS and navigation technologies, like those provided by the SpaceX constellation, are also common uses for satellites.

SATELLITES LAUNCHED BY PURPOSE

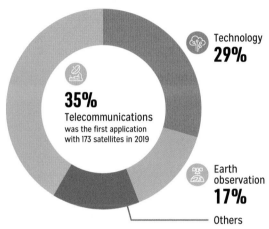

35%
Telecommunications
was the first application
with 173 satellites in 2019

Technology
29%

Earth observation
17%

Others

Source: Euroconsult, 2019

SHIFTING PRIORITIES

TOP THREE APPLICATIONS BY SATELLITE MANUFACTURING AND LAUNCH VALUE

Telecommunications   Earth observation   Security

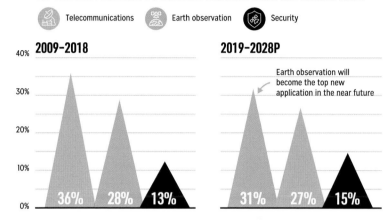

2009–2018

36%	28%	13%

2019–2028P

Earth observation will become the top new application in the near future

31%	27%	15%

Source: Euroconsult, 2019

ALL OPERATIONAL COMMERCIAL SATELLITES BY USE TYPE

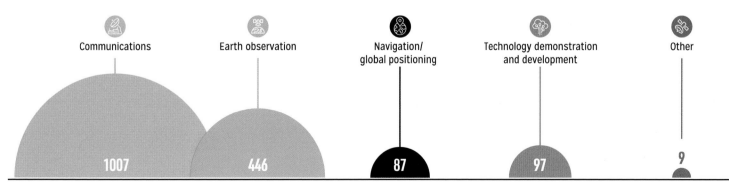

Communications	Earth observation	Navigation/ global positioning	Technology demonstration and development	Other
1007	446	87	97	9

Source: UCS, 2020

SHOOTING FOR THE STARS

GLOBAL SPACE INDUSTRY REVENUE IMPACT
PAST AND FUTURE

Beyond Earth-based applications for satellite technology, the impact of the world's demand for connectivity will continue to spread. Sectors like manufacturing and launch services, and associated technologies, are also expected to experience huge revenue boosts.

● 2009-2018   ○ 2019-2028P

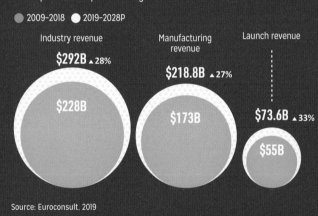

Industry revenue
$292B ▲28%
$228B

Manufacturing revenue
$218.8B ▲27%
$173B

Launch revenue
$73.6B ▲33%
$55B

Source: Euroconsult, 2019

THE SMALLSAT BOOM

From CubeSats that are smaller than a loaf of bread, to 1,000-pound smallsats—small-satellite operators like Planet Labs will continue to leverage economies of scale with their growing constellations.

SMALLSAT LAUNCH FORECAST

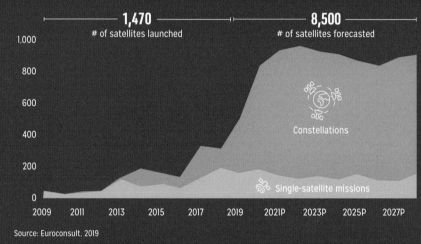

1,470
# of satellites launched

8,500
# of satellites forecasted

Constellations

Single-satellite missions

2009 2011 2013 2015 2017 2019 2021P 2023P 2025P 2027P

Source: Euroconsult, 2019

MISSED CONNECTIONS
MORE FIXED COVERAGE VIA SATELLITE

Connectivity is arguably a basic human right. With developing nations working toward increased prosperity, the growing need for fixed internet coverage is expected to be filled by satellite-led connection. Trailing markets, such as Pakistan, Bolivia, and many African nations, are unlikely to gain widespread advanced connectivity in the near term.

Source: Grijpink et al., 2020

Coverage
% of global population

● Advanced (>100 Mbps) e.g., fiber, DOCSIS 3.x   ● Intermediate (<100 Mbps) eg. VDSL   ● Basic or no coverage (<50 Mbps) eg. DSL

2018 44% 3% 52%

2030P ~55% ~45%

Low-earth orbit (LEO) has the potential to massively increase fixed connectivity coverage, although affordability could limit its adoption.

THE SPACEX EFFECT

SpaceX, founded by Elon Musk, has been changing the economics of rocket launches. The company has been able to recover major pieces of its Falcon 9 rockets, which results in a significant cost savings.

COST OF LAUNCHING A ROCKET INTO GEOSYNCHRONOUS ORBIT COST PER KG

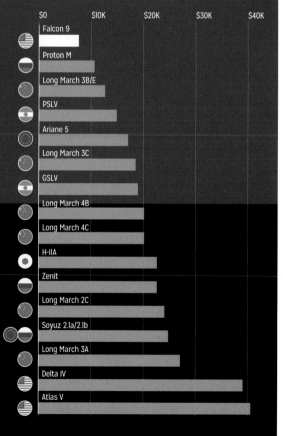

	$0	$10K	$20K	$30K	$40K
Falcon 9					
Proton M					
Long March 3B/E					
PSLV					
Ariane 5					
Long March 3C					
GSLV					
Long March 4B					
Long March 4C					
H-IIA					
Zenit					
Long March 2C					
Soyuz 2.1a/2.1b					
Long March 3A					
Delta IV					
Atlas V					

Source: Data from Federal Aviation Association, via Bloomberg 2018

ENTER THE NEW SPACE RACE.

While the media is often distracted by dreams of asteroid mining or space tourism, they seem to have missed the big picture. The new space race is already under way, and it's going to be a lucrative business fueled by the rush for more connectivity and data.

Discovery of DNA structure

DNA sequencing

Microbial DNA

 Discovery of Cas9 protein

New gene editing tools

Discovery of unique, repeating DNA sequences

The discovery of clustered DNA repeats was made independently in three parts of the world.

Netherlands

Japan

Spain

Source: Zimmer, 2015

Stem cell research

 Dolly the sheep

Dolly becomes the world's first cloned sheep.

Source: Weintraub, 2016

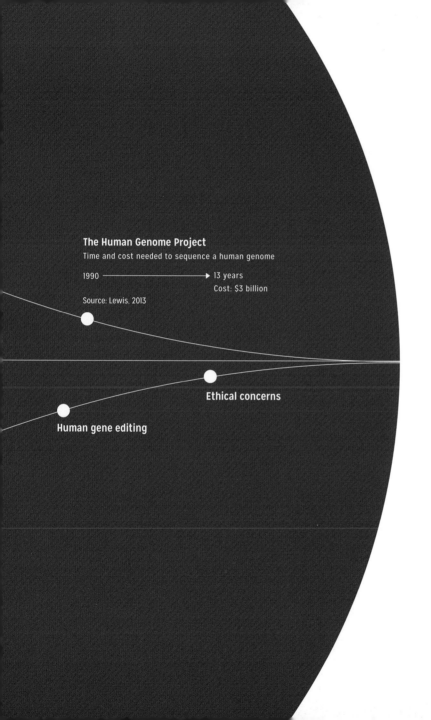

The Human Genome Project
Time and cost needed to sequence a human genome

1990 ——————————▶ 13 years
Cost: $3 billion

Source: Lewis, 2013

Human gene editing

Ethical concerns

CRISPR: GENE EDITING AT SCALE

CRISPR: GENE EDITING AT SCALE

 SIGNAL RANGE
Very broad (5/5)

 **SIGNAL-TO-NOISE RATIO**
Very high (5/5)

The speed of genetic sequencing is growing exponentially. CRISPR*—a series of DNA sequences in bacteria and archaea—has become synonymous with a type of gene editing technology.

SEQUENCING COST PER HUMAN GENOME LOGARITHMIC

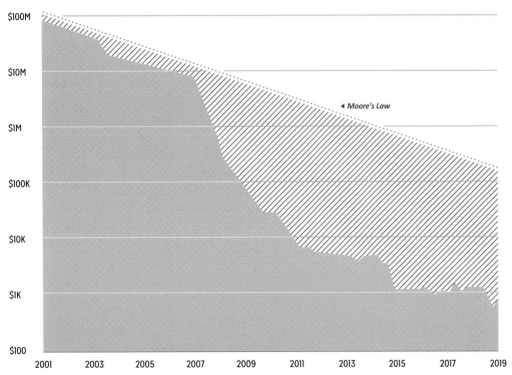

◄ Moore's Law

WHEN PEOPLE HEAR CRISPR, they think of diseases—but the scope and applications of gene editing are much wider. New tools make editing DNA cheap and easy, and more scientific advantages in the field could inevitably lead to a very different world.

WHY CRISPR MATTERS

CRISPR gene editing technology is:

 Simple, cheap, and easy to use

 4x more efficient than the next best tool (TALEN)

 More precise at targeting specific genes than previous technologies

*This technology is often referenced as CRISPR-Cas9, but we'll refer to it as CRISPR throughout this chapter.

Source: Data from Wetterstrand, KA. 2020

HOW DOES IT WORK?

CRISPR – a family of DNA sequences
Clustered **R**egularly **I**nterspaced **S**hort **P**alindromic **R**epeats

THE TOOLS

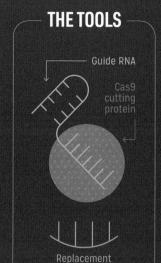

Guide RNA

Cas9 cutting protein

Replacement DNA sequence
Contains repair enzymes

Source: The Economist, 2015

STEP 1

Guided RNA finds target DNA in cell

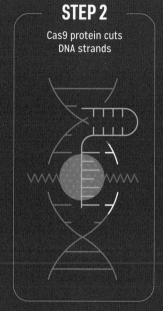

Target DNA

STEP 2

Cas9 protein cuts DNA strands

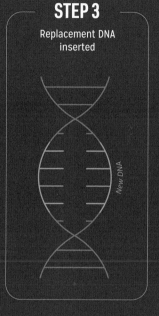

STEP 3

Replacement DNA inserted

New DNA

ⓘ *Cas9 = CRISPR associated protein 9. It acts as molecular scissors, cutting strands of DNA*

POTENTIAL APPLICATIONS

Source: Hsu, et al., 2014

Medicine

Gene surgery

Drug development

Biology

Animal models

Genetic variation

Biotech

Fuel

Food

Materials

HOW HAS CRISPR BEEN USED SO FAR?

Rising to prominence as a potential gene editing tool in a 2012 research paper, CRISPR has already been leveraged to accomplish impressive scientific and medical feats.

ANIMALS

 Reducing the severity of genetic deafness in mice

 Editing bone marrow cells in mice to treat sickle-cell anemia

 Shrinking tumors in mice caused by human prostate and liver cancer cells

 Editing out Huntington disease from mice

 Treating muscular dystrophy in dogs

CROPS

 Combining desired traits of modern and ancient tomatoes

 Desirable traits from wild tomato species were combined to create a fruit 3x larger in size and 10x larger in quantity.

 Doubling the amount of biofuel produced by algae

 Creating mushrooms that don't brown easily

HUMANS

 Removing HIV from human immune cells

 Editing the genes of twin human baby girls to resist HIV

The world's first gene-edited babies, born in China in 2018, have sparked intense debate, particularly about the ethics of gene editing.

 Editing human embryo to remove a gene that causes a form of heart disease

 Starting human trials for CRISPR cancer treatments

PHARMA

 Rapidly screening for new drug candidates

 Creating COVID-19 diagnostic tests

CRISPR can speed up the discovery process, enabling faster development of some diagnostics.

 Slowing the growth of cancerous cells

 Making 13,000 gene edits in a single cell

THE FUTURE OF CRISPR

Experts believe we have just scratched the surface with CRISPR, and they see it being used in the future to potentially:

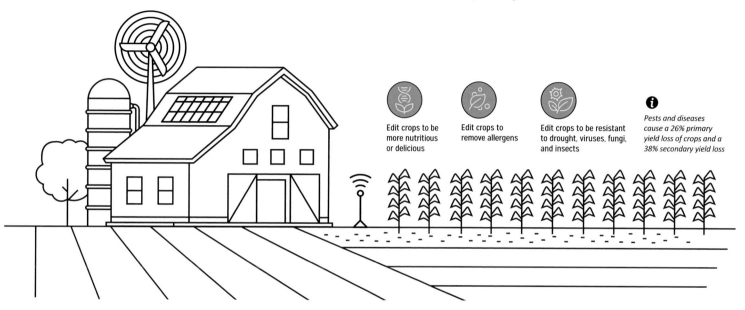

Edit crops to be more nutritious or delicious

Edit crops to remove allergens

Edit crops to be resistant to drought, viruses, fungi, and insects

Pests and diseases cause a 26% primary yield loss of crops and a 38% secondary yield loss

Control entire populations of disease-spreading animals (mosquitoes, mice, etc.)

MALARIA CASES WORLDWIDE:

228 MILLION *2018*

90%
of these in Africa

Edit the human genome to stop genetic diseases

Scientists have identified more than 10,000 inherited diseases caused by a single defective gene, including cystic fibrosis, hemophilia, and muscular dystrophy.

Create "designer babies"

This is subject to massive ethical questions and concerns, but is feasible.

Develop cells immune to cancer

Cancer was the cause of 9.6 million deaths globally in 2018.

Rewire pathogens to "destroy themselves"

Develop more powerful antivirals and antibiotics

Sources: Data from Bergan 2017

INCREDIBLE PROMISE, GROWING SCRUTINY

TOP 10 COUNTRIES BY NUMBER OF CRISPR PATENT APPLICATIONS 2019

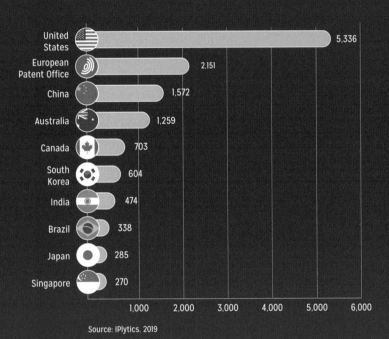

United States	5,336
European Patent Office	2,151
China	1,572
Australia	1,259
Canada	703
South Korea	604
India	474
Brazil	338
Japan	285
Singapore	270

Source: IPlytics, 2019

PUBLISHED ACADEMIC PAPERS ON CRISPR

2011	2018
<100	**>17,000**

Source: Plumer et al., 2018

"

Scientists should consult the public before applying gene editing to humans.

Percentage of people who agree with the statement above

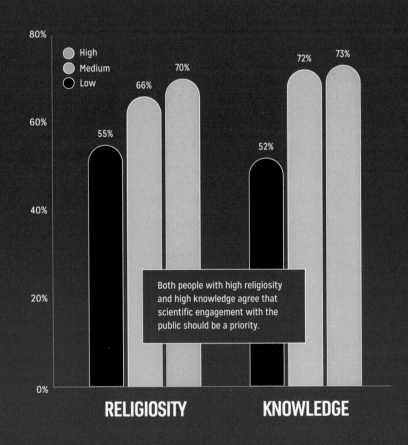

- High
- Medium
- Low

RELIGIOSITY
- 55%
- 66%
- 70%

KNOWLEDGE
- 52%
- 72%
- 73%

Both people with high religiosity and high knowledge agree that scientific engagement with the public should be a priority.

Source: Scheufele, et al., 2017

OBSTACLES TO OVERCOME

PRECISION

Even though CRISPR is more accurate than other gene editing technologies, it is still not perfect. If it "mistargets" the wrong gene, it could lead to defects or cancer, which is why human uses are limited so far.

ETHICAL

If the human germline is edited, future generations would not be able to opt out of those changes, creating an ethical dilemma. Current public opinion also is divided on human gene editing.

ⓘ *A germline is the source DNA for all other cells in the human body. Germlines that are mutated can pass directly from parent to child and become present in the offspring's cell DNA too.*

71% of U.S. adults support gene editing to protect babies from inherited diseases

12% of U.S. adults support gene editing to enhance intelligence or athletic ability

Source: AP-NORC, 2018

POLITICAL

In a 2016 report, the Obama Administration listed gene editing as a top threat to the country, under the category of potential weapons of mass destruction. Some scientists have speculated that in the wrong hands, CRISPR could be used to create plagues that wipe out staple crops or even a virus that attacks human DNA.

IS CRISPR WORTH THE RISK?

This rapidly evolving gene editing technology continues to receive growing scrutiny, and more research needs to be done to curb potential abuse.

However, over the last decade, scientists have discovered potential applications ranging from farming to pharma—and there's more to come.

05

MONEY & MARKETS

NUMBER OF SIGNALS / 06

The stock market is a prolific source of data that receives more attention and analysis than almost anything else around. There are people who spend every waking hour thinking about how to make use of this data—and at the same time, computers and automated algorithms are processing this information at breakneck speeds, just to gain the slightest edge on the competition.

However, markets are also the source of massive amounts of noise. As Benjamin Graham described, in the short-term markets can be a "voting machine" that tallies up which firms are popular and unpopular. Prices are subject to the feelings of the herd, and sentiment can swing up or down for seemingly no reason.

Over time, key data-driven signals reveal the trends that are shaping the future of money and markets. In this chapter we look at everything from monetary policy and central banks to a growing saturation in stock market indices. We highlight a crucial 700-year trend in interest rates, as well as why the life span of iconic companies is shortening.

As trends affecting global markets come to a steam in the post-COVID era, there will likely be more questions than answers going forward. But by using these signals, you can arm yourself with knowledge to be prepared for almost anything.

Credit cards are introduced in the 1950s

Corporate debt

Low borrowing costs

Insufficient profits

% of businesses with
interest expenses higher
than revenues

2016
12%

1987
2%

Low yields on corporate bonds

Highly leveraged companies

Across 14 advanced economies
Source: Banerjee and Hofmann, 2018

Federal budget deficits

Government debt

Rising debt-to-GDP ratio

Government debt, as a % of GDP.
G7 countries, average

1995 | **87%**
2018 | **134%**

100%

Source: Data from OCED 2020

Credit cards

The Diners Club Card, created in
1950, claims the title of the first
credit card in widespread use.

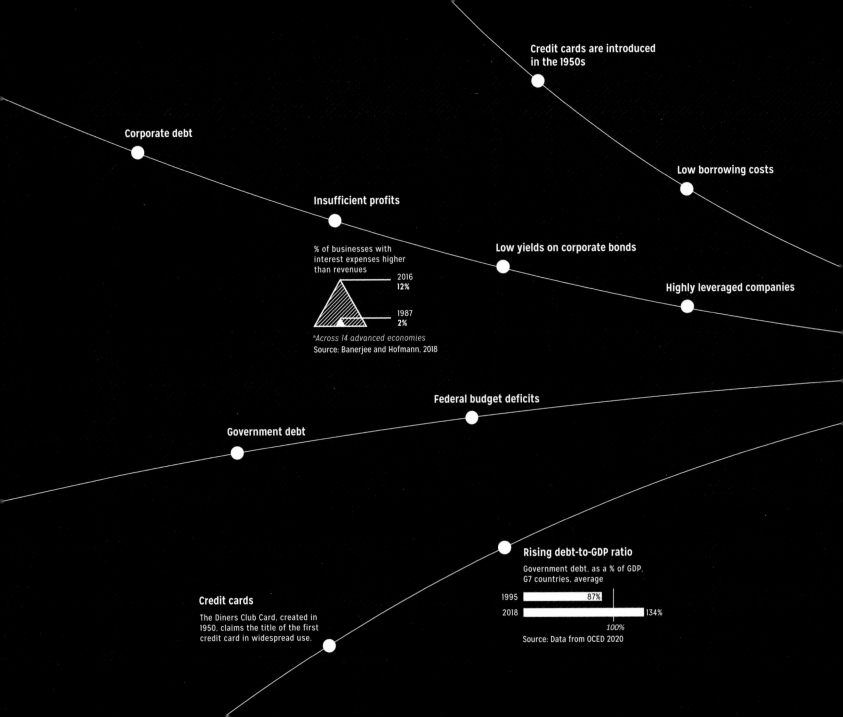

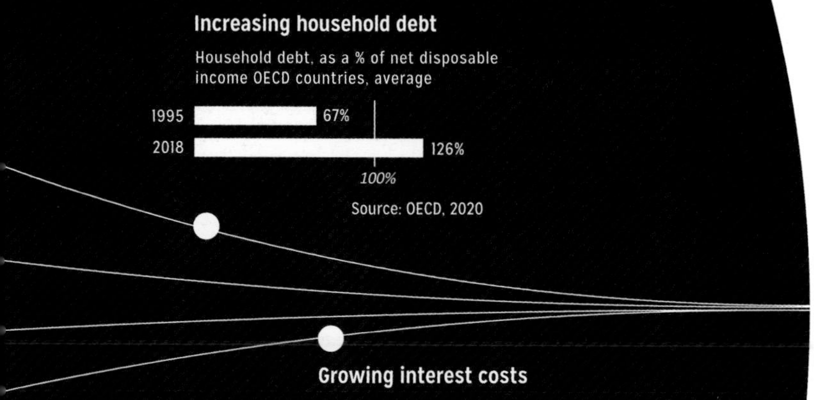

Increasing household debt

Household debt, as a % of net disposable
income OECD countries, average

1995	67%
2018	126%

100%

Source: OECD, 2020

Growing interest costs

SIGNAL 16

INDEBTED WORLD

INDEBTED WORLD

Since the 2008 Global Financial Crisis, the world has borrowed money at an alarming rate. Global debt now sits at $289T, a figure representing more than three times the world's GDP.

 SIGNAL RANGE
Very Broad (5/5)

 **SIGNAL-TO-NOISE RATIO**
High (4/5)

RISING DEBT AROUND THE WORLD

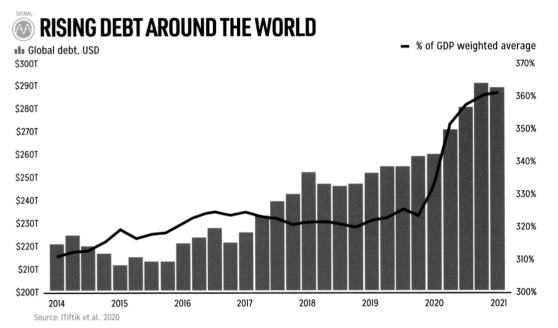

▪▪ Global debt, USD

— % of GDP weighted average

Source: ITiftik et al., 2020

CONSISTENTLY LOW INTEREST RATES have enabled governments, companies, and households to borrow at the highest levels measured since the 1970s. In the past, similar waves of debt accumulation have ended in crises.

This issue is unlikely to resolve itself anytime soon, despite the worst of the pandemic being behind us.

GLOBAL DEBT BY SECTOR USD, Q1 2021 ● Households ● Non-financial corporates ● Government ● Financial sector

Mature markets $47.4T	Emerging markets $37.1T	
Mature markets $54.9T	Emerging markets $12.6T	

Global	$53.3T	$84.5T	$83.5T	$67.5T	Total $288.8T

Mature markets $37.0T | Emerging markets $16.3T

Mature markets $63.3T | Emerging markets $20.2T

Source: Data from Tiftik et al. 2020

RISING GOVERNMENT DEBT

Many countries have seen their debt loads increase to over 90% of their GDP.

ℹ How to read this
2020 debt
2007 debt

Change in public debt from 2007 to 2020, %

-50%   0%   50%   100%   200%

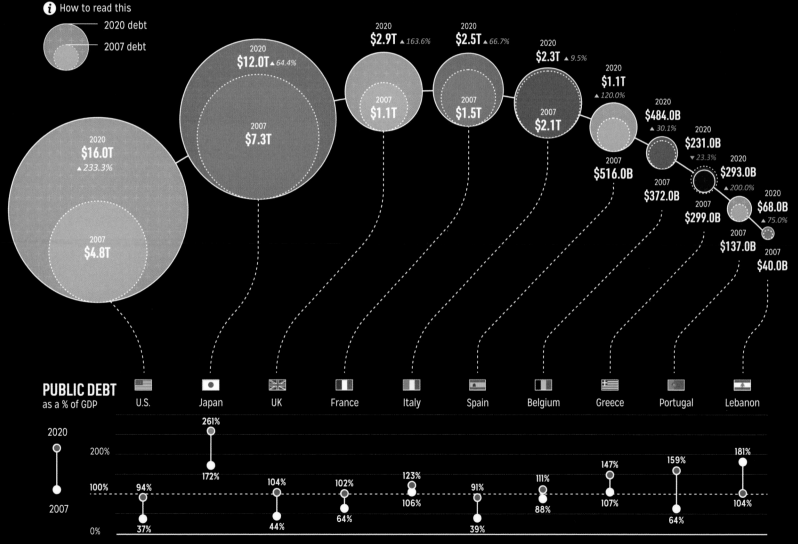

2020
$16.0T
▲ 233.3%

2007
$4.8T

2020
$12.0T ▲ 64.4%

2007
$7.3T

2020
$2.9T ▲ 163.6%

2007
$1.1T

2020
$2.5T ▲ 66.7%

2007
$1.5T

2020
$2.3T ▲ 9.5%

2007
$2.1T

2020
$1.1T
▲ 120.0%

2007
$516.0B

2020
$484.0B
▲ 30.1%

2007
$372.0B

2020
$231.0B
▼ 23.3%

2007
$299.0B

2020
$293.0B
▲ 200.0%

2007
$137.0B

2020
$68.0B
▲ 75.0%

2007
$40.0B

PUBLIC DEBT
as a % of GDP

U.S.   Japan   UK   France   Italy   Spain   Belgium   Greece   Portugal   Lebanon

2020

200%

100%

2007

0%

U.S.	Japan	UK	France	Italy	Spain	Belgium	Greece	Portugal	Lebanon
94%	261%	104%	102%	123%	91%	111%	147%	159%	181%
37%	172%	44%	64%	106%	39%	88%	107%	64%	104%

Source: Economist Intelligence Unit, 2012
2020 data as of July 2020.

COVID-19: A NEW WAVE OF GOVERNMENT BORROWING

Costly pandemic relief measures have forced governments to greatly expand their already growing debts.

ANNUAL CHANGE IN GLOBAL GOVERNMENT DEBT AS % OF GLOBAL GDP

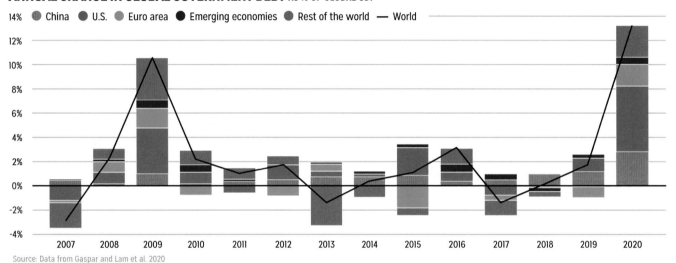

● China ● U.S. ● Euro area ● Emerging economies ● Rest of the world — World

Source: Data from Gaspar and Lam et al. 2020

FUTURE IMPLICATIONS

The increasing costs of servicing this debt could cannibalize future investment in areas such as healthcare and education.

NET INTEREST COSTS ON U.S. GOVERNMENT DEBT

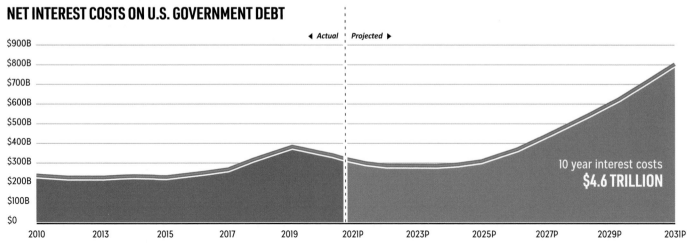

◀ Actual ┊ Projected ▶

10 year interest costs
$4.6 TRILLION

Source: Peter G. Peterson Foundation, 2020

HIGHLY LEVERAGED COMPANIES

Businesses are also taking advantage of low interest rates, evidenced by a rise in debt relative to equity.

TOTAL DEBT TO EQUITY IN THE U.S.

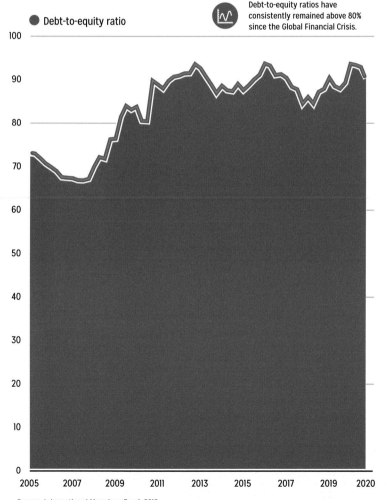

● Debt-to-equity ratio

Debt-to-equity ratios have consistently remained above 80% since the Global Financial Crisis.

WEAKENING CORPORATE CREDIT QUALITY

Riskier segments of the credit market such as high-yield bonds have expanded significantly since the Global Financial Crisis.

GLOBAL HIGH-YIELD BONDS OUTSTANDING

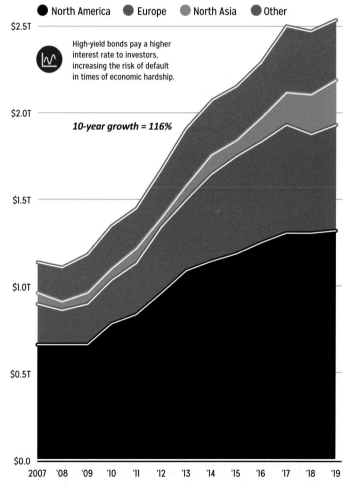

● North America ● Europe ● North Asia ● Other

High-yield bonds pay a higher interest rate to investors, increasing the risk of default in times of economic hardship.

10-year growth = 116%

Source: International Monetary Fund, 2019

Source: Data from International Monetary Fund 2020

HOUSEHOLD DEBT

Global household debt has grown to a record $48 trillion, with households in emerging markets leading the way.

HOUSEHOLD DEBT BY REGION AS % OF GLOBAL GDP

% of global GDP, mature markets

% of global GDP, emerging and frontier markets

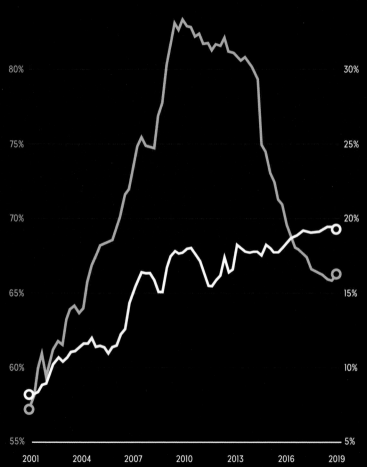

Source: Tiftik and Guardia, 2020

YOUNGER GENERATIONS AT HIGHER RISK

Younger generations are having to borrow more as they pursue an education or purchase real estate. Their growing debts could be a cause for concern if interest rates were to increase in the future.

AVERAGE AMERICAN DEBT BY GENERATION

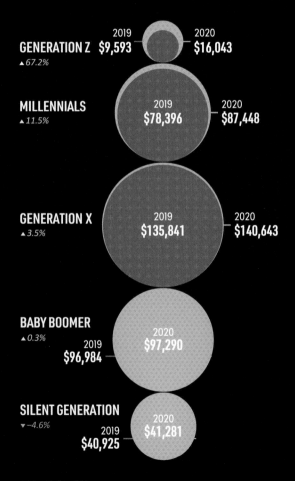

GENERATION Z $9,593
▲67.2%
2019
2020 $16,043

MILLENNIALS
▲11.5%
2019 $78,396
2020 $87,448

GENERATION X
▲3.5%
2019 $135,841
2020 $140,643

BABY BOOMER
▲0.3%
2020 $97,290
2019 $96,984

SILENT GENERATION
▼−4.6%
2020 $41,281
2019 $40,925

Source: Stolba, 2020
Generation Z (age 18-23); Millennials (age 24-39); Generation X (40-55); Baby boomers (age 56-74); Silent generation (age 75+)

PUSHING THE STAKES FURTHER

Excessive debt relative to GDP can cause volatility and impair growth. By 2019, the debt burden across three of four sectors had already surpassed their pre-Global Financial Crisis levels.

DEBT BY SECTOR
AS % OF GDP

- Non-fin. corporates
- Government
- Financial sector
- Household

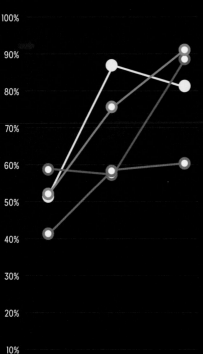

Source: Tiftik and Mahmood, 2020

THE WORLD HAS DEVELOPED AN INSATIABLE APPETITE FOR DEBT.

Since the Global Financial Crisis, low interest rate regimes have enabled global debt to rise at an alarming rate. This puts consumers, businesses, and governments at a higher risk of insolvency.

Policymakers will be hard-pressed to find ways of easing this burden in a non-disruptive fashion, and there's no clear path for returning to normal.

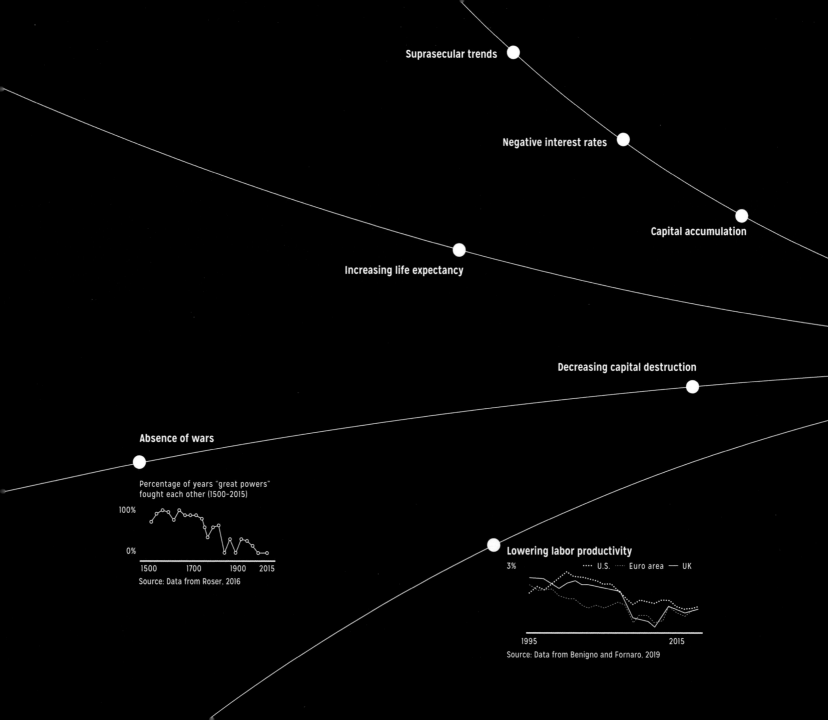

Suprasecular trends

Negative interest rates

Capital accumulation

Increasing life expectancy

Decreasing capital destruction

Absence of wars

Percentage of years "great powers" fought each other (1500–2015)

100%

0%

1500   1700   1900   2015

Source: Data from Roser, 2016

Lowering labor productivity

3%

······ U.S.   ······ Euro area   —— UK

1995   2015

Source: Data from Benigno and Fornaro, 2019

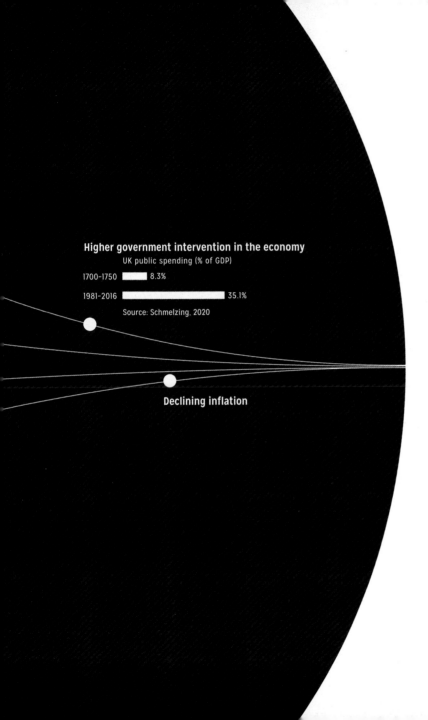

Higher government intervention in the economy

UK public spending (% of GDP)

1700-1750 8.3%

1981-2016 35.1%

Source: Schmelzing, 2020

Declining inflation

SIGNAL 17

FALLING INTEREST RATES

FALLING INTEREST RATES

Interest rates have been falling for seven centuries, and this trend is projected to continue over the next several decades.

SIGNAL RANGE
Very Broad (5/5)

SIGNAL-TO-NOISE RATIO
Medium (3/5)

CENTENNIAL AVERAGES OF REAL LONG-TERM "SAFE ASSET" RATES*

BY PERCENTAGE, GLOBAL

ℹ️ **How to read this**
The real rate of interest is calculated by subtracting the inflation rate from the nominal rate

Nominal rate

Real rate   Inflation rate

OVER 700 YEARS, real interest rates have declined an average of 1.59 basis points (0.0159%) per year. Despite such a long track record, the exact reasons behind this trend remain unclear.

Research has suggested that a variety of factors such as growing capital accumulation, increasing life expectancies, and increased public spending could all be playing a role.

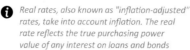

3.5% — 2000s — 1.3%
5.0% — 1900s — 2.0%
3.5% — 1800s — 3.4%
4.1% — 1700s — 3.5%
5.4% — 1600s — 4.6%
7.8% — 1500s — 6.1%
11.2% — 1400s — 9.1%
7.3% — 1300s — 5.1%

ℹ️ *Real rates, also known as "inflation-adjusted" rates, take into account inflation. The real rate reflects the true purchasing power value of any interest on loans and bonds*

*Safe assets are issued from global financial powers
Source: Schmelzing, 2020

HISTORICAL INTEREST RATES 1317-2018

GLOBAL REAL RATE IN PERCENTAGE

—— Global real rate, 7-year moving average

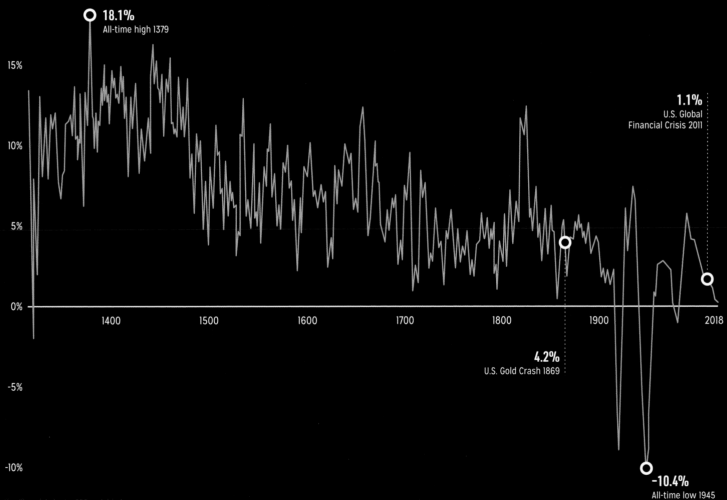

18.1%
All-time high 1379

1.1%
U.S. Global
Financial Crisis 2011

4.2%
U.S. Gold Crash 1869

-10.4%
All-time low 1945

Headline global rate. GDP-weighted.
Source: Data from Schmelzing 2020

INTEREST RATES SELECTED OECD COUNTRIES

From a short-term perspective, the results are equally striking. Since 1990, interest rates across several countries have dropped from double-digit to single-digit numbers.

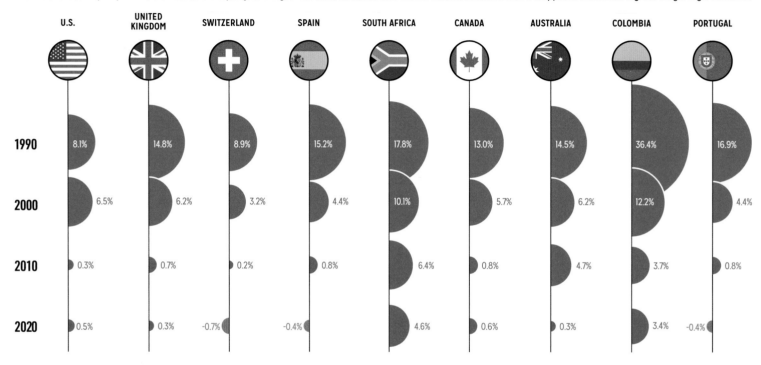

	U.S.	UNITED KINGDOM	SWITZERLAND	SPAIN	SOUTH AFRICA	CANADA	AUSTRALIA	COLOMBIA	PORTUGAL
1990	8.1%	14.8%	8.9%	15.2%	17.8%	13.0%	14.5%	36.4%	16.9%
2000	6.5%	6.2%	3.2%	4.4%	10.1%	5.7%	6.2%	12.2%	4.4%
2010	0.3%	0.7%	0.2%	0.8%	6.4%	0.8%	4.7%	3.7%	0.8%
2020	0.5%	0.3%	-0.7%	-0.4%	4.6%	0.6%	0.3%	3.4%	-0.4%

Short-term interest rates, based on three-month money market rates when available.
Source: OECD, 2021

U.S. MORTGAGE RATES 1990-2020

U.S. mortgage rates have also fallen significantly over the past 30 years.

January 1990	August 2020
10.1%	**3.0%**

30 Year Fixed Rate Mortgage. Data as of August 19, 2020.
Source: Data from Mortgage Rates 2020

DECLINING BOND YIELDS 1314-2018

Bond yields are following a similar downward path. The present bond market,
which began in 1981, is the second longest in 700 years.

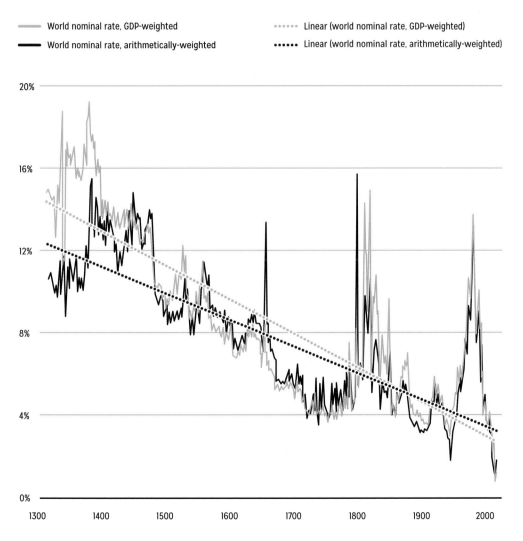

- ——— World nominal rate, GDP-weighted
- **——— World nominal rate, arithmetically-weighted**
- ·········· Linear (world nominal rate, GDP-weighted)
- •••••• Linear (world nominal rate, arithmetically-weighted)

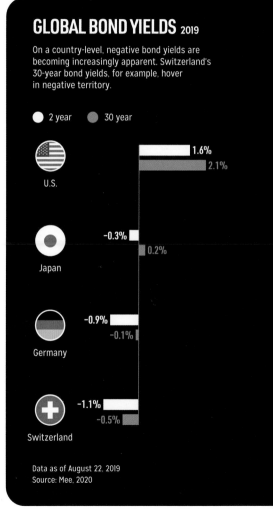

GLOBAL BOND YIELDS 2019

On a country-level, negative bond yields are
becoming increasingly apparent. Switzerland's
30-year bond yields, for example, hover
in negative territory.

● 2 year ● 30 year

U.S.
- 1.6%
- 2.1%

Japan
- -0.3%
- 0.2%

Germany
- -0.9%
- -0.1%

Switzerland
- -1.1%
- -0.5%

Data as of August 22, 2019
Source: Mee, 2020

DIMINISHING SAVINGS AND PENSION RETURNS

Evidence suggests that falling interest rates will likely have implications for deposit rates, resulting in the gradual erosion of individual savings.

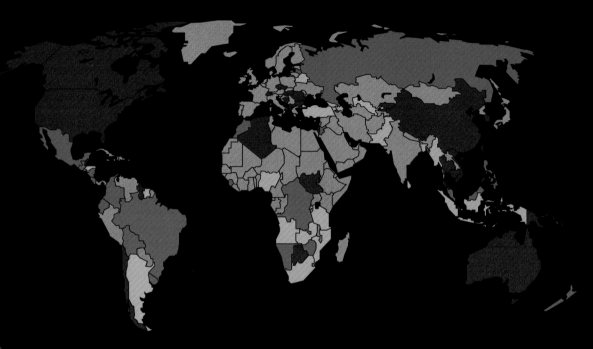

DEPOSIT INTEREST RATES

- Under 2.59%
- 2.59–5.71%
- 5.71–9.70%
- 9.70–16.16%
- Over 16.16%
- Not available

DEPOSIT RATES AROUND THE WORLD

— European Central Bank ···· Danish National Bank — Swiss National Bank — Swedish Riksbank ···· Bank of Japan

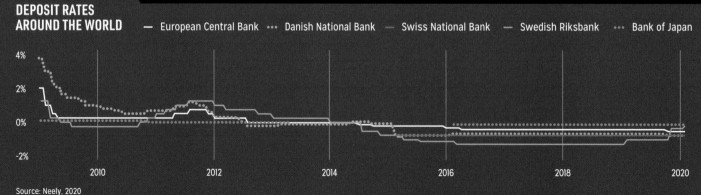

4%
2%
0%
-2%

2010   2012   2014   2016   2018   2020

Source: Neely, 2020

PROPORTION OF CASHFLOW NEGATIVE PENSION PLANS IN THE UK

There are also stark implications for pension funds. In the UK, the proportion of cashflow negative pension funds in 2018 topped 64%.

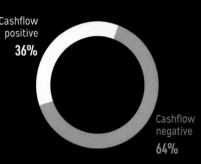

Cashflow positive
36%

Cashflow negative
64%

EXPECTED TIME TO BECOME CASHFLOW NEGATIVE

UK PENSION PLANS IN 2018

Within 10 years, it's expected that 72% of the remaining cashflow-positive UK pension funds will make the flip to cashflow negative.

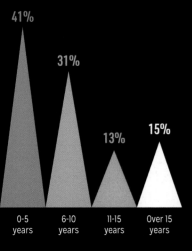

41%	31%	13%	15%
0-5 years	6-10 years	11-15 years	Over 15 years

Source: Mercer, 2019

NEGATIVE INTEREST RATES COULD SOON BECOME A GLOBAL REALITY.

To date, there has been little indication of a reversal in their long-term decline.

The implications of this milestone could be wide-reaching, affecting the financial decisions of individuals, businesses, and governments.

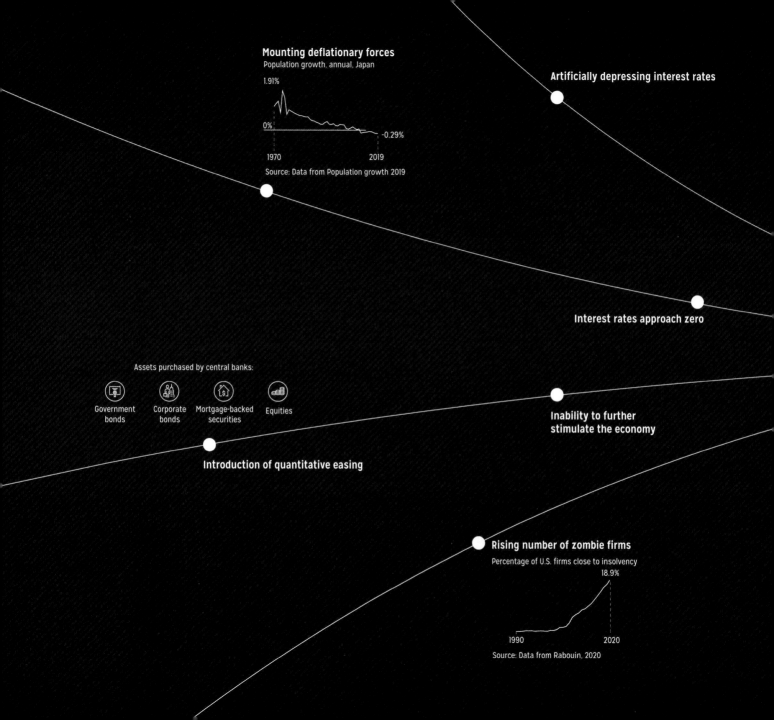

Mounting deflationary forces
Population growth, annual, Japan

1.91%

0%

-0.29%

1970   2019

Source: Data from Population growth 2019

Artificially depressing interest rates

Interest rates approach zero

Assets purchased by central banks:

Government bonds   Corporate bonds   Mortgage-backed securities   Equities

Introduction of quantitative easing

Inability to further stimulate the economy

Rising number of zombie firms
Percentage of U.S. firms close to insolvency

18.9%

1990   2020

Source: Data from Rabouin, 2020

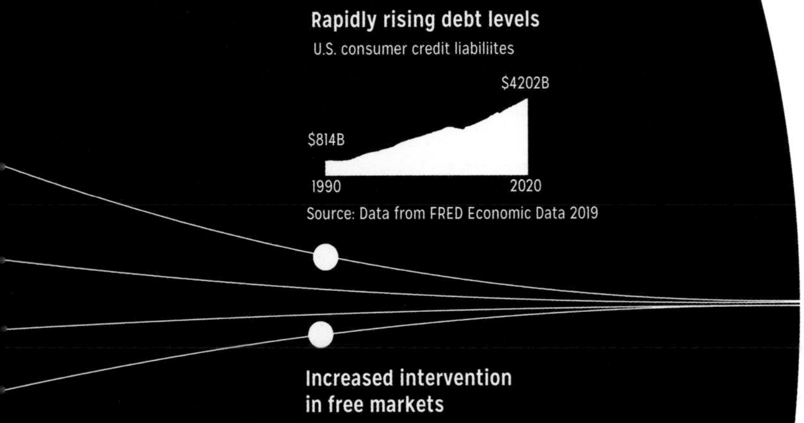

Rapidly rising debt levels

U.S. consumer credit liabiliites

$4202B

$814B

1990   2020

Source: Data from FRED Economic Data 2019

Increased intervention in free markets

SIGNAL 18

CENTRAL BANK IMPOTENCE

CENTRAL BANK IMPOTENCE

Following the Global Financial Crisis, central banks have struggled to stimulate growth with traditional monetary policy.

SIGNAL RANGE
Broad (4/5)

SIGNAL-TO-NOISE RATIO
Moderate (3/5)

CENTRAL BANKS BALANCE SHEETS USD

- Bank of Japan (BoJ)
- European Central Bank (ECB)
- U.S. Federal Reserve (Fed)
- Swiss National Bank (SNB)
- Bank of England (BoE)

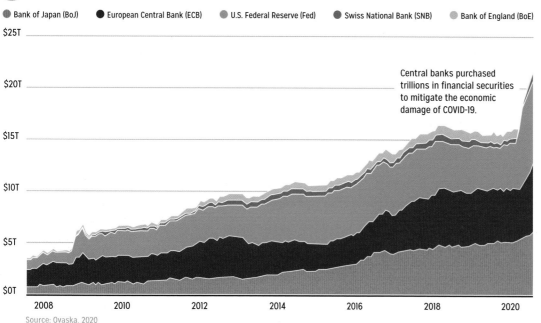

Central banks purchased trillions in financial securities to mitigate the economic damage of COVID-19.

Source: Ovaska, 2020

LOW INTEREST RATES are intended to make it easier for businesses and consumers to access loans, thereby increasing investment and large purchases. An issue arises, however, when rates approach zero.

Unable to cut rates any further, central banks are relying on an unconventional policy known as quantitative easing (QE) to boost the economy. This results in massive increases in central bank liabilities, causing many to question if these institutions have gone too far.

CENTRAL BANK POLICY RATES

— Bank of Japan — European Central Bank — U.S. Federal Reserve — Swiss National Bank — Bank of England

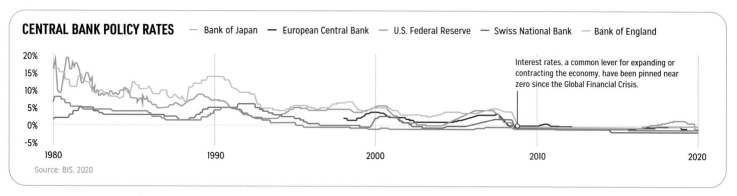

Interest rates, a common lever for expanding or contracting the economy, have been pinned near zero since the Global Financial Crisis.

Source: BIS, 2020

THE CENTRAL BANK'S TRADITIONAL TOOLKIT

Rapid inflation can erode the purchasing power of a currency and make it difficult for businesses to set prices. As a result, many central banks set a target inflation rate to promote steady growth.

TARGET INFLATION RATES

 2%
Bank of England
Bank of Japan
U.S. Federal Reserve

 <2%
Swiss National Bank
European Central Bank

Source: Central Bank News, 2020

SETTING THE POLICY RATE

To meet inflation targets, central banks will adjust their policy rate to boost or slow the economy. This influences other rates, such as those for mortgages.

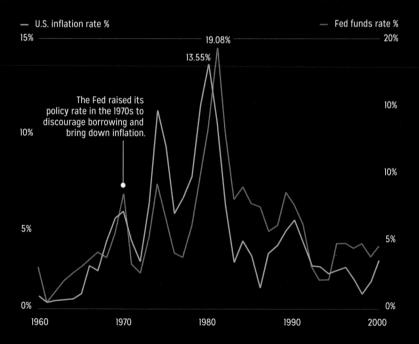

— U.S. inflation rate %   — Fed funds rate %

19.08%

13.55%

The Fed raised its policy rate in the 1970s to discourage borrowing and bring down inflation.

Source: Federal Reserve of Dallas, 2020

OPEN MARKET OPERATIONS

Central banks can buy or sell short-term government bonds to influence interest rates. This works because of the inverse relationship between a bond's price and yield.

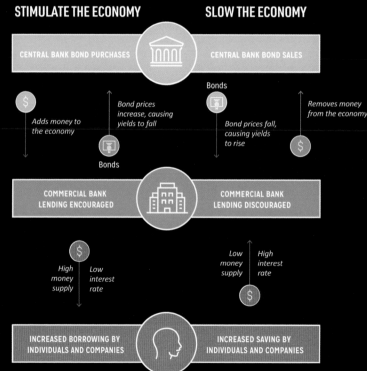

STIMULATE THE ECONOMY

CENTRAL BANK BOND PURCHASES

$ — Adds money to the economy

Bond prices increase, causing yields to fall

Bonds

COMMERCIAL BANK LENDING ENCOURAGED

$ — *High money supply* | *Low interest rate*

INCREASED BORROWING BY INDIVIDUALS AND COMPANIES

SLOW THE ECONOMY

CENTRAL BANK BOND SALES

Bonds

Bond prices fall, causing yields to rise

Removes money from the economy — $

COMMERCIAL BANK LENDING DISCOURAGED

Low money supply | *High interest rate* — $

INCREASED SAVING BY INDIVIDUALS AND COMPANIES

JAPAN'S DEFLATION BATTLE

The Bank of Japan was one of the first to struggle with impotency. It has had limited success in overcoming decades of low or negative inflation, both of which can be detrimental to economic growth. Falling prices can cause businesses and consumers to postpone new investment and expenditures.

JAPAN'S INFLATION VS. BANK OF JAPAN POLICY RATE

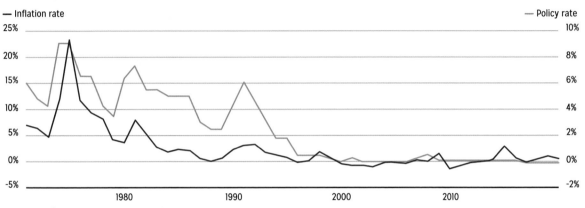

— Inflation rate   — Policy rate

Source: Data from World Bank, via Macrotrends 2020

Rate increases have decreased inflation in the past, but this tool isn't as potent when used the opposite way.

With its policy rate at zero, the Bank of Japan required additional stimulus. In 2001, it began **quantitative easing**—the purchase of longer-term securities to further increase the money supply and depress long-term rates.

ASSETS HELD BY THE BANK OF JAPAN USD

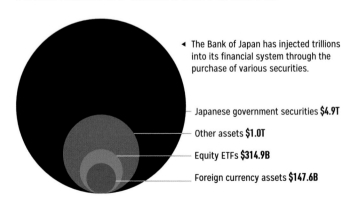

◄ The Bank of Japan has injected trillions into its financial system through the purchase of various securities.

Japanese government securities **$4.9T**

Other assets **$1.0T**

Equity ETFs **$314.9B**

Foreign currency assets **$147.6B**

Source: Japan Macro Advisors, 2020

STAGNATING WAGES

The results of Japan's quantitative easing have been inconclusive. Deflationary forces, such as stagnating wages, may be negating some of its effect.

Average annual real wages in million Japanese yen

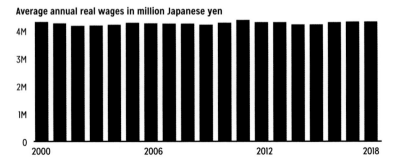

Source: Data from Statista Research Department 2020

U.S. FEDERAL RESERVE: OPERATING WITHOUT BOUNDARIES

The U.S. Fed has insisted it will do whatever necessary to support the economy. Its liberal use of quantitative easing, however, may have undesirable side effects.

INFLATING EQUITY MARKETS

TOTAL FED ASSETS VS. S&P 500

— Total Fed assets

The Fed has purchased trillions in government and corporate bonds since 2008, driving the yields of these securities to historic lows. These low yields are likely pushing investors into equities, increasing the risk of a price bubble.

— S&P 500 index value

◄ Shading indicates a U.S. recession

Source: Federal Reserve of St. Louis, 2020

Unprecedented levels of stimulus are a likely factor for the S&P 500's immense growth in recent years.

EXCESS BANK RESERVES

Excess reserves held with the Fed

In 2008, the Fed began to pay interest on excess reserves that commercial banks held with it. This policy can incentivize banks to keep deposits with the Fed, rather than increase lending to consumers and businesses.

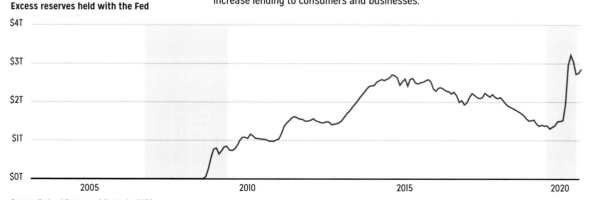

Source: Federal Reserve of St. Louis, 2020

Efforts to increase the money supply are less efficient when trillions of dollars sit idle at the Fed.

THE LOW RATE DILEMMA

Central banks are using quantitative easing to depress interest rates as much as possible. According to traditional theory, this should encourage consumers to spend, rather than save. In practice, these ultra-low rates may be doing the opposite.

ULTRA-LOW YIELDS BOOST HOUSEHOLD SPENDING, UP TO A THRESHOLD

Monthly value ● 1980-2000 ● 2001-2020

↑ Household spending as % of disposable income

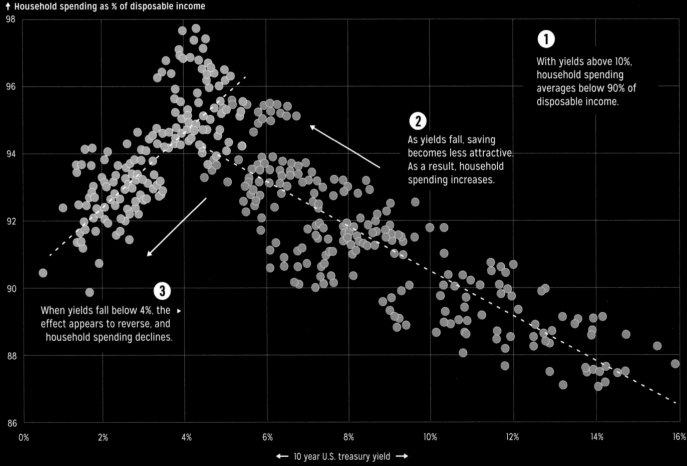

1 With yields above 10%, household spending averages below 90% of disposable income.

2 As yields fall, saving becomes less attractive. As a result, household spending increases.

3 When yields fall below 4%, the effect appears to reverse, and household spending declines.

← 10 year U.S. treasury yield →

Source: Data from Bank of America Research Investment Committee and Haver Analytics, via Zerohedge 2020

s the rate of return from safer fixed-income
securities plummets, households may have
to cut back on spending in order to prepare
or retirement.

This dilemma could lock central banks into a
cycle of providing continuous stimulus, as
een in Japan.

30% OF JAPAN'S ETFs ARE
OWNED BY ITS CENTRAL BANK

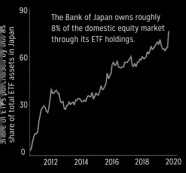

The Bank of Japan owns roughly
8% of the domestic equity market
through its ETF holdings.

Source: Data from Deutsche Bank, via Zerohedge 2020

CRUMBLING YIELDS ON
JAPANESE TREASURY BONDS

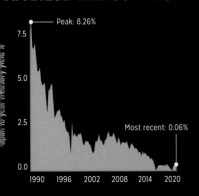

Source: CNBC, 2020

CENTRAL BANKS REMAIN COMMITTED TO STIMULATING THEIR ECONOMIES.

This has resulted in years of ultra-low interest rates and numerous rounds
of quantitative easing. Critics claim that these types of interventions are
counterintuitive to the concept of free markets and are causing more harm
than good.

Whether a truly free market would have performed better in the years
following 2008, however, remains a mystery.

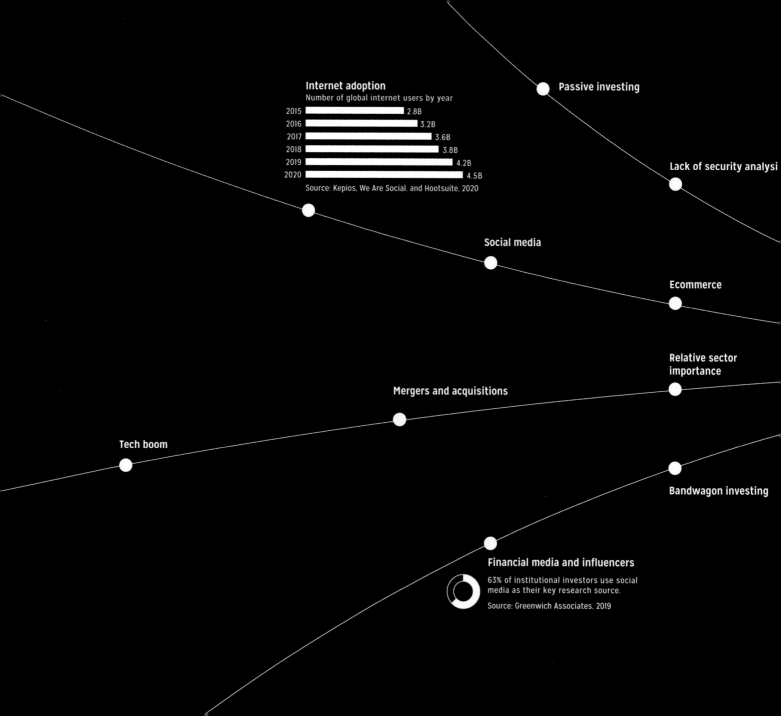

Internet adoption
Number of global internet users by year

Year	Users
2015	2.8B
2016	3.2B
2017	3.6B
2018	3.8B
2019	4.2B
2020	4.5B

Source: Kepios, We Are Social, and Hootsuite, 2020

Passive investing

Lack of security analysi

Social media

Ecommerce

Relative sector
importance

Mergers and acquisitions

Tech boom

Bandwagon investing

Financial media and influencers

63% of institutional investors use social
media as their key research source.

Source: Greenwich Associates, 2019

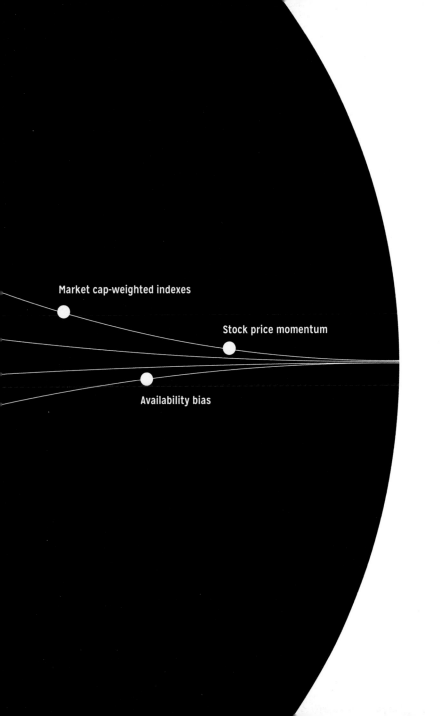

Market cap-weighted indexes

Stock price momentum

Availability bias

STOCK MARKET CONCENTRATION

STOCK MARKET CONCENTRATION

A handful of successful companies dominate the stock market, and their oversized weighting is growing over time.

PERCENTAGE OF S&P 500'S MARKET CAP
REPRESENTED BY 5 LARGEST STOCKS

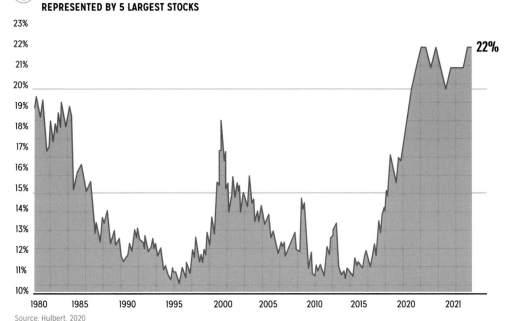

Source: Hulbert, 2020

SIGNAL RANGE
Moderate (3/5)

SIGNAL-TO-NOISE RATIO
Very high (5/5)

THE FIVE LARGEST STOCKS represent almost a quarter of the S&P 500's value, the highest concentration since at least 1980. Consequently, these stocks have a large influence on the performance of the index—and by association, the $11.2T in investor funds indexed or benchmarked to the S&P 500.

FAAMG STOCKS CONTRIBUTION TO S&P 500 RETURN MAY 2015-MAY 2020

🍎 Apple   ⬛ Microsoft   a, Amazon   f Facebook   G Alphabet

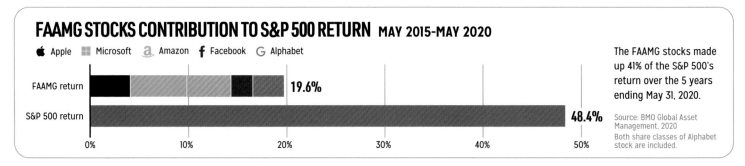

FAAMG return — **19.6%**

S&P 500 return — **48.4%**

The FAAMG stocks made up 41% of the S&P 500's return over the 5 years ending May 31, 2020.

Source: BMO Global Asset Management, 2020
Both share classes of Alphabet stock are included.

A GLOBAL COMPARISON

Compared to other stock markets globally, the U.S. is less concentrated.
However, the S&P 500 has more constituents than most broad market indexes used in other countries.

MARKET CAPITALIZATION OF TOP 5 FIRMS AS % OF TOTAL MARKET CAPITALIZATION

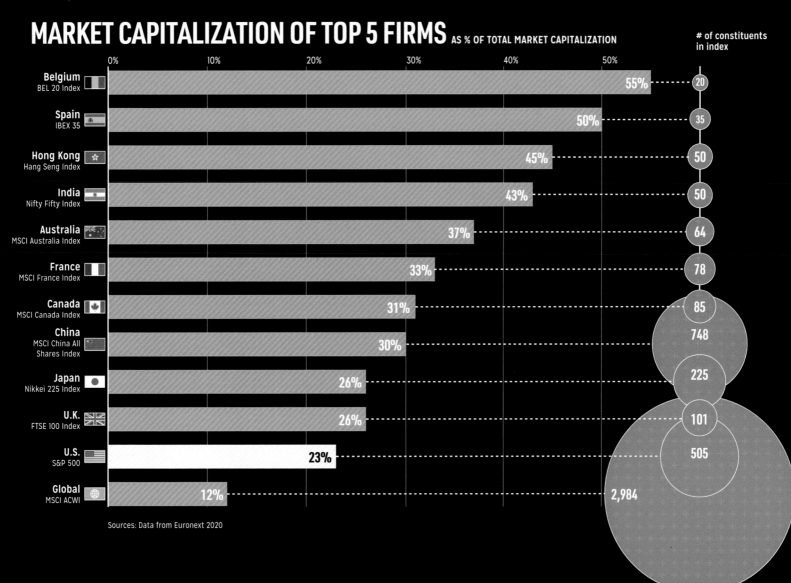

# of constituents in index

Country	Index	Top 5 %	# Constituents
Belgium	BEL 20 Index	55%	20
Spain	IBEX 35	50%	35
Hong Kong	Hang Seng Index	45%	50
India	Nifty Fifty Index	43%	50
Australia	MSCI Australia Index	37%	64
France	MSCI France Index	33%	78
Canada	MSCI Canada Index	31%	85
China	MSCI China All Shares Index	30%	748
Japan	Nikkei 225 Index	26%	225
U.K.	FTSE 100 Index	26%	101
U.S.	S&P 500	23%	505
Global	MSCI ACWI	12%	2,984

Sources: Data from Euronext 2020

TECH'S MOMENTUM

The tech sector has been driving index concentration in recent years, but this wasn't always the case. For example, energy stocks reigned supreme in 1980, when the top 5 stocks represented 19% of the S&P 500.

TOP 5 STOCKS IN THE S&P 500 OVER TIME BY MARKET CAPITALIZATION

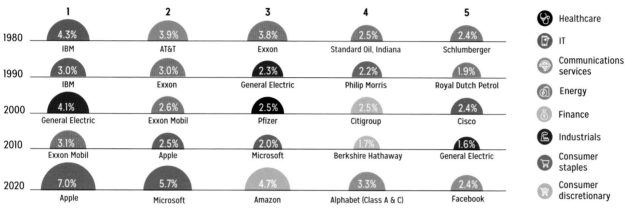

	1	2	3	4	5
1980	4.3% IBM	3.9% AT&T	3.8% Exxon	2.5% Standard Oil, Indiana	2.4% Schlumberger
1990	3.0% IBM	3.0% Exxon	2.3% General Electric	2.2% Philip Morris	1.9% Royal Dutch Petrol
2000	4.1% General Electric	2.6% Exxon Mobil	2.5% Pfizer	2.5% Citigroup	2.4% Cisco
2010	3.1% Exxon Mobil	2.5% Apple	2.0% Microsoft	1.7% Berkshire Hathaway	1.6% General Electric
2020	7.0% Apple	5.7% Microsoft	4.7% Amazon	3.3% Alphabet (Class A & C)	2.4% Facebook

Legend:
- Healthcare
- IT
- Communications services
- Energy
- Finance
- Industrials
- Consumer staples
- Consumer discretionary

Source: Data from S&P 500 via Slickcharts 2020

Today, all of the top 5 stocks are known as Big Tech, although some are officially classified under another sector according to S&P Dow Jones Indices.

BIG TECH MARKET CAP OVER TIME

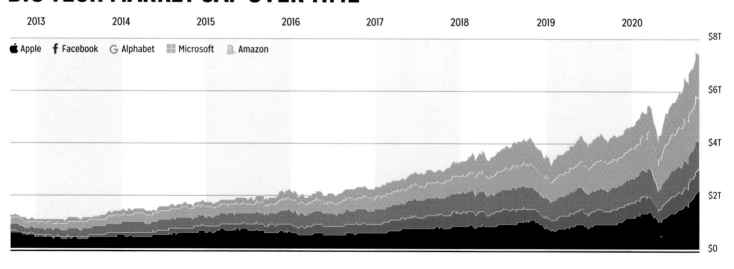

 Apple   f Facebook   G Alphabet   ▦ Microsoft   a Amazon

Source: Data from S&P 500 via Slickcharts. 2020

PASSIVE INVESTING

The rise of passive investing has also contributed to stock market saturation. In the U.S., the top 10 ETFs account for 28% of total assets under management.

Source: Gurdus, 2019

Since many of the top funds track market cap-weighted indexes, whose components are weighted according to their total share value, the biggest stocks attract even more money as their prices increase.

Source: Aviva Investors, 2018

ACTIVE-PASSIVE FUND FLOWS AND MARKET SHARE

ESTIMATED NET FLOWS, USD
- Active flows
- Passive flows

MARKET SHARE
— Active market share — Passive market share

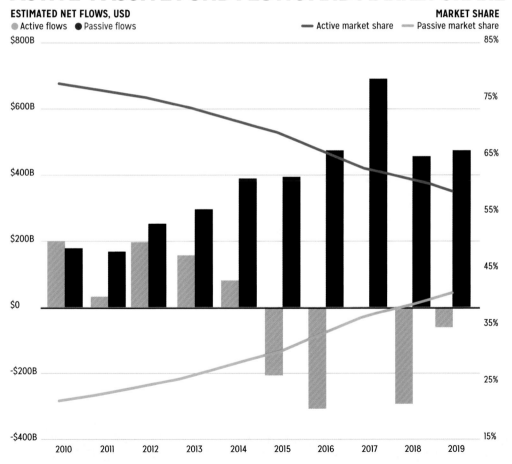

Michael Burry, portrayed in the movie **The Big Short** for accurately predicting the Global Financial Crisis, believes there is a passive investing bubble. He argues that indexed funds do not require true security-level analysis, and when investors realize stock prices are distorted, there will be problematic outflows.

Other industry experts disagree, however, arguing that active investors will arbitrage price discrepancies out of the market, and that ETFs have sufficient liquidity.

Source: Divine, 2019

Source: McDevitt and Watson, 2020

For investors, stock market concentration can cause a high level of unsystematic risk, which affects only a particular company or sector.

As an example, regulatory action has historically had a negative impact on sector performance.

SECTOR PERFORMANCE FOLLOWING REGULATORY ATTENTION

Performance differential (sector-S&P 500 index, indexed to 100)

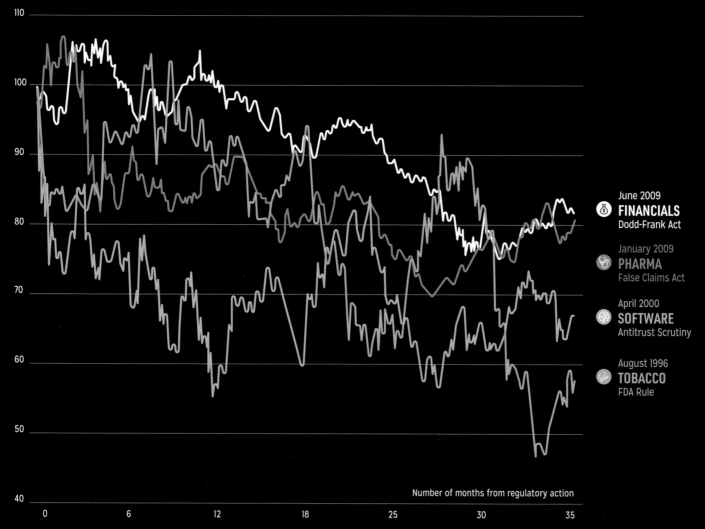

June 2009
FINANCIALS
Dodd-Frank Act

January 2009
PHARMA
False Claims Act

April 2000
SOFTWARE
Antitrust Scrutiny

August 1996
TOBACCO
FDA Rule

Number of months from regulatory action

Source: Data from Goldman Sachs Asset Management Connect 2020

At the same time, however, this additional risk has the potential to deliver higher returns.

Compared to the S&P 500 Equal Weight Index, which weights all companies evenly to increase diversification, the S&P 500 has historically outperformed.

ANNUALIZED TOTAL RETURNS

As of August 31, 2020

● S&P 500 Equal weight
● S&P 500

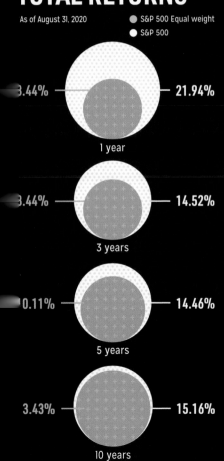

3.44% — 21.94%

1 year

3.44% — 14.52%

3 years

0.11% — 14.46%

5 years

3.43% — 15.16%

10 years

Source: S&P Dow Jones Indices, 2020

—

STOCK MARKET CONCENTRATION ALSO AFFECTS THE ECONOMY AS A WHOLE.

Using three decades of data from 47 countries, researchers found that concentrated stock markets are associated with declines in economic growth, IPOs, innovation, and funding for new firms.

As profits, sales, and employment become clustered in the most successful firms, competition and creativity may suffer.

Source: Bae, 2020

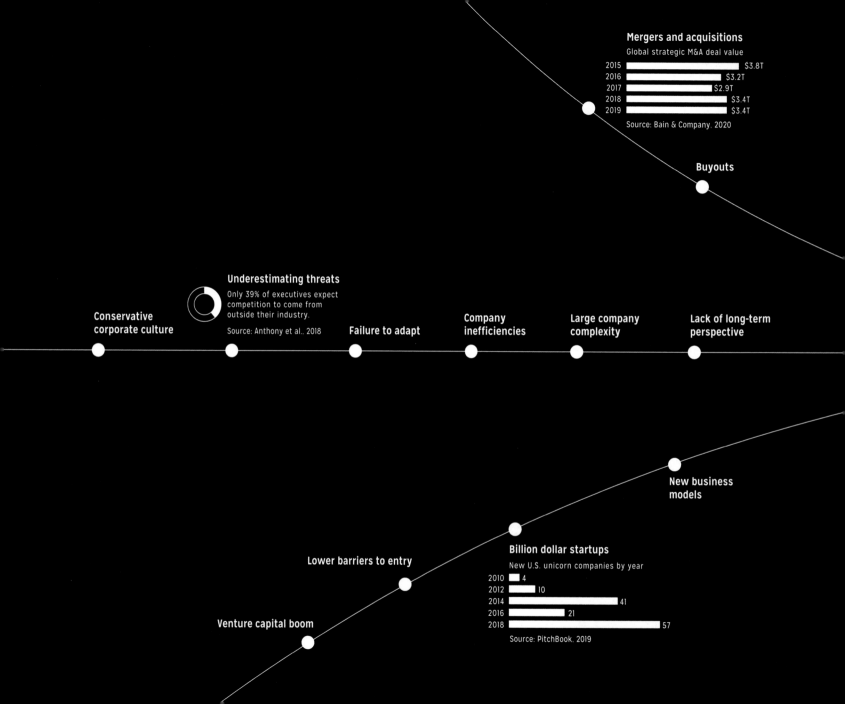

Mergers and acquisitions
Global strategic M&A deal value

2015	$3.8T
2016	$3.2T
2017	$2.9T
2018	$3.4T
2019	$3.4T

Source: Bain & Company, 2020

Buyouts

Underestimating threats
Only 39% of executives expect competition to come from outside their industry.

Source: Anthony et al., 2018

Conservative corporate culture

Failure to adapt

Company inefficiencies

Large company complexity

Lack of long-term perspective

New business models

Lower barriers to entry

Billion dollar startups
New U.S. unicorn companies by year

2010	4
2012	10
2014	41
2016	21
2018	57

Source: PitchBook, 2019

Venture capital boom

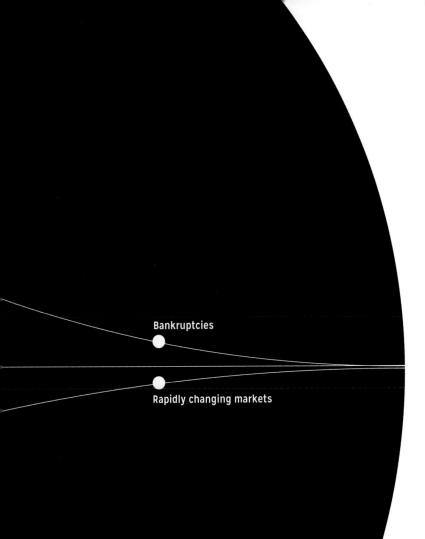

Bankruptcies

Rapidly changing markets

DWINDLING CORPORATE LONGEVITY

DWINDLING CORPORATE LONGEVITY

Companies have shorter life spans than they did in previous decades, and they are projected to become even shorter in the future.

AVERAGE COMPANY LIFE SPAN ON S&P 500 INDEX*

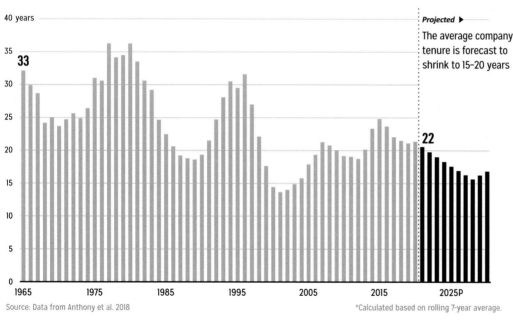

40 years

Projected ▶

The average company tenure is forecast to shrink to 15–20 years

35

33

30

25

22

20

15

10

5

0

1965　1975　1985　1995　2005　2015　2025P

Source: Data from Anthony et al. 2018

*Calculated based on rolling 7-year average.

SIGNAL RANGE
Narrow (2/5)

SIGNAL-TO-NOISE RATIO
Moderate (3/5)

INCREASINGLY, ICONIC FIRMS ARE DYING OUT.
To get an indication of how long businesses last, the average company life span on the S&P 500 Index rolling 7-year average is used as a proxy measure. Life spans vary cyclically along with economic cycles and technology breakthroughs, but are trending down overall.

LESS STAYING POWER

50%
of S&P 500 companies could be replaced from 2018–2027 at current churn rates.

Source: Data from Anthony et al. 2018

What's causing shorter corporate life spans?
Looking at the companies that have been removed
from the S&P 500 Index can provide some insight:

FAILURE
- Bankruptcies
- Market cap reductions

M&A
- Mergers
- Acquisitions

SELECT DELETIONS AND ADDITIONS TO THE S&P 500

2016-2020

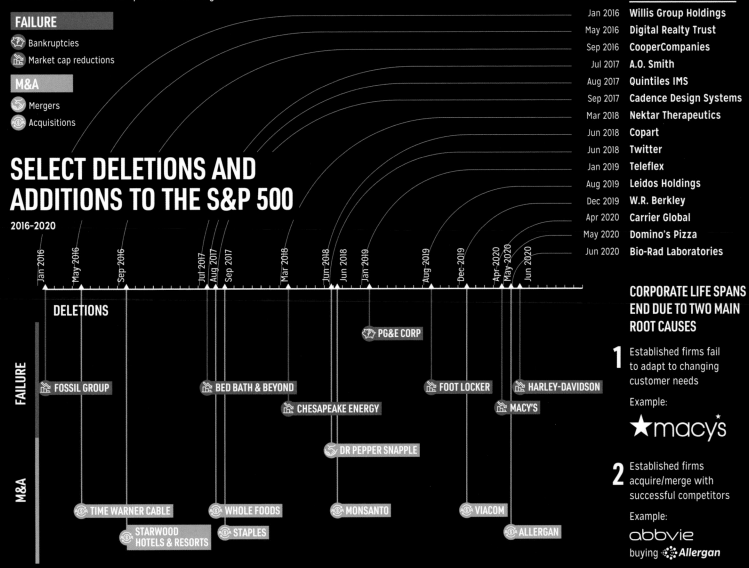

ADDITIONS

Jan 2016	**Willis Group Holdings**
May 2016	**Digital Realty Trust**
Sep 2016	**CooperCompanies**
Jul 2017	**A.O. Smith**
Aug 2017	**Quintiles IMS**
Sep 2017	**Cadence Design Systems**
Mar 2018	**Nektar Therapeutics**
Jun 2018	**Copart**
Jun 2018	**Twitter**
Jan 2019	**Teleflex**
Aug 2019	**Leidos Holdings**
Dec 2019	**W.R. Berkley**
Apr 2020	**Carrier Global**
May 2020	**Domino's Pizza**
Jun 2020	**Bio-Rad Laboratories**

DELETIONS

FAILURE

- FOSSIL GROUP
- BED BATH & BEYOND
- PG&E CORP
- CHESAPEAKE ENERGY
- FOOT LOCKER
- HARLEY-DAVIDSON
- MACY'S

M&A

- TIME WARNER CABLE
- STARWOOD HOTELS & RESORTS
- WHOLE FOODS
- STAPLES
- DR PEPPER SNAPPLE
- MONSANTO
- VIACOM
- ALLERGAN

CORPORATE LIFE SPANS END DUE TO TWO MAIN ROOT CAUSES

1 Established firms fail to adapt to changing customer needs

Example:

★macy's

2 Established firms acquire/merge with successful competitors

Example:

abbvie
buying Allergan

Source: Data from S&P Dow Jones Indices. 2020

VENTURE CAPITAL MEGA-DEALS

Venture capital mega-deals ($100M+) have likely contributed to dwindling corporate life spans. Startups are large enough to be formidable competition or are merged with/acquired by existing companies.

In particular, merger and acquisition (M&A) activity is directly correlated with turnover in the S&P 500—and by proxy, corporate longevity.

U.S. VENTURE CAPITAL MEGA-DEAL ACTIVITY
USD, BILLIONS

● Deal value ●— Deal count

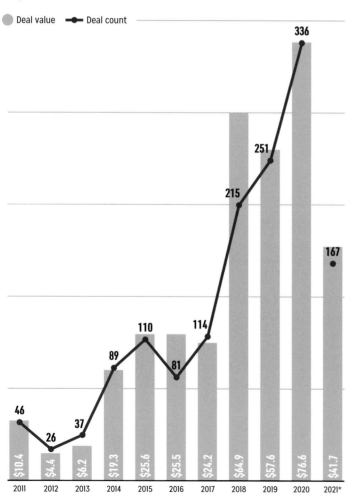

Year	Deal value	Deal count
2011	$10.4	46
2012	$4.4	26
2013	$6.2	37
2014	$19.3	89
2015	$25.6	110
2016	$25.5	81
2017	$24.2	114
2018	$64.9	215
2019	$57.6	251
2020	$76.6	336
2021*	$41.7	167

Source: PitchBook, 2021   *As of March 31, 2020

S&P 500 TURNOVER AND U.S. M&A VOLUME
1990–2016, 2015 USD

● U.S. M&A volume   —— S&P 500 annual turnover

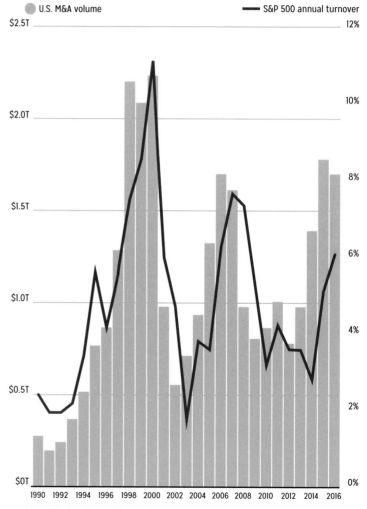

Source: Data from Thomson Reuters, S&P Dow Jones Indices via Credit Suisse 2017

ACCELERATING TECHNOLOGY

PERCENTAGE OF U.S. HOUSEHOLDS USING TECHNOLOGY

1860–2019, ADOPTION RATE

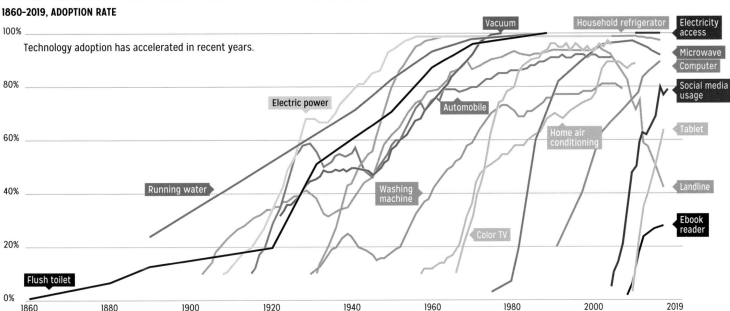

Technology adoption has accelerated in recent years.

Labels on chart: Vacuum · Household refrigerator · Electricity access · Microwave · Computer · Social media usage · Electric power · Automobile · Tablet · Running water · Washing machine · Home air conditioning · Landline · Color TV · Ebook reader · Flush toilet

Y-axis: 100%, 80%, 60%, 40%, 20%, 0%
X-axis: 1860, 1880, 1900, 1920, 1940, 1960, 1980, 2000, 2019

Source: Ritchie, 2017

This constant change has caused a swell in startup innovation that can push established firms out if they fail to adapt.

Kodak failed to recognize how the digital camera would completely revolutionize their industry.

Blockbuster turned down an early partnership offer with Netflix and eventually went bankrupt.

Source: Anthony, 2016; Satell, 2014

Retail is one sector particularly affected by technology adoption, as consumers go online in increasing numbers.

ESTIMATED U.S. ECOMMERCE SALES USD

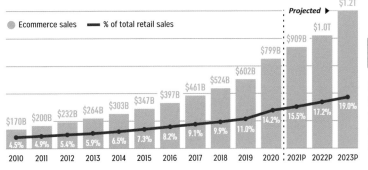

● Ecommerce sales —— % of total retail sales

Projected ▶

Year	Ecommerce sales	% of total retail sales
2010	$170B	4.5%
2011	$200B	4.9%
2012	$232B	5.4%
2013	$264B	5.9%
2014	$303B	6.5%
2015	$347B	7.3%
2016	$397B	8.2%
2017	$461B	9.1%
2018	$524B	9.9%
2019	$602B	11.0%
2020	$799B	14.2%
2021P	$909B	15.5%
2022P	$1.0T	17.2%
2023P	$1.2T	19.0%

Ecommerce has led to the downfall of iconic retail giants, a trend exacerbated by COVID-19.

Source: Data from US Census Bureau via Business Insider 2020 and eMarketer 2021

SIGNAL 20 > DECODE > IMPACT

As companies scramble to keep up, their focus has shifted from advertising to research and development (R&D).

R&D SPENDING OUTSTRIPS ADVERTISING SPENDING

% OF COMPANY EXPENSES

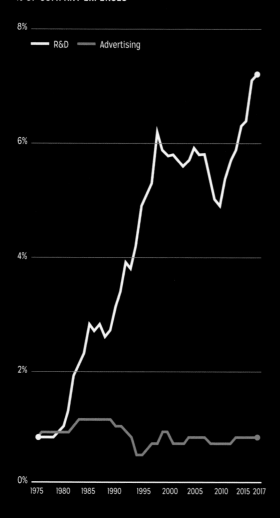

Source: Data from Anthony 2016

With a focus on innovation, companies will need a workforce that continuously evolves as well—but skills remain a concern.

GLOBAL CEOs' CONCERNS OVER SKILL AVAILABILITY

RESPONDED "SOMEWHAT CONCERNED" OR "EXTREMELY CONCERNED"

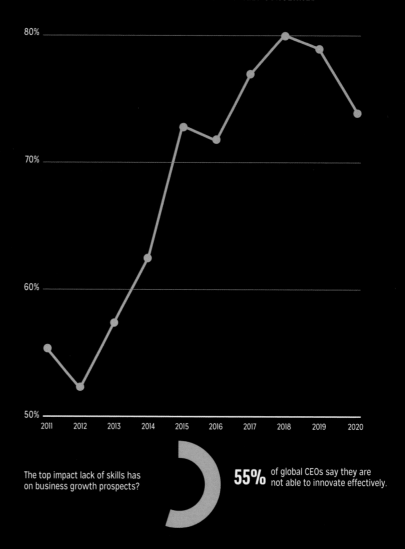

The top impact lack of skills has on business growth prospects?

55% of global CEOs say they are not able to innovate effectively.

Source: PwC, 2019

When companies invest in upskilling programs to teach their employees new skills, innovation and other strong gains result.

EFFECTIVENESS OF UPSKILLING PROGRAMS

% OF GLOBAL CEOs WHO RESPONDED "VERY EFFECTIVE"

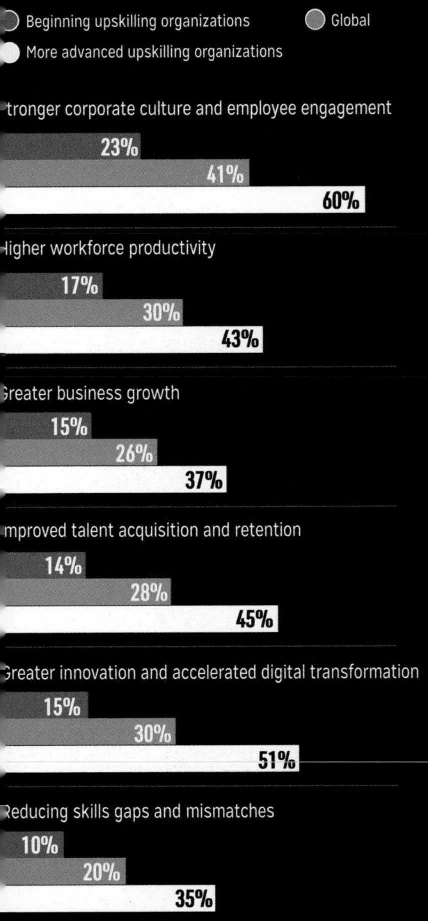

- Beginning upskilling organizations
- Global
- More advanced upskilling organizations

Stronger corporate culture and employee engagement
- 23%
- 41%
- 60%

Higher workforce productivity
- 17%
- 30%
- 43%

Greater business growth
- 15%
- 26%
- 37%

Improved talent acquisition and retention
- 14%
- 28%
- 45%

Greater innovation and accelerated digital transformation
- 15%
- 30%
- 51%

Reducing skills gaps and mismatches
- 10%
- 20%
- 35%

Source: PwC, 2020

COMPANIES THAT FAIL TO ADAPT RISK BEING LEFT BEHIND.

It's harder now than ever for elite companies to maintain their position on top of the food chain.

This raises the stakes for investors, employees, and business leaders, but it also creates vast amounts of opportunity for ambitious startups.

Source: Garelli, 2016; Reeves, 2015

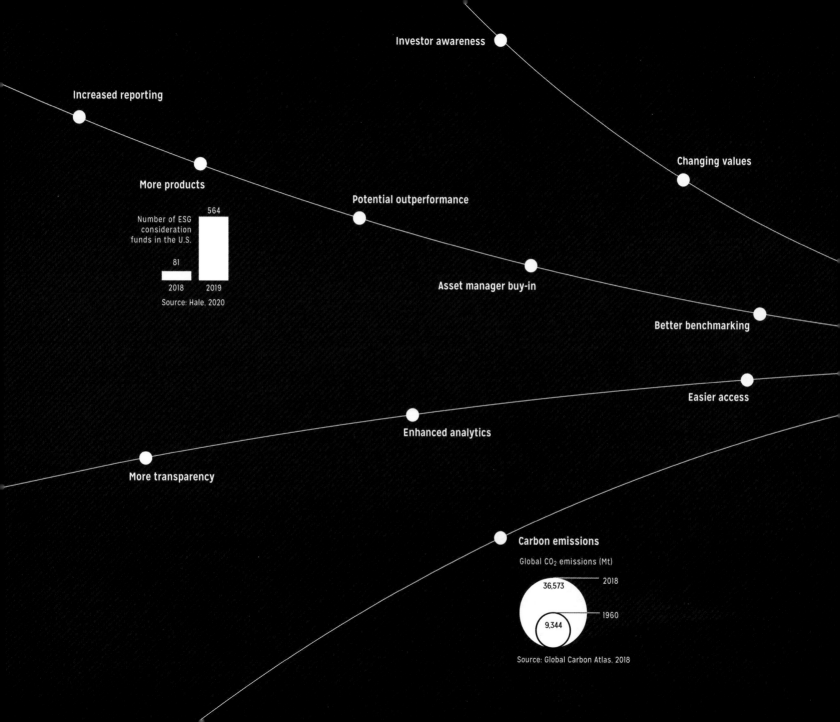

Investor awareness

Increased reporting

Changing values

More products

Potential outperformance

Number of ESG
consideration
funds in the U.S.

564

81

2018   2019

Source: Hale, 2020

Asset manager buy-in

Better benchmarking

Easier access

Enhanced analytics

More transparency

Carbon emissions

Global CO₂ emissions (Mt)

36,573   2018

1960

9,344

Source: Global Carbon Atlas, 2018

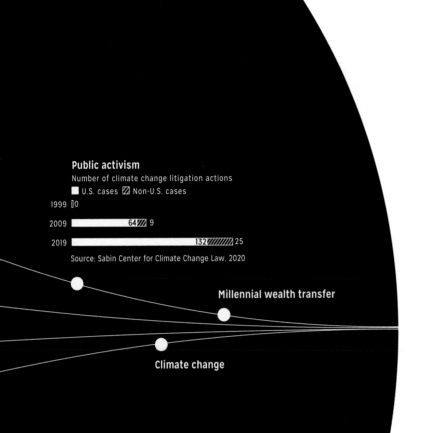

Public activism

Number of climate change litigation actions

■ U.S. cases ▨ Non-U.S. cases

1999 ▮0

2009 ▬▬▬▬▬ 64 ▨ 9

2019 ▬▬▬▬▬▬▬▬ 132 ▨ 25

Source: Sabin Center for Climate Change Law, 2020

Millennial wealth transfer

Climate change

SUSTAINABLE INVESTING

SUSTAINABLE INVESTING

Sustainable assets have grown significantly in recent years, and this shift is projected to continue in the coming decades.

SIGNAL RANGE
Moderate (3/5)

SIGNAL-TO-NOISE RATIO
Very high (5/5)

GLOBAL ASSETS UNDER MANAGEMENT FALLING UNDER AN ESG MANDATE USD

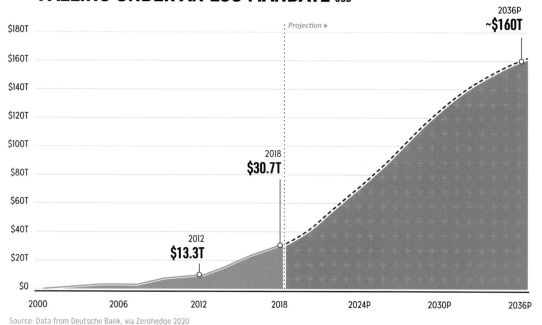

Projection ▶

2036P
~$160T

2018
$30.7T

2012
$13.3T

$180T						
$160T						
$140T						
$120T						
$100T						
$80T						
$60T						
$40T						
$20T						
$0						
	2000	2006	2012	2018	2024P	2030P	2036P

Source: Data from Deutsche Bank, via Zerohedge 2020

AS CALLS FOR EQUALITY, CLIMATE ACTION, AND CORPORATE ACCOUNTABILITY GROW LOUDER, the popularity of sustainable investing has grown. However, these strategies are about more than personal values. Sustainable investing also helps investors manage environmental, social, and governance risks. As a result the investment strategy has proliferated around the world.

ESG ASSETS AS PERCENTAGE OF TOTAL ASSETS

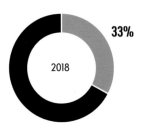

2018 — 33%

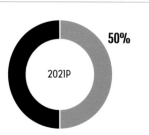

2021P — 50%

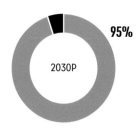

2030P — 95%

Source: Deutsche Bank, 2019; Global Sustainable Investment Alliance, 2019

SUSTAINABLE INVESTING ASSETS BY REGION 2012 AND 2018

▲ CAGR

Europe
2018
$14.08T
2012
$8.76T

Canada
2018
$1.70T
2012
$0.59T
19.3%

U.S.
2018
$12.00T
2012
$3.74T
21.5%

8.2%

Japan
2018
$2.18T
2012
$0.01T
145.3%

Australia & New Zealand
2012
$0.18T
2018
$0.73T
26.3%

SUSTAINABLE ASSETS RELATIVE TO TOTAL MANAGED ASSETS ● 2012 ● 2018

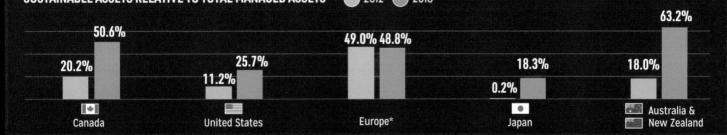

	Canada	United States	Europe*	Japan	Australia & New Zealand
2012	20.2%	11.2%	49.0%	0.2%	18.0%
2018	50.6%	25.7%	48.8%	18.3%	63.2%

*At least part of the market share decline in Europe stems from a shift to stricter standards and definitions for sustainable investing.

Source: Global Sustainable Investment Alliance, 2018

INTEREST AND ADOPTION
BY U.S. INDIVIDUAL INVESTORS

PROJECTED ANNUAL AGGREGATE INCOME
BY GENERATION

INTEREST IN SUSTAINABLE INVESTING

● Millennial population ● General population

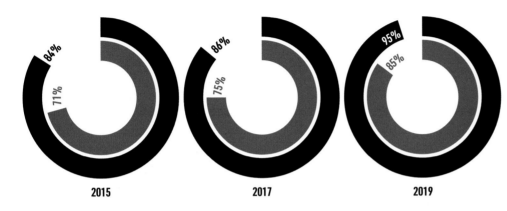

84% 71% **2015**

86% 75% **2017**

95% 85% **2019**

ADOPTION OF SUSTAINABLE INVESTING

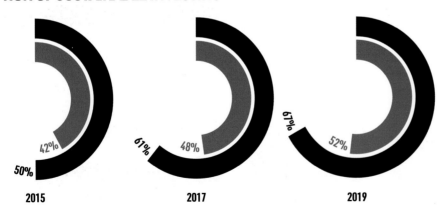

50% 42% **2015**

61% 48% **2017**

67% 52% **2019**

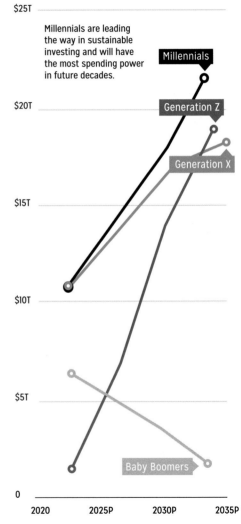

Millennials are leading the way in sustainable investing and will have the most spending power in future decades.

$25T

$20T — Generation Z

Millennials

$15T — Generation X

$10T

$5T

Baby Boomers

0

2020   2025P   2030P   2035P

Source: Data from Morgan Stanley Institute for Sustainable Investing 2019

Source: Data from Brookings 2020
Generation Z refers to individuals born 2000–2020.

INVESTOR IMPLICATIONS

ESG investing minimizes sustainability risks, and can lead to higher returns and less volatility for investors.

CUMULATIVE ALL COUNTRY WORLD INDEX PERFORMANCE GROSS RETURNS

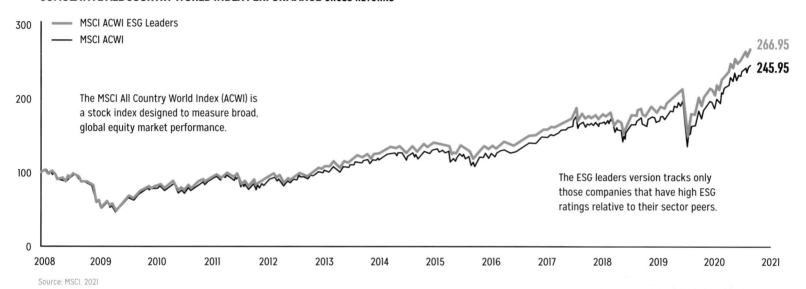

— MSCI ACWI ESG Leaders
— MSCI ACWI

The MSCI All Country World Index (ACWI) is a stock index designed to measure broad, global equity market performance.

The ESG leaders version tracks only those companies that have high ESG ratings relative to their sector peers.

266.95
245.95

Source: MSCI, 2021

GROSS RETURNS ANNUALIZED

● MSCI ACWI ESG Leaders   ● MSCI ACWI

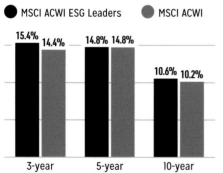

	3-year	5-year	10-year
MSCI ACWI ESG Leaders	15.4%	14.8%	10.6%
MSCI ACWI	14.4%	14.8%	10.2%

Source: MSCI, 2021

RISK ANNUALIZED STANDARD DEVIATION

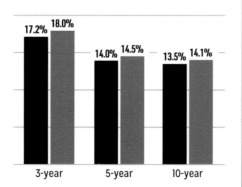

	3-year	5-year	10-year
MSCI ACWI ESG Leaders	17.2%	14.0%	13.5%
MSCI ACWI	18.0%	14.5%	14.1%

S&P 500 COMPANIES SUSTAINABILITY REPORTING

2011 — 20%
2019 — 90%

As the popularity of ESG investing grows, more companies are providing sustainability reports. This provides more transparency to investors and the public, and increases corporate accountability.

Source: Governance and Accountability Institute, 2019

INFLUENCING CHANGE

Over time, more investors have become signatories of the UN Principles for Responsible Investment (PRI). This has translated into more support for environmental and social proposals.

GROWING SUPPORT FOR SUSTAINABILITY

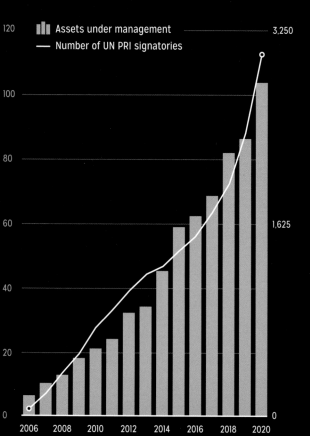

Focusing capital on environmental, social, and governance issues has widespread societal impacts. For example, environmental investments have potentially contributed to an increase in renewable electricity generation.

WORLD NET ELECTRICITY GENERATION
1990–2050

 Hydro   Wind   Solar Other renewables All other fossil fuels

The U.S. Energy Information Administration (2019) projects that renewables will provide 49% of world electricity by 2050, up from 28% in 2018.

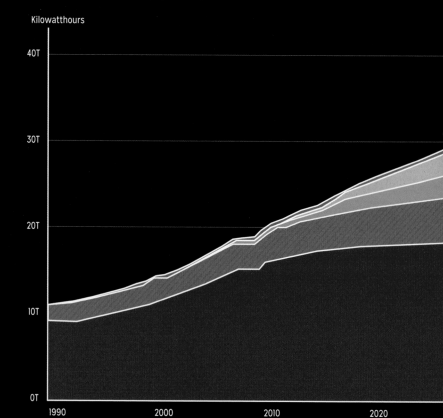

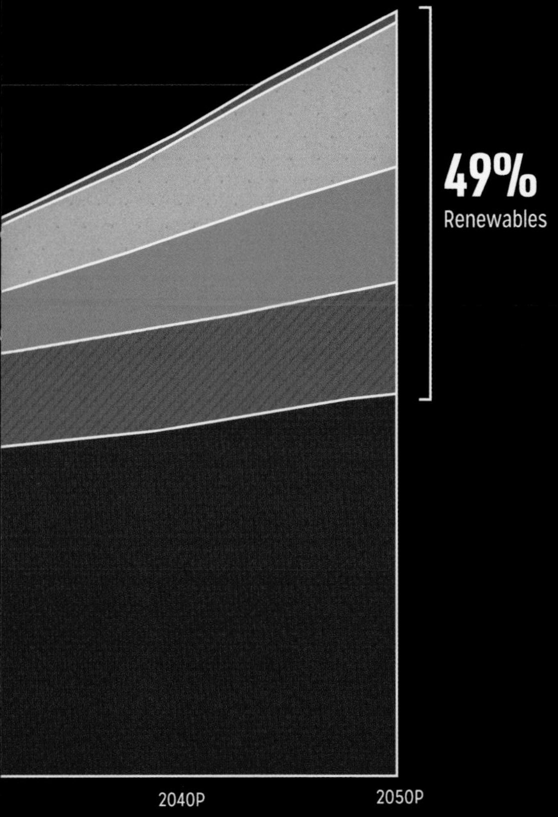

49%
Renewables

2040P   2050P

Projected net electricity generation ▶

SUSTAINABLE INVESTING IS FIRMLY IN THE MAINSTREAM.

With younger, more socially conscious generations set to inherit a wealth of spending power in the near future, sustainable investing practices represent a compelling opportunity for investors to create a positive impact while still generating strong returns.

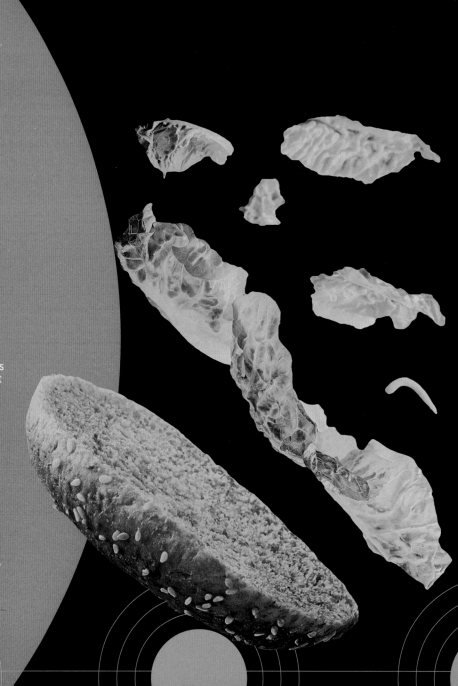

CHAPTER 06

CONSUMER BEHAVIOR

NUMBER OF SIGNALS / 03

Technology may help drive innovation, but it is ultimately the consumers who grease the wheels of commercialization. In this chapter, we look at three emerging trends in very different sectors that are capturing both the minds and wallets of consumers.

The first signal touches on the evolution of retail, in which consumers are gravitating toward a frictionless experience where barriers to transactions, logistics, and personalization are being eroded away by seamless technologies.

Then, we move to the rise of meatless meat—a consumer phenomenon taking place through technological advancements intersecting with environmental concerns and changing social attitudes. Finally, we end with a paradigm shift in healthcare, where discontent with the status quo is leading to a new vision of consumer-centric health.

As demand rapidly grows for products in these consumer-led segments, it's possible that slow-moving businesses in the retail, food, and healthcare spaces are at risk of being left behind.

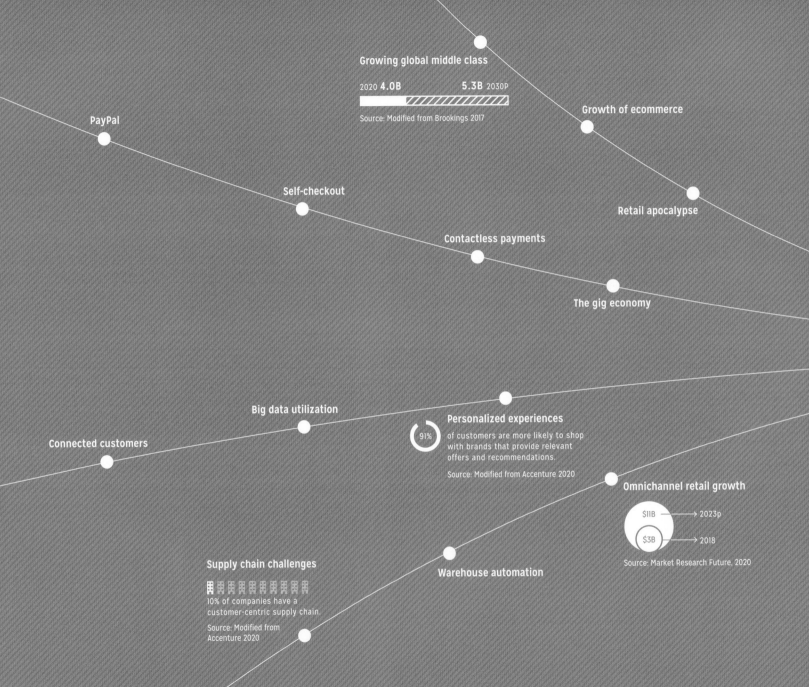

PayPal

Growing global middle class

2020 **4.0B**   **5.3B** 2030P

Source: Modified from Brookings 2017

Growth of ecommerce

Self-checkout

Retail apocalypse

Contactless payments

The gig economy

Big data utilization

Personalized experiences

91% of customers are more likely to shop with brands that provide relevant offers and recommendations.

Source: Modified from Accenture 2020

Connected customers

Omnichannel retail growth

$11B → 2023p

$3B → 2018

Source: Market Research Future, 2020

Supply chain challenges

10% of companies have a customer-centric supply chain.

Source: Modified from Accenture 2020

Warehouse automation

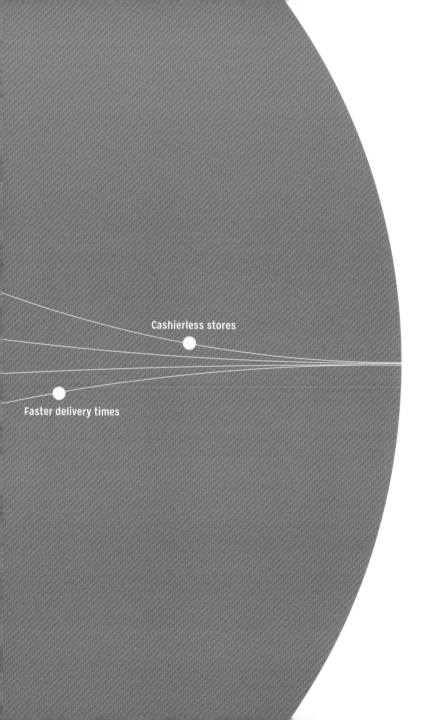

Faster delivery times

Cashierless stores

FRICTIONLESS RETAIL

FRICTIONLESS RETAIL

The retail world is undergoing a massive digital transformation. The confluence of innovations will remove friction from the customer experience and make buying things faster and easier than ever before.

SIGNAL RANGE
Moderate (3/5)

SIGNAL-TO-NOISE RATIO
Moderate (3/5)

SIGNAL

SMART RETAIL INVESTMENT GROWTH
GLOBAL IN-STORE RETAIL TECH COMPANY DEALS AND FINANCING
Source: CBInsights, 2020

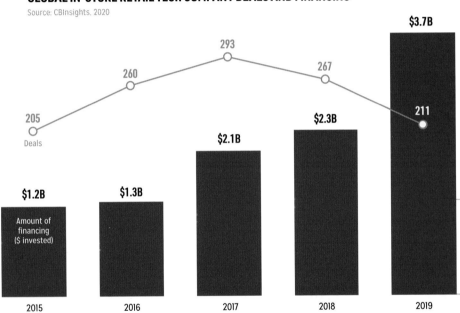

$3.7B

293

260

267

205
Deals

211

$2.3B

$2.1B

$1.2B

Amount of
financing
($ invested)

$1.3B

2015   2016   2017   2018   2019

TECHNOLOGICAL BREAKTHROUGHS, intense competition for customer dollars, and changing consumer tastes have all left their mark on the retail sector.

Retail brands are demanding ruthless efficiency on the supply chain side, and hunting for innovative new approaches to the customer experience in both the physical and digital realms.

Despite a 21% reduction in the number of deals in 2019, dollars invested increased by almost **60% to $3.7 billion**, with a median deal size of $7 million.

KEY FUNCTIONS among companies that use AI across retail and consumer packaged goods include:

 Merchandising   Inventory management   Checkout-free store tech   Point-of-sale shrinkage monitoring   Omnichannel marketing   Retail supply chain optimization   Ecommerce search

THE TECHNOLOGY PIPELINE

Piece-picking robots—which perform repetitive actions like loading boxes—will be a key component of ecommerce supply chain automation.

WAREHOUSE PIECE-PICKING ROBOTS MARKET FORECAST

REVENUE USD

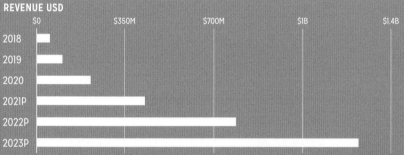

	$0	$350M	$700M	$1B	$1.4B
2018					
2019					
2020					
2021P					
2022P					
2023P					

Source: Modified from Interact analysis 2020

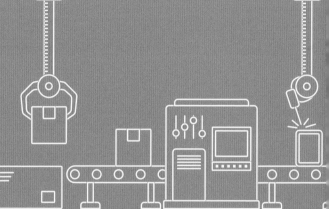

Warehouse automation is a magnet for investment, but technology is set to transform the retail landscape in other ways as well. Here is what the industry is investing in.

PERCENTAGE OF RETAIL, MANUFACTURING, AND LOGISTICS FIRMS

who are currently investing in the following technologies

Source: Hadwick, 2019

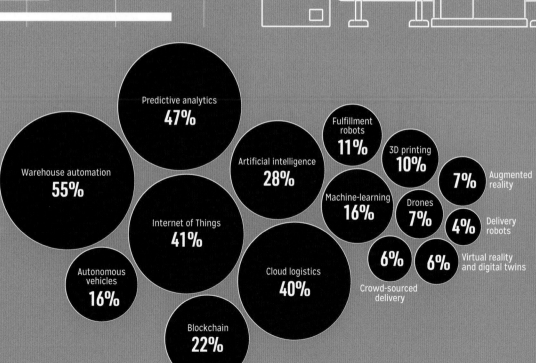

Predictive analytics
47%

Warehouse automation
55%

Artificial intelligence
28%

Fulfillment robots
11%

3D printing
10%

7% Augmented reality

Machine-learning
16%

Drones
7%

4% Delivery robots

Internet of Things
41%

Cloud logistics
40%

6% 6% Virtual reality and digital twins

Crowd-sourced delivery

Autonomous vehicles
16%

Blockchain
22%

THE AMAZON EFFECT

Amazon is closing the gap between online and offline shopping by delivering instant gratification and a seamless experience for its customers.

AMAZON PRIME MEMBERSHIPS

Source: Modified from Ali 2021

Number of members in the U.S.

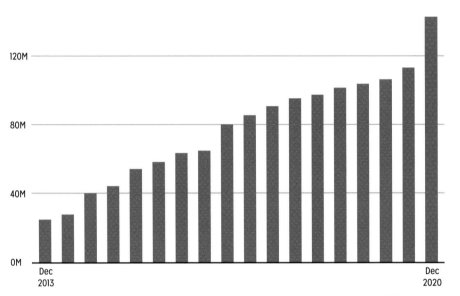

Dec 2013 — Dec 2020

CLICK-TO-DOOR TIMES FOR ONLINE ORDERS 2020
By days — Not Amazon — Amazon

As a powerful second-order effect, Amazon's shipping times have had a major impact on how quickly other retailers serve their customers. Other ecommerce brands have been forced to keep pace.

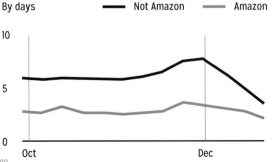

Oct — Dec

Source: Modified from Rakuten Intelligence 2019

The company is also launching cashierless stores called Amazon Go.

HERE'S HOW AMAZON GO WORKS:

1. Shopper scans an app to enter the store

2. Ceiling-mounted cameras and shelf censors track what items have been picked

3. Shopper leaves the store and their account is charged for the selected items

Amazon Go is only one example of "invisible payment" technologies, which are projected to grow to a value of $78 billion by 2022.

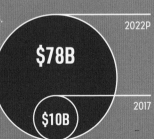

$78B — 2022P

$10B — 2017

Source: Smith, 2018

FRICTIONLESS SHOPPING

Consumer attitudes toward innovation in retail will continue to improve as new technologies become more commonplace. The majority of consumers are already willing to change their behavior if it makes their shopping experience easier.

% OF CONSUMERS WHO ARE WILLING TO SHIFT THEIR IN-STORE PURCHASES TO A RETAILER WHO USES AUTOMATION TECHNOLOGY

59% Agree	**22%** Neutral	**19%** Disagree

67% of those comfortable with automation are millennials

Interestingly, over half of consumers are willing to spend more in cashierless stores if it means that they can avoid speaking with a retail clerk.

Digital wallets appear to be the gateway for consumers to embrace cashierless shopping.

78% of consumers who made their most recent purchases using digital wallets are interested in making purchases via unattended channels.

Source: Modified from Bridges 2020

More brands will embrace augmented shopping, which enables customers to engage with brands and products via digital experiences. These experiences help deliver more detailed, intuitive product information than standard websites.

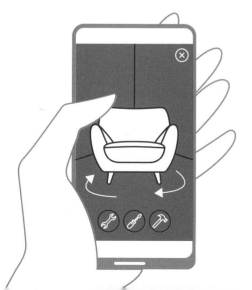

AUGMENTED SHOPPING OPPORTUNITY MATRIX

◯ Experimentation   ◯ Early technical successes   ◯ Positive ROI, spreading adoption

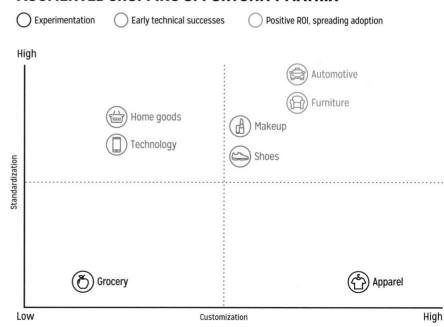

Source: Cook et al., 2020

THE BENEFITS OF INNOVATION

Along with providing an elevated customer experience, better employee engagement, and more efficient processes overall, the use of innovative technology could double store profitability.

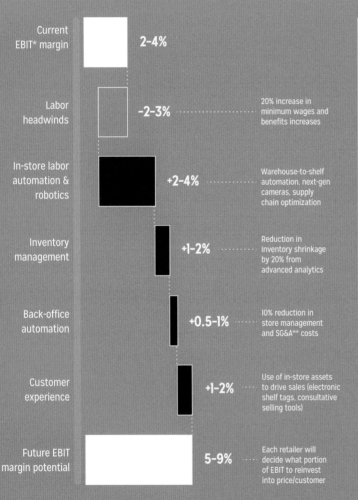

Current EBIT* margin	**2–4%**
Labor headwinds	**−2–3%** — 20% increase in minimum wages and benefits increases
In-store labor automation & robotics	**+2–4%** — Warehouse-to-shelf automation, next-gen cameras, supply chain optimization
Inventory management	**+1–2%** — Reduction in inventory shrinkage by 20% from advanced analytics
Back-office automation	**+0.5–1%** — 10% reduction in store management and SG&A** costs
Customer experience	**+1–2%** — Use of in-store assets to drive sales (electronic shelf tags, consultative selling tools)
Future EBIT margin potential	**5–9%** — Each retailer will decide what portion of EBIT to reinvest into price/customer

*Earnings before interest and taxes **Sales, general, and administrative
Source: McKinsey, 2020

As an industry, retail lags behind when it comes to businesses achieving digital maturity and creating long-term digital initiatives when compared to other industries like IT & technology.

Dwindling consumer loyalty and higher expectations for seamless experiences may put retailers in a tough spot if they don't prioritize innovation.

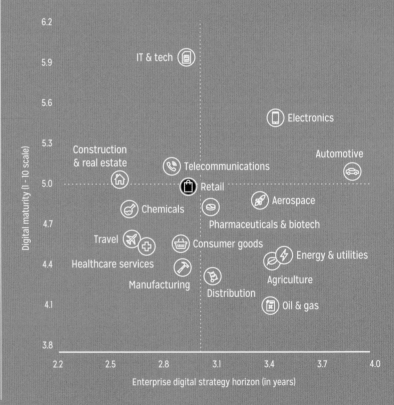

Source: Wellener et al., 2018

DISRUPTING THE WORKFORCE

The rapid pace of innovation across the supply chain will unlock a wealth of opportunities for retail brands, including solving consumer pain points and trimming operational costs. That said, automation in both the retail and distribution settings could ultimately lead to the displacement of millions of employees the world over.

RETAIL RELATED OCCUPATIONS ACCORDING TO THEIR PROBABILITY OF AUTOMATION

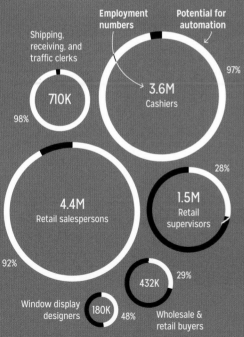

Employment numbers

Potential for automation

Shipping, receiving, and traffic clerks

710K — 98%

3.6M Cashiers — 97%

4.4M Retail salespersons — 92%

1.5M Retail supervisors — 28%

432K — 29%

Window display designers

180K — 48%

Wholesale & retail buyers

Source: U.S. Bureau of Labor Statistics 2020; Frey and Osborne, 2013

FRICTIONLESS RETAIL IS THE RESULT OF THE RELENTLESS PURSUIT OF CONVENIENCE.

This phenomenon is neither an online or offline outcome. Instead, the lines are being erased as consumers demand an experience that permeates both channels. Retailers that embrace technology to improve efficiency and eliminate pain points will reap the benefits. For customers, making day-to-day purchases will be easier than ever before.

Global population growth

7.7B | 9.7B

2020 | 2050P

Source: Modified from United Nations 2019

Food security

Innovation in food technology

Changing values

Diversified alternatives

Plant-based startup Beyond Meat goes public in 2019

Increase in share price of plant-based startup Beyond Meat on its first day of trading.
Source: Modified from Our World in Data 2019

Unsustainable supply chains

Animal welfare

Carbon footprint

Beef's carbon footprint is over 15x higher than tofu's.
Source: Based on BBC News 2019

Health conscious consumers

 40% of 18-30 year olds in the UK consume a diet consistent with clean eating.

Source: Based on Allen et al. 2018

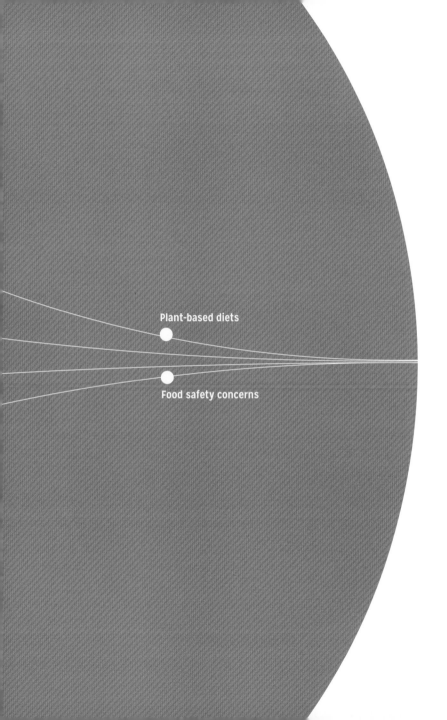

Plant-based diets

Food safety concerns

THE RISE OF MEATLESS MEAT

THE RISE OF MEATLESS MEAT

SIGNAL RANGE
Moderate (3/5)

SIGNAL-TO-NOISE RATIO
Moderate (3/5)

Meat alternatives are rapidly growing in popularity worldwide. Research shows that the widespread adoption of faux meat could bring about benefits for both people and the planet, and potentially disrupt the conventional meat industry.

GLOBAL MEAT ALTERNATIVES MARKET FORECAST, USD

By 2040, sales of meat alternatives are estimated to overtake sales of conventional meat.

● Conventional meat ● Meat alternatives

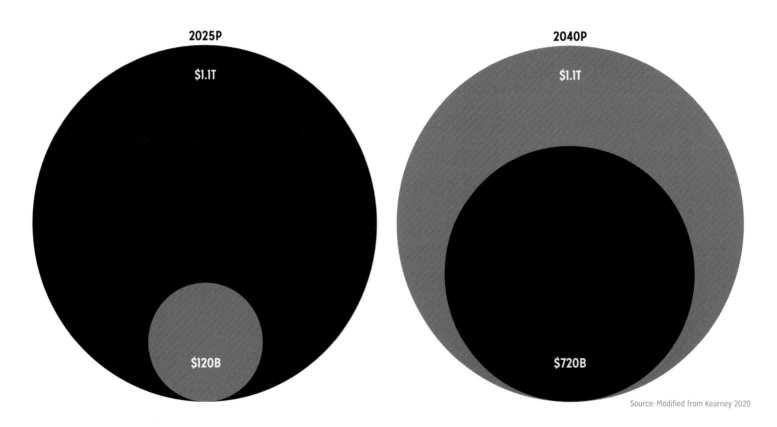

2025P

$1.1T

$120B

2040P

$1.1T

$720B

Source: Modified from Kearney 2020

GLOBAL MEAT CONSUMPTION USD

Consumption of conventional meat could decline by more than 33% over the same time period.

- ● Conventional meat
- ◐ Cultured meat
- ○ Novel vegan meat replacement

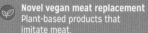

Cultured meat
Engineered in a lab using animal cells.

Novel vegan meat replacement
Plant-based products that imitate meat.

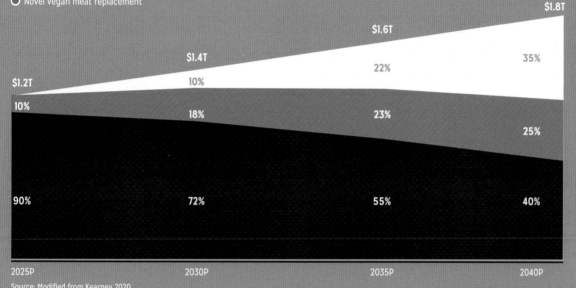

$1.2T $1.4T $1.6T $1.8T

	10%	22%	35%
10%	18%	23%	25%
90%	72%	55%	40%

2025P   2030P   2035P   2040P

Source: Modified from Kearney 2020

CAGR (2025–2040)

+41%

+9%

-3%

Technological advancements and changing consumer preferences could result in cultured meat overtaking novel vegan meat by 2040.

Demand for conventional meat is estimated to decline by about 3% each year despite meat consumption increasing by 3% each year.

INTEREST IN PROTEIN DIETS

Consumer interest in alternative proteins has skyrocketed since 2016.

Internet queries normalized to highest point (based off of internet searches)

○ Vegan   ○ Vegetarian   ● High protein   ○ Dairy free

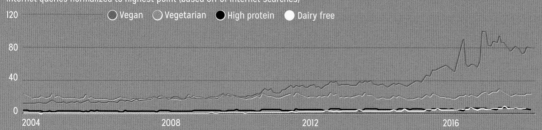

120
80
40
0

2004   2008   2012   2016

Source: Modified from Google Trends 2019

TOTAL U.S. PLANT BASED MEAT MARKET USD

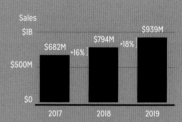

Sales
$1B
$500M
$0

$682M   +16% $794M   +18% $939M

2017   2018   2019

This demand is reflected in plant-based meat sales, as the U.S. experienced 38% growth in alternatives between 2017 and 2019, while overall retail food sales grew by just 4%.

Source: Modified from Good Food Institute 2020

IMPACT ON HEALTH

Foods that have a negative impact on the environment are also associated with significant reductions in mortality.

HEALTH AND ENVIRONMENTAL IMPACT PER SERVING OF FOOD PER DAY

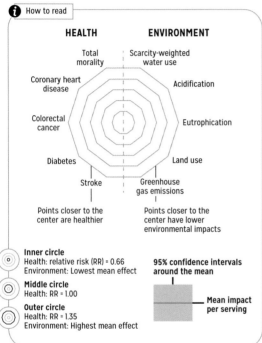

How to read

HEALTH — **ENVIRONMENT**

- Total morality
- Coronary heart disease
- Colorectal cancer
- Diabetes
- Stroke

- Scarcity-weighted water use
- Acidification
- Eutrophication
- Land use
- Greenhouse gas emissions

Points closer to the center are healthier

Points closer to the center have lower environmental impacts

Inner circle
Health: relative risk (RR) = 0.66
Environment: Lowest mean effect

Middle circle
Health: RR = 1.00

Outer circle
Health: RR = 1.35
Environment: Highest mean effect

95% confidence intervals around the mean

Mean impact per serving

The environmental impact of foods is heavily influenced by agricultural production. For example, organic foods typically require more landmass and cause more pollution per unit of food compared to nonorganic foods.

Water use for nuts depends on the type, and regional availability.

WHOLE GRAINS

FRUITS

VEGETABLES

NUTS

LEGUMES

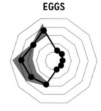

POTATOES

REFINED GRAINS

No data

FISH

DAIRY

EGGS

UNPROCESSED MEAT

PROCESSED RED MEAT

ALL FOODS

CHICKEN

Producing one serving of chicken causes more environmental damage than most other foods

No data

SSBs

OLIVE OIL

No data

While consuming both meat types is associated with a significant increase in disease risk, it is higher for processed red meat.

Both types also have the highest mean environmental impact of all foods studied, due in part to high greenhouse gas emissions.

Source: Modified from Springman et al. 2019

ANIMAL WELFARE

The number of animals killed for meat production could see a decline if more people embrace a predominantly plant-based diet.

TOTAL NUMBER OF ANIMALS KILLED FOR MEAT EACH YEAR 2018

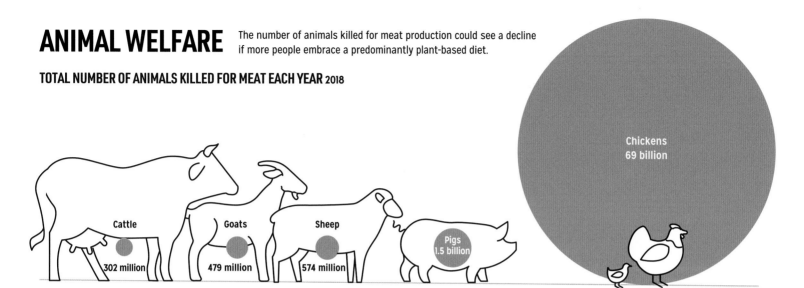

Cattle
302 million

Goats
479 million

Sheep
574 million

Pigs
1.5 billion

Chickens
69 billion

Source: Modified from UN FAO 2020

A CLOSER LOOK AT LAND USE

An increase in plant-based diets would mean less livestock would need to be raised, freeing up land for other uses. Currently, over 127 million acres of land in the U.S. is used to feed livestock, which is roughly the size of California.

Source: Merrill et al., 2018

DISRUPTION OF THE MEAT MARKET

ANIMAL REVENUE OF MEAT COMPANIES

Global meat behemoths, who rely on animal-based products for a majority of their total revenue, could be vulnerable to the growth of meat alternatives.

Company	Market Cap (2019 USD)	Animal revenue, 2016
Hormel Foods	$22.6B	67%
Tyson	$20.6B	82%
JBS	$8.7B	69%
Pilgrim's	$4.1B	94%
Sanderson Farms	$2.4B	100%
Bachoco	$2.1B	78%

Several of these companies are already investing in alternative protein startups and new product development that will allow them to compete in the space.

Source: Modified from CB Insights 2019

A TIPPING POINT FOR THE WIDER ALTERNATIVES MARKET

Aside from meat, there has been a huge amount of innovation in other plant-based alternative markets, and they are also poised for growth in the coming years.

GLOBAL DAIRY ALTERNATIVES MARKET PROJECTION USD

$21B 2020

$37B 2025P

CAGR 11.4%

Source: Modified from McKinsey 2019

TOUGH COMPETITION

The plant-based ecosystem is becoming more and more competitive each year as new products enter the market.

○ Vegan ◐ Vegetarian ○ Dairy free ◐ High protein ● Ethical

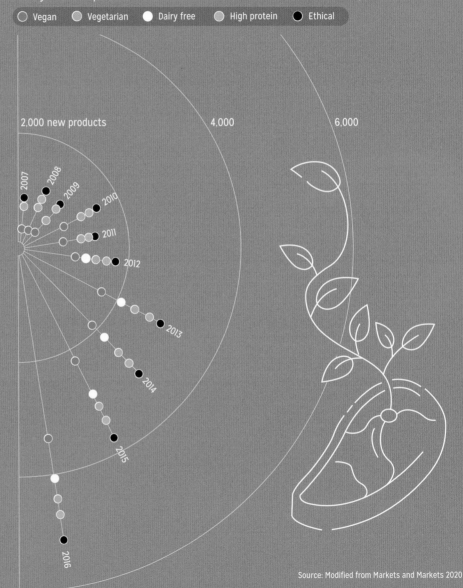

2,000 new products   4,000   6,000

2007 2008 2009 2010 2011 2012 2013 2014 2015 2016

Source: Modified from Markets and Markets 2020

THE NEED TO SCALE

If the market is to succeed, pricing for alternatives will need to see a substantial decrease to appeal to a broader audience.

MEAT PRICING IN THE U.S. PER 100G, 2018

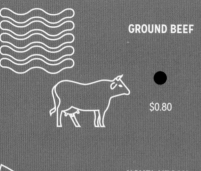

GROUND BEEF

$0.80

NOVEL VEGAN ALTERNATIVE

$2.50

CULTURED MEAT

$80.00

Source: Based on Kearney 2020

As the saying goes,

"WE ARE WHAT WE EAT."

While the benefits of meat-based diets have been debated for decades, research studies in favor of reducing meat consumption are growing.

The global shift toward plant-based diets could prove significant when it comes to not only improving health outcomes, but tackling climate change as well.

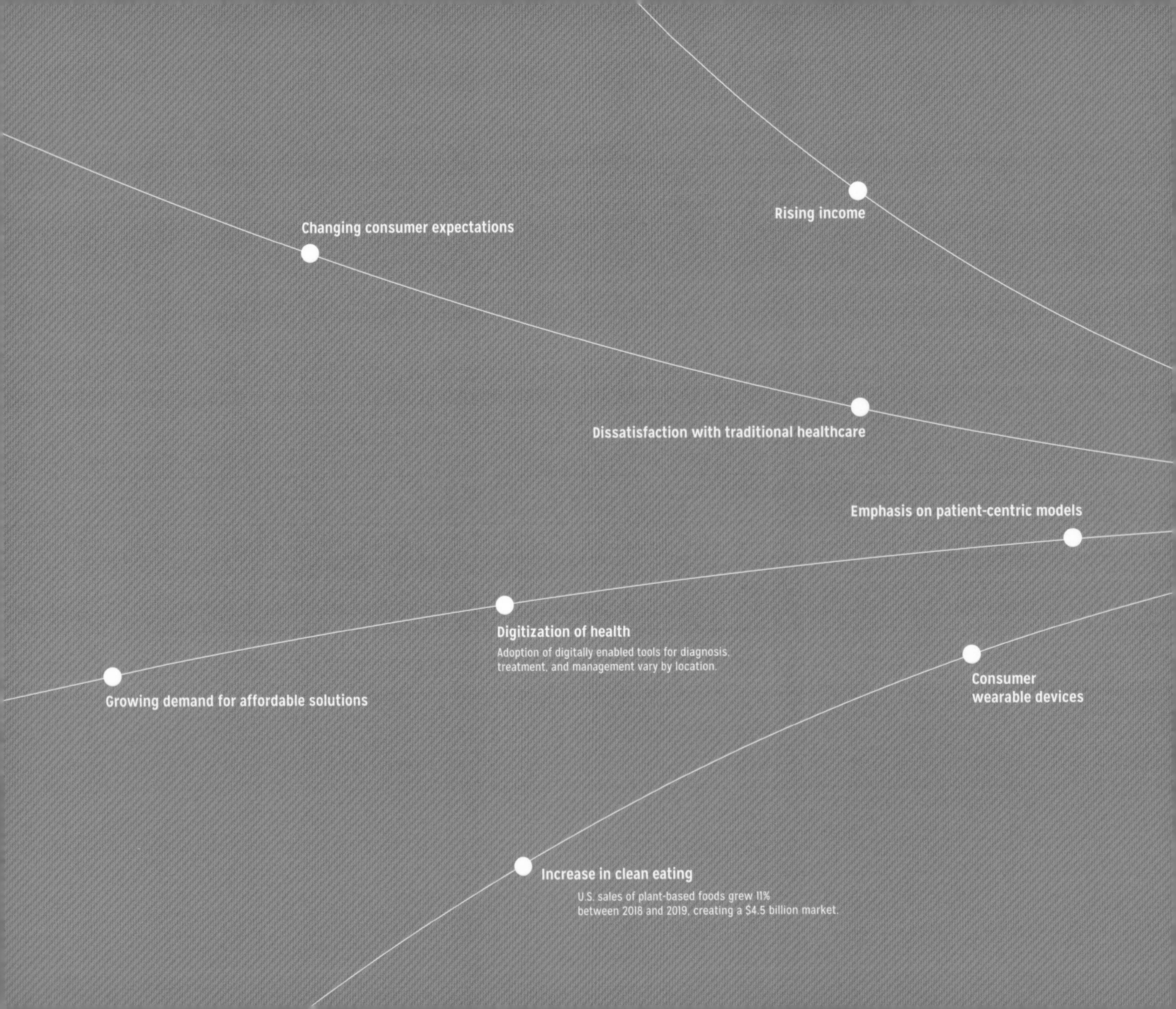

Changing consumer expectations

Rising income

Dissatisfaction with traditional healthcare

Emphasis on patient-centric models

Digitization of health
Adoption of digitally enabled tools for diagnosis,
treatment, and management vary by location.

Growing demand for affordable solutions

**Consumer
wearable devices**

Increase in clean eating
U.S. sales of plant-based foods grew 11%
between 2018 and 2019, creating a $4.5 billion market.

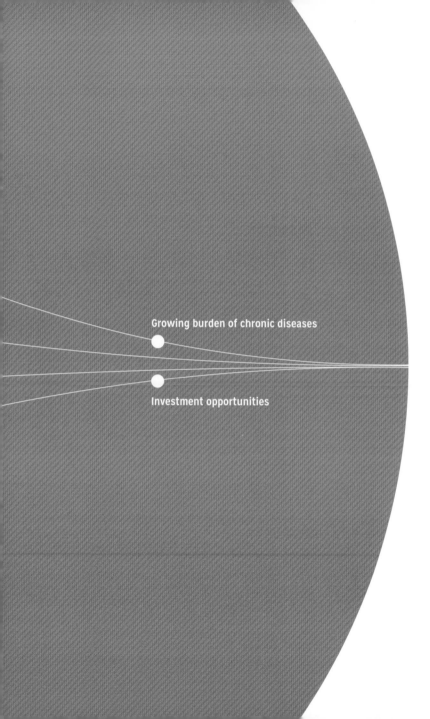

Growing burden of chronic diseases

Investment opportunities

CONNECTED HEALTH

CONNECTED HEALTH

SIGNAL RANGE	SIGNAL-TO-NOISE RATIO
Broad (4/5)	Moderate (3/5)

Dissatisfied with traditional healthcare systems, consumers are armed with information about their health, and ready to take matters into their own hands.

ADOPTION OF DIGITAL HEALTH TOOLS ● 2015 ● 2019

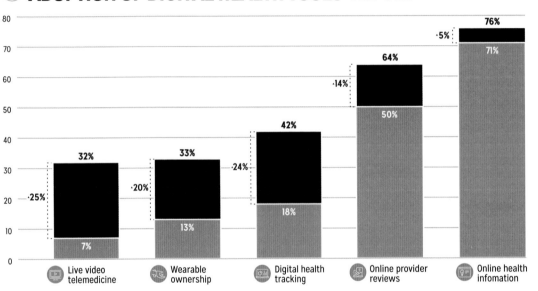

- Live video telemedicine: 32% (2019), 7% (2015), +25%
- Wearable ownership: 33% (2019), 13% (2015), +20%
- Digital health tracking: 42% (2019), 18% (2015), +24%
- Online provider reviews: 64% (2019), 50% (2015), +14%
- Online health infomation: 76% (2019), 71% (2015), +5%

Source: Modified from Rock Health 2020

MORE AND MORE consumers are adopting innovative health management tools such as wearables in an attempt to prevent chronic illnesses.

This proactive approach to health is decreasing their reliance on traditional forms of healthcare, which is forcing healthcare services to reassess how they engage with their patients.

PERCENTAGE OF CONSUMERS WHO HAVE VISITED A PRIMARY CARE PHYSICIAN IN THE LAST 12 MONTHS

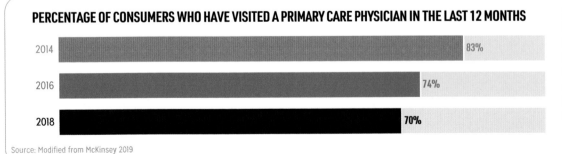

- 2014: 83%
- 2016: 74%
- 2018: 70%

Source: Modified from McKinsey 2019

Fewer consumers are visiting their doctor each year. However, they continue to use emergency services for several reasons, from not being able to make a doctor's appointment at a suitable time, to the doctor's office not being open when they need them.

FRUSTRATION WITH THE STATUS QUO

Consumers from every age group are willing to try nontraditional services, but younger generations are particularly dissatisfied with the quality of their healthcare, and are consequently fueling the demand for more digital capabilities.

PERCENTAGE OF PEOPLE WHO ARE DISSATISFIED WITH ASPECTS OF TRADITIONAL HEALTHCARE

● Gen Z   ○ Millennials   ● Gen X   ○ Baby Boomers   ○ Silent Generation

Effectiveness of treatment

- 32%
- 12%
- 5%
- 4%
- 5%

Convenience of the location or channel

- 24%
- 13%
- 8%
- 4%
- 4%

Transparency about care

- 23%
- 13%
- 9%
- 9%
- 3%

Efficient operations (i.e., e-billing)

- 18%
- 16%
- 11%
- 8%
- 5%

Source: Modified from Accenture 2019

CONNECTED HEALTH DEVICES GROWING IN POPULARITY

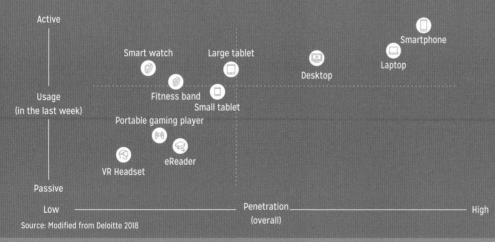

Active

Smart watch   Large tablet   Smartphone

Fitness band   Desktop   Laptop

Usage (in the last week)

Small tablet

Portable gaming player

VR Headset   eReader

Passive

Low ———— Penetration (overall) ———— High

Source: Modified from Deloitte 2018

Consumers are integrating newer digital devices such as wearables into their everyday lives more often. Wearables could even overtake more mature products such as tablets and desktops in terms of relevance, as they continue to play an increasingly large role in consumers managing their overall health.

In fact, wearable devices could gain even more traction with the help of high speed 5G networks, which will enhance data precision and allow for smaller, and less obtrusive, models.

WHAT IS CONNECTED HEALTH?

Connected health leverages the use of digital technology, such as telehealth or remote patient monitoring, to create integrated care solutions that revolve around patients, rather than practitioners.

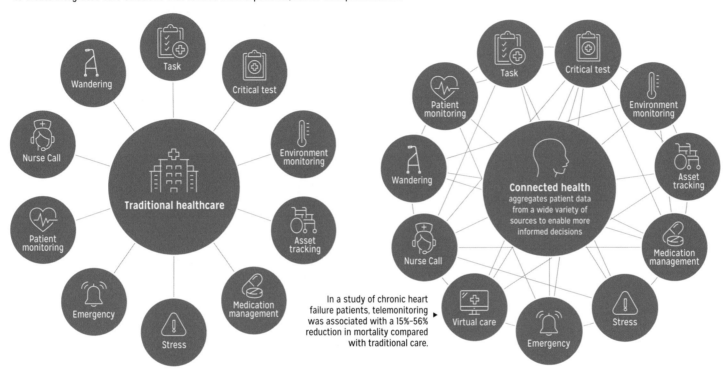

In a study of chronic heart failure patients, telemonitoring was associated with a 15%–56% reduction in mortality compared with traditional care. ▸

Source: VMware, 2017; Drobac et al., 2014

POTENTIAL COST SAVINGS

By 2040, global GDP could increase by roughly $12 trillion, as a result of health improvements aided by digital innovation. For example, artificial intelligence (AI) systems could be revolutionary for certain molecular technologies, such as gene editing, which could unlock huge cost savings.

Souce: Remes et al., 2020

POTENTIAL ECONOMIC BENEFITS FROM HEALTH IMPROVEMENTS, GDP

Potential GDP 2040 **$153.7T**

- Base case GDP in 2040 **$142T**
- Fewer early deaths **$1.4T**
- Fewer health conditions **$4.2T**
- Expanded participation **$4.1T**
- Increase in productivity **$2.0T**

THE EXPLOSION OF THE HEALTH TECH INDUSTRY

The demand for connected healthcare has created a market that is set to grow to $884 billion between 2020 and 2030 at a CAGR of 21.8%.

PERCENTAGE OF EXECUTIVES WHO BELIEVE DATA AND INTEROPERABILITY WILL BE THE INDUSTRY NORM BY 2030

94% agree

Next-generation data-sharing and interoperability solutions enable clinical care teams to share most of their patients' data.

88% agree

Widespread use of personal health technology by consumers is integrated with care delivery and results in more personalized, tailored care.

86% agree

Patient-generated data is automatically integrated into electronic health records and made available to clinicians and patients for decision-making.

BIG TECH MEETS BIG HEALTHCARE

Since 2010, the biggest tech companies* in the U.S. have been investing in digital health applications, with Google being the most active.

THE BIGGEST CATEGORIES, BY NUMBER OF DEALS

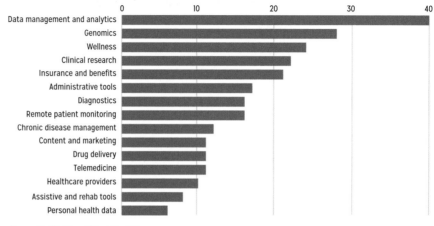

Source: Modified from CB Insights 2019
*By market capitalization as of 2018

As the level of investment activity grows, so too does the body of evidence that proves the efficacy of using digital health tools.

PUBLISHED DIGITAL HEALTH EFFICACY STUDIES

● Observational study ● Randomized control trial ● Systematic review or critically appraised topics ● Meta analysis

Number of studies — 571 efficacy studies between 2007 and 2017

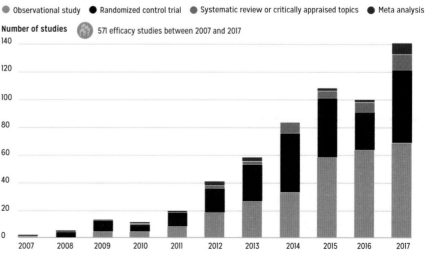

Source: Iqvia Institute, 2017

THE HEALTH AND WELLNESS ECOSYSTEM

The rise in conscientious health consumers has opened the floodgates to an entire health and wellness ecosystem that's valued at trillions of dollars.

WELLNESS ECONOMY SECTORS

 **$1T**
Personal care, beauty, & anti-aging

 $702B
Healthy eating, nutrition, & weight loss

 $639B
Wellness tourism

 $595B
Fitness & mind-body

 $575B
Preventive & personalized medicine & public health

 $360B
Traditional & complementary medicine

 $134B
Wellness real estate

 $119B
Spa economy

 $56B
Thermal/mineral springs

$48B
Workplace wellness

Source: Modified from Global Wellness Institute 2018

UNPRECEDENTED FUNDING

In 2020, digital health companies in the U.S. raised $14 billion in venture funding, almost double the amount in 2019.

DIGITAL HEALTH VENTURE FUNDING IN THE U.S.

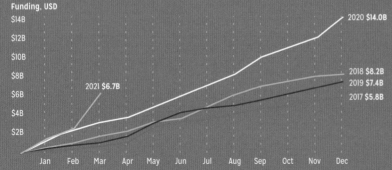

Funding, USD

2020 $14.0B
2018 $8.2B
2019 $7.4B
2021 $6.7B
2017 $5.8B

$14B $12B $10B $8B $6B $4B $2B

Jan Feb Mar Apr May Jun Jul Aug Sep Oct Nov Dec

Source: Modified from Rock Health 2021

DISRUPTIVE INNOVATION IN HEALTHCARE

Experts predict that digital health solutions will completely transform the healthcare industry by creating affordable, effective, and accessible patient solutions.

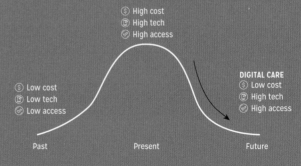

($) High cost
High tech
High access

($) Low cost
Low tech
Low access

DIGITAL CARE
($) Low cost
High tech
High access

Past   Present   Future

Source: Goldman Sachs, 2015

DATA PRIVACY CONCERNS

Consumers are apprehensive about sharing their personal data with companies, which suggests that building trust will be a significant challenge going forward.

COMFORT LEVEL WITH SHARING PERSONAL DATA, U.S. AND UK

- ● I feel **very comfortable**
- ● I feel **somewhat comfortable**
- ○ **I am not sure** how I feel about it
- ◐ I feel **somewhat uncomfortable**
- ○ I feel **very uncomfortable**
- ● Prefer not to say

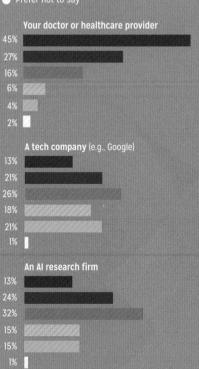

Your doctor or healthcare provider

45%	
27%	
16%	
6%	
4%	
2%	

A tech company (e.g., Google)

13%	
21%	
26%	
18%	
21%	
1%	

An AI research firm

13%	
24%	
32%	
15%	
15%	
1%	

Source: Modified from Global Web Index 2020

"AN OUNCE OF PREVENTION IS WORTH A POUND OF CURE."

—Benjamin Franklin

Although consumers are asserting their position on connected, patient-focused healthcare, conventional healthcare systems may face significant challenges in adapting to these needs.

Regardless, digital technology is proving to be a relentless force with the power to create a sustainable healthcare system for the world's rapidly growing population.

GEOPOLITICAL LANDSCAPE

NUMBER OF SIGNALS / 03

The election cycle is short, and political power can swing at the drop of a hat.

However, outside of the ebb and flow of politics as usual, there are actually much more powerful forces in the background that shape the geopolitical landscape. These economic, monetary, and cultural shifts occur at a more gradual pace, but they are also much more potent in the long run.

In particular, this chapter focuses on the ripple effects of one of the more persistent trends affecting the global economy—the economic rise of China.

Not only has this surge in Chinese economic strength led to two distinct spheres of global trade influence, but it has even split the internet into two competing visions. We look at the data on these clear signals, as well as how the very nature of globalization itself is changing.

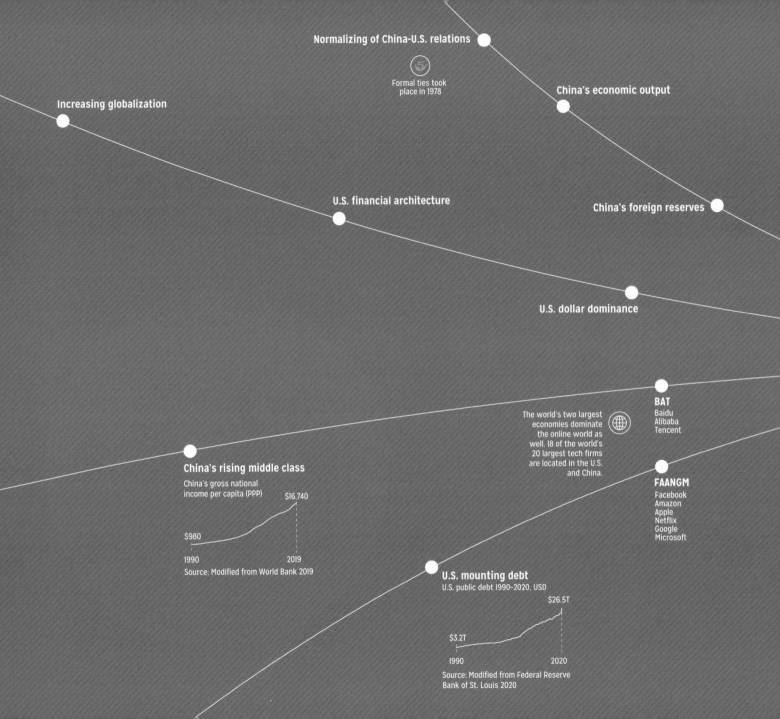

Normalizing of China-U.S. relations

Formal ties took
place in 1978

China's economic output

Increasing globalization

U.S. financial architecture

China's foreign reserves

U.S. dollar dominance

The world's two largest
economies dominate
the online world as
well. 18 of the world's
20 largest tech firms
are located in the U.S.
and China.

BAT
Baidu
Alibaba
Tencent

China's rising middle class

China's gross national
income per capita (PPP)

$16,740

$980

1990   2019

Source: Modified from World Bank 2019

FAANGM
Facebook
Amazon
Apple
Netflix
Google
Microsoft

U.S. mounting debt
U.S. public debt 1990–2020, USD

$26.5T

$3.2T

1990   2020

Source: Modified from Federal Reserve
Bank of St. Louis 2020

Belt and Road Initiative

BIPOLAR WORLD

BIPOLAR WORLD

China is challenging America's role as the world's sole superpower. As a result of China's widening influence, twin spheres of global dominance are projected for the future.

SIGNAL RANGE
Broad (4/5)

SIGNAL-TO-NOISE RATIO
Very High (5/5)

QUANTIFYING POWER

PURCHASING POWER PARITY (PPP) / SHARE OF GLOBAL TOTAL, 1980–2020

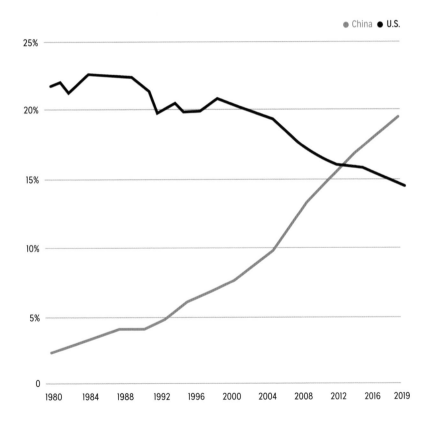

● China ● U.S.

TWO PILLARS are shaping the world's trade and financial architecture. Since WWII, the U.S. has maintained its foothold as a global superpower, underscored by its dollar dominance, multilateralism, and military prowess. At the same time, China is increasingly solidifying its power.

Since market liberalizations in 1978, China's economy has doubled every eight years. Four of the largest banks in the world (by assets) are located in China—and in the age of easy money, it is one of the largest creditors in the world.

Depending on the measurement, the most powerful economy in the world oscillates between China and the U.S. The era of America's singular dominance is being challenged across multiple strategic domains, with several second-order outcomes.

NOMINAL GDP 2019

One reason why China's economy is smaller in nominal GDP terms is its lower price of goods.

China nominal GDP | U.S. nominal GDP

$14.3 TRILLION | $21.4 TRILLION

Source: Morrison, 2019

WHO IS THE LARGER TRADING PARTNER? BY GEOGRAPHIC REGION IN 2018

In a short period of time, China has overtaken the U.S. as the largest trading partner across 128 of 190 countries. In fact, 90 countries traded with China nearly twice as much as they did with the U.S. in 2018.

○ Traded more than twice as much with China   ○ Traded mainly with China   ○ Traded mainly with the U.S.   ● Traded twice as much with the U.S.   ○ No data

NORTH AMERICA

EUROPE

ASIA

AFRICA

LATIN AMERICA & THE CARIBBEAN

AUSTRALIA & NEW ZEALAND

Source: Modified from Lowy Institute calculations 2019

% OF COUNTRIES TRADING MORE WITH U.S. OR CHINA

China 20%
U.S. 80%
2001

China 70%
U.S. 30%
2018

YUAN: A GROWING TRADE CURRENCY

China's expanding trade presence could foreshadow a shift toward the yuan. In other words, the yuan could replace the dollar as a major trade currency. Cross-border trade settlement in renminbi (RMB), instead of U.S. dollars, has risen exponentially since 2010.

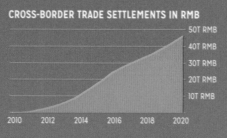

CROSS-BORDER TRADE SETTLEMENTS IN RMB

50T RMB
40T RMB
30T RMB
20T RMB
10T RMB

2010 2012 2014 2016 2018 2020

Source: Modified from CEIC, The People's Bank of China 2020

CHINA-U.S. TRADE DYNAMICS

At the same time, trade between the U.S. and China has grown over tenfold in the last 30 years. Of course, recent trade wars have caused fractures between the two nations' trade relationship.

BILATERAL TRADE BETWEEN CHINA AND U.S.

1980 | $5B
2018 | $660B

Source: Congressional Research Service, 2019

FOREIGN POLICY & THE BELT AND ROAD INITIATIVE

As its formative foreign policy initiative, China's Belt & Road Initiative (BRI) has signed infrastructure agreements with 138 countries, many of which are developing. Increasingly, BRI countries are accounting for a greater share of China's trade volumes.

TRADE VOLUME ACROSS BRI COUNTRIES

Source: Modified from Steil and Della Rocca 2019

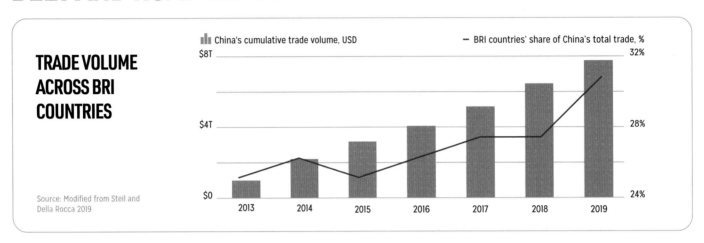

China's cumulative trade volume, USD — BRI countries' share of China's total trade, %

GROWING ECONOMIC TIES

The bilateral relationship between BRI countries and China can also be illustrated in key economic indicators: imports from China and external debt to China.

● Imports from China ● Debt to China

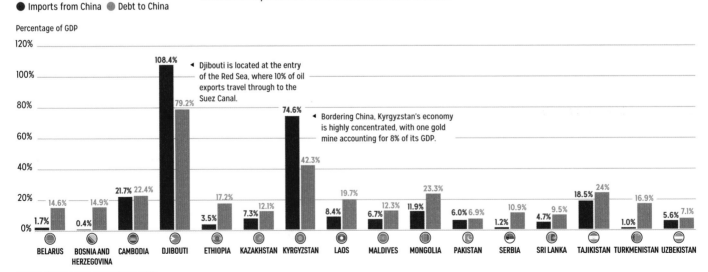

Djibouti is located at the entry of the Red Sea, where 10% of oil exports travel through to the Suez Canal.

Bordering China, Kyrgyzstan's economy is highly concentrated, with one gold mine accounting for 8% of its GDP.

Source: Modified from Ding and Xiao 2020

CHINA'S 25 LARGEST MEGAPROJECTS

China's sophisticated infrastructure projects are a pivotal part of its financial diplomacy maneuvers. Globally, there are over 3,485 megaprojects backed by China's government, many of which fall under the BRI. Overall, they are valued in excess of $350 billion.

Largest 25 officially financed Chinese projects by financial amount, in millions of constant 2009 USD

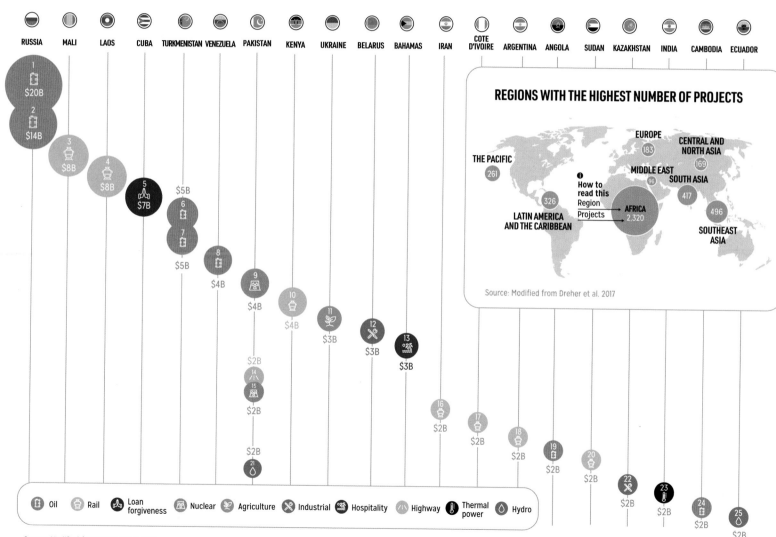

REGIONS WITH THE HIGHEST NUMBER OF PROJECTS

THE PACIFIC — 261
EUROPE — 183
CENTRAL AND NORTH ASIA — 169
MIDDLE EAST — 96
SOUTH ASIA — 417
LATIN AMERICA AND THE CARIBBEAN — 326
AFRICA — 2,320
SOUTHEAST ASIA — 496

How to read this
Region
Projects

Source: Modified from Dreher et al. 2017

Countries (left to right): RUSSIA, MALI, LAOS, CUBA, TURKMENISTAN, VENEZUELA, PAKISTAN, KENYA, UKRAINE, BELARUS, BAHAMAS, IRAN, COTE D'IVOIRE, ARGENTINA, ANGOLA, SUDAN, KAZAKHSTAN, INDIA, CAMBODIA, ECUADOR

Legend: Oil, Rail, Loan forgiveness, Nuclear, Agriculture, Industrial, Hospitality, Highway, Thermal power, Hydro

Source: Modified from Dreher et al. 2017

GLOBAL IMPLICATIONS

As China's bilateral relationships proliferate, the RMB is gaining a noticeable foothold. Although the dollar reserve currency bloc still accounts for the largest share globally, the RMB bloc accounts for a 30% share of global GDP.

RESERVE CURRENCY BLOCS BY REGION

● EUR ◐ GBP ○ JPY ● USD ● RMB ● No data

i Reserve currency blocs are the reserve currency that wields the most authority over a given country. In turn, these can influence global exchange rates

NORTH AMERICA

EUROPE

ASIA

AFRICA

LATIN AMERICA & THE CARIBBEAN

AUSTRALIA & NEW ZEALAND

Source: Modified from Nor and Mora 2018

RESERVE CURRENCY BLOCS % SHARE OF GLOBAL GDP

40%
Dollar bloc

30%
RMB bloc

20%
Euro bloc

CHALLENGING U.S. FINANCIAL DOMINANCE

Despite China's formidable rise, the global financial fabric is still dominated by America.

Since the end of WWII, with the emergence of the International Monetary Fund and World Bank, the U.S. has controlled the world's financial plumbing. For instance, SWIFT's 11,000 global members send over 37 million interbank transactions daily.

At the same time, the dollar remains the safest store of value in the world. It underpins the majority of foreign exchange reserves, global supply chains, and international loans—for now at least.

Source: Gourinchas, 2019; SWIFT, 2020

USD 62%
EUR 20%
JPY 5%
GBP 4%
RMB 2%

FOREIGN EXCHANGE RESERVES

USD 59%
EUR 21%
JPY 4%

INTERNATIONAL LOANS

USD 63%
EUR 22%
JPY 3%

INTERNATIONAL DEBTS

CURRENCY CENTRALITY

Crucially, 40% of global payments are conducted in the dollar, while 2% are conducted in renminbi. This will likely take years to shift.

GLOBAL PAYMENT CURRENCY

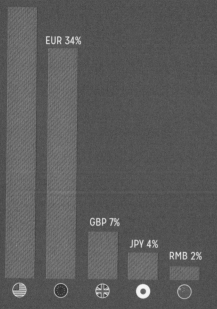

USD 40%

EUR 34%

GBP 7%

JPY 4%

RMB 2%

Source: Gourinchas, 2019; Carney, 2019

USD 44%
EUR 16%
JPY 11%
GBP 6%
RMB 2%

FOREIGN EXCHANGE TURNOVER

"GREAT POWERS HAVE GREAT CURRENCIES."

—Robert Mundell, Nobel Laureate in 1993

Thanks to its sprawling trade network and powerful currency, China's position as an emerging superpower is gaining speed.

However, the U.S. has deep roots embedded in the financial architecture of the world, and whether or not China will gain enough ground to take over as the number-one global superpower remains to be seen.

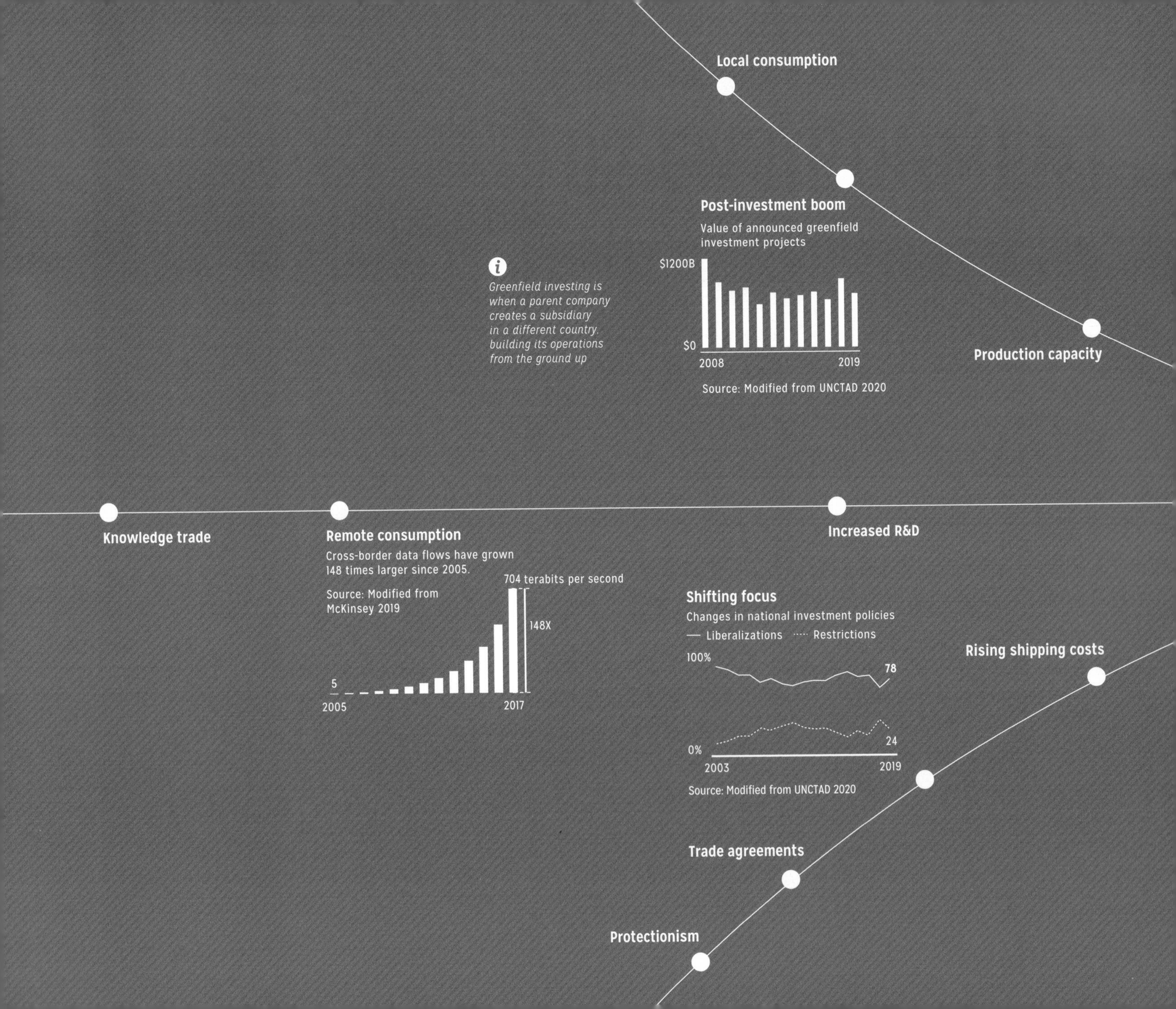

Local consumption

Post-investment boom

Value of announced greenfield
investment projects

ⓘ
*Greenfield investing is
when a parent company
creates a subsidiary
in a different country,
building its operations
from the ground up*

$1200B

$0

2008   2019

Source: Modified from UNCTAD 2020

Production capacity

Knowledge trade

Increased R&D

Remote consumption

Cross-border data flows have grown
148 times larger since 2005.

Source: Modified from
McKinsey 2019

704 terabits per second

148X

5

2005   2017

Shifting focus

Changes in national investment policies
— Liberalizations   ⋯⋯ Restrictions

100%   78

0%   24
2003   2019

Source: Modified from UNCTAD 2020

Rising shipping costs

Trade agreements

Protectionism

Lower labor exports

Only 18% of global goods trade is driven by labor-cost arbitrage.

Source: Modified from McKinsey 2019

Labor-cost arbitrage refers to exports from countries where the GDP per capita is one-fifth or less than that of the importing country

Post-COVID safety

SIGNAL 26

PEAK GLOBALIZATION

PEAK GLOBALIZATION

Decades of runaway growth were rudely interrupted by the Global Financial Crisis in 2008. Since then, global trade has undergone a transformation and it seems that globalization will take a different turn in the imminent future.

SIGNAL RANGE
Broad (4/5)

SIGNAL-TO-NOISE RATIO
Medium (3/5)

GLOBAL TRADE AS A % OF GDP

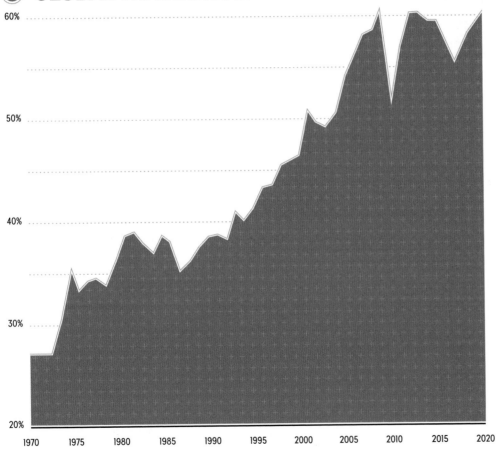

GLOBALIZATION IS NEITHER STATIC NOR CONSTANT. A plethora of factors influence the complex web of international trade. Despite the complexity, one thing is becoming clear—globalization's rapid ascent has stalled out. This shift has major implications for the global economy and geopolitics.

TRADE VOLUME GROWTH AVERAGE

1990–2007

2.1X FASTER
than real GDP

SINCE 2011

1.1X FASTER
than real GDP

Source: Modified from Kuznetsov 2019

PROTECTIONISM IS ON THE UPSWING

Market protectionism has been a rising trend since the financial crisis, with the United States leading the way.

PROTECTIONIST MEASURES TAKEN BY G20 COUNTRIES

Number of discriminatory interventions imposed since Nov. 2008

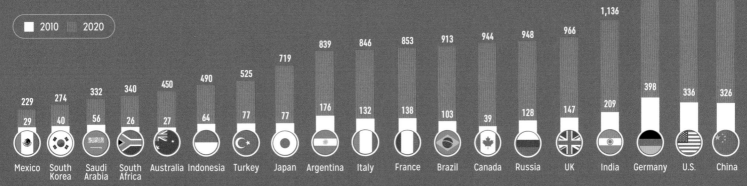

- 2010
- 2020

Country	2010	2020
Mexico	29	229
South Korea	40	274
Saudi Arabia	56	332
South Africa	26	340
Australia	27	450
Indonesia	64	490
Turkey	77	525
Japan	77	719
Argentina	176	839
Italy	132	846
France	138	853
Brazil	103	913
Canada	39	944
Russia	128	948
UK	147	966
India	209	1,136
Germany	398	1,968
U.S.	336	2,480
China	326	2,952

Source: Modified from Evenett and Fritz 2020

IS TRADE LIBERALIZATION REVERSING?

Effective U.S. tariff rate

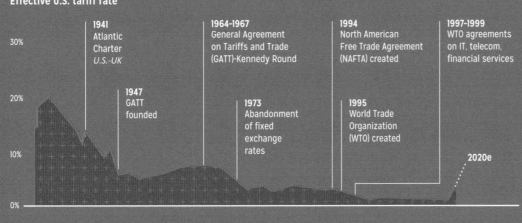

1941
Atlantic Charter
U.S.-UK

1947
GATT founded

1964–1967
General Agreement on Tariffs and Trade (GATT)-Kennedy Round

1973
Abandonment of fixed exchange rates

1994
North American Free Trade Agreement (NAFTA) created

1995
World Trade Organization (WTO) created

1997–1999
WTO agreements on IT, telecom, financial services

2020e

30%
20%
10%
0%

Source: Modified from Credit Suisse 2019

By late 2019, 40% of world goods trade was affected by populist era trade distortions.

Source: Modified from Baldwin and Evenett 2020

"THE RISING TIDE LIFTS ALL BOATS"

GLOBALIZATION'S HEYDAY

By the turn of the century, globalization appeared to be an unstoppable force on the world stage. Thanks in part to significant technological advancements and geopolitical developments—globalization continued to advance and trade as a percentage of GDP marched ever upward.

CONTAINERIZATION

The standardized shipping container turned the world economy on its head by driving the cost of shipping down and drastically increasing the efficiency of ports.

THE FALL OF THE IRON CURTAIN

The collapse of the Soviet Union in 1991 allowed Eastern Europe to begin the long convergence process with Western Europe. For the first time since WWII, the newly independent states were free to explore new trade relationships.

MARKET REFORMS IN INDIA AND CHINA

After experiencing a financial crisis in the early 1990s, the government of India made sweeping policy changes—including the easing of regulation and licensing controls, as well as currency devaluation, in order to encourage competitive trade.

Over in China, economic reforms were picking up steam, and a number of free trade and economic zones were established around the country. China joined the WTO in 2001, and emerged as the "factory of the world" by the 2000s, hot on the heels behind U.S. as an emerging global superpower.

U.S. ECONOMIC DOMINANCE

Globalization and free trade received a boost under Bill Clinton's presidency. Also, in the wake of the post-Soviet depression and Asian Financial Crisis, the U.S. was well positioned to cement its leadership in global affairs.

ACCESSIBLE AIR TRAVEL

When flights became more affordable for a wider portion of the world's population, it greatly increased the spread of people through tourism and immigration.

THE INTERNET

The growth of the internet helped supercharge the speed of cross-border communication, and paved the way for the rise of e-commerce.

Sources: Fitch Solutions, 2016; Altman, 2020; WTO, 2019; Baldwin and Evenett, 2020; Lund et al., 2019

THE ERA OF FLAT GROWTH

After the crash of 2008, economic recovery has been patchy,
and the expansion of world trade has leveled out.
What factors have played into this plateauing of globalization?

BUTTING HEADS

The bilateral relationship between the U.S and China is perceived by many to be the most consequential in the world, but that relationship has been strained in recent times. An ongoing trade war and tit-for-tat actions against specific companies is causing dysfunction and uncertainty in the global economy.

RISING PROTECTIONISM

Over the past decade, market protectionism has been on the rise around the world. In fact, since 2008, there have been over **14,000 policy interventions** involving discrimination against foreign goods producers.

COVID-19

While the pandemic certainly made a sizable dent in the global economy, there does not appear to be a collapse of international market integration taking place. That said, COVID-19 has exposed vulnerabilities in the global supply chain. As the pandemic took hold in China, disruptions shed light on just how reliant many countries are on the world's top exporter.

REGIONALIZATION

In response to protectionism and issues with the WTO, countries have increasingly been building regional trade blocs. One prominent example is the China-led Regional Inter-sessional Comprehensive Economic Partnership (RCEP).

WANING WAGE-COST ARBITRAGE

Today, only 14% of goods trade is from low-wage to high-wage countries, signaling that wage-cost arbitrage is becoming a less important factor.

THE SHIFTING NATURE OF GLOBAL TRADE

GLOBALIZATION CAN BE DESCRIBED AS HAVING FOUR DISTINCT PILLARS.

TRADE   **CAPITAL**   **INFORMATION**   **PEOPLE**

While most categories have experienced flat or uneven growth, the impact of the information pillar has been climbing for as long as it's been measured.

Global Connectedness Index

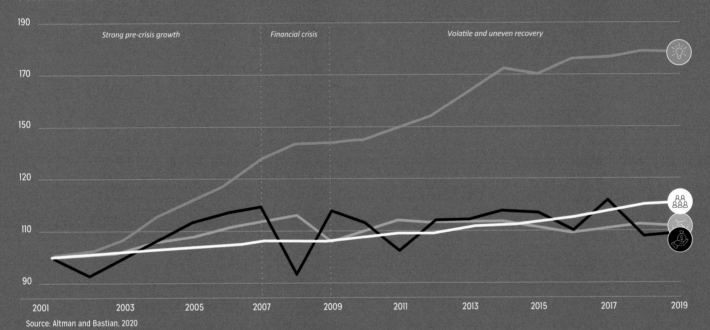

Strong pre-crisis growth   *Financial crisis*   *Volatile and uneven recovery*

Source: Altman and Bastian, 2020

Services trade is growing 60% faster than goods trade.

Goods
2.4%

Services
3.9%

Source: Modified from Lund et al. 2019

Services are also undervalued in international trade statistics. Viewed an alternative way, trade in services may already be more valuable than trade in goods.

Source: Modified from Lund et al. 2019

**GOODS
(TRADE IN VALUE ADDED)**

$13.0T

$13.0T

**SERVICES
(TRADE IN VALUE ADDED)**

$5.1T Gross services trade

$4.3T Services embedded in goods trade

$3.2T Intangibles provided to foreign affiliates

$0.8T Free cross-border digital services

$13.4T

GLOBALIZATION'S NEXT CHAPTER

A different mix of countries, companies, and workers will benefit from the next chapter of globalization.

LIKELY TO BENEFIT

ADVANCED ECONOMIES

DEVELOPING ECONOMIES
With close proximity to large consumer markets

NEED TO ADAPT

DEVELOPING ECONOMIES
That are less connected

Source: Modified from Lund et al. 2019

BY TRADITIONAL MEASURES, GLOBALIZATION APPEARS TO HAVE PEAKED.

However, global trade continues to evolve in new and unpredictable ways, and globalization is evolving along with it. Policymakers and business leaders must understand how the trade landscape is shifting so they can prepare for globalization's next chapter—and the opportunities and challenges it will present.

ARPANET

In 1969, the "internet" only consisted of four nodes: The University of California Los Angeles (UCLA), the University of California Santa Barbara (UCSB), the University of Utah, and the Stanford Research Institute (SRI).

Source: Modified from Smithsonian Magazine 2013

TCP/IP standard

Development of ICANN

Russia passes strict data localization laws

U.S. passes Section 230

Section 230 was passed in 1996. It released internet services providers and web-hosting companies from legal responsibility for information their customers posted or shared online.

Source: Modified from Cornell Law School 2020

EU's GDPR is enacted

General Data Protection Regulation

China's Golden Shield Project

China passes CL97

A law that regulated two broad categories of "cybercrime": those targeting computer networks and those carried out over computer networks.

Undersea cable network

The first intercontinental fiber optic cable—known as TAT-8—was strung across the floor of the Atlantic Ocean in 1988.

Source: Modified from Reuters 1988

China Internet
Security Law (2016)

SIGNAL 27

SPLINTERNET

SPLINTERNET

The global internet is growing increasingly fragmented, with restrictiveness increasing in many regions.

SIGNAL RANGE
Broad (4/5)

SIGNAL-TO-NOISE RATIO
Moderate (3/5)

INTERNET FREEDOM STATUS % OF THE GLOBAL ONLINE POPULATION

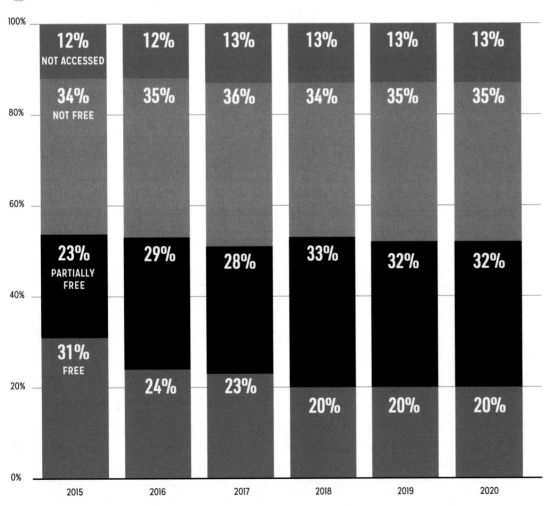

	2015	2016	2017	2018	2019	2020
NOT ACCESSED	12%	12%	13%	13%	13%	13%
NOT FREE	34%	35%	36%	34%	35%	35%
PARTIALLY FREE	23%	29%	28%	33%	32%	32%
FREE	31%	24%	23%	20%	20%	20%

A NUMBER OF FORCES are working against a free and open internet, but perhaps the most alarming trend is the continued rise of digital authoritarianism. Over time, more of the global online population are living in countries considered not free.

Freedom House applies a score to each country using a methodology that measures obstacles to access, limits on content, and violations of user rights. A high score means a country has a high level of internet freedom.

● Free (70–100)
● Partially free (40–69)
● Not free (0–39)

Source: Modified from Freedom House 2020

PULLING THE PLUG

As opposed to one globally connected internet, we are now a growing number of national intranets, where censorship, content filtering, and tracking occur. Many countries now have the ability to completely shut down internet services at their convenience.

NUMBER OF NETWORK DISRUPTIONS GLOBALLY ARE INCREASING 2016-2019

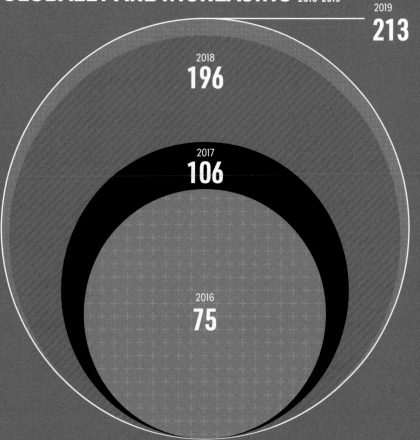

2019
213

2018
196

2017
106

2016
75

Source: Modified from Taye 2020

SOME OF THE REASONS INTERNET SHUTDOWNS OCCUR:

Protests

Elections

Exams

Repression

HOW DO GOVERNMENTS SHUT THE INTERNET DOWN?

Internet service providers

Government-controlled infrastructure

Government

DIVIDED DIGITAL WORLD

Here are some examples of internet surveillance, restrictions, and outright shutdowns around the world.

❶ FRAGMENTATION

The EU's GDPR rules enhance privacy, but create new layers of compliance that could restrict access to information and digital services.

❷ SHUTDOWN

WiFi on the London Underground transit system was shutdown during a protest in 2019.

❸ BLOCKING

Chad's block on social media and messaging platforms lasted well over a year.

❹ SHUTDOWN

Following a failed coup attempt, Ethiopia shut down the internet for over 100 million people.

❺ NATIONAL INTRANET

Iran has expressed interest in implementing a "national network" separate from the global Internet, possibly in partnership with China.

❻ THROTTLING

Tajikistan has admitted to throttling most social networks, including Facebook, Twitter, and Instagram, saying they were "vulnerable to terrorist activity."

❼ SHUTDOWN

Local authorities restrict connectivity routinely in India, justifying shutdowns on the basis of protests, misinformation, exams, and to maintain public order.

❽ NATIONAL INTRANET

People in North Korea are only able to venture online using Kwangmyong, the country's officially sanctioned intranet. Only a tiny core of elites have access to the global internet.

❾ CONTENT FILTERING

South Korea routinely blocks websites deemed to be a threat to national security and public morality.

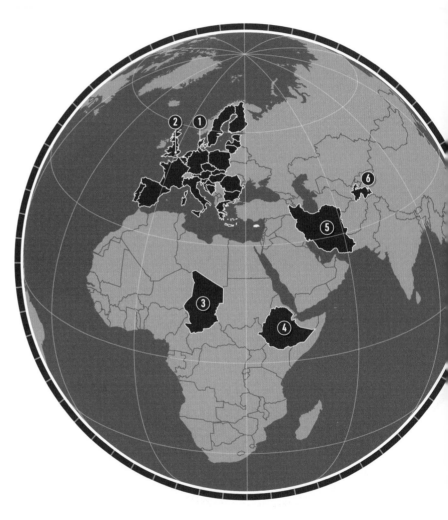

Source: Modified from Huang 2019

HOW CHINA CONTROLS THE INTERNET

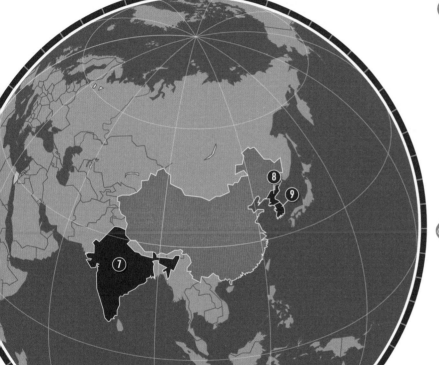

DATA SOVEREIGNTY

Data localization has been a de facto requirement in China since the 1990s, and has since been formalized by law. This means that any business operating within China must store personal data of Chinese citizens and other "important data" on domestic servers. Any data leaving the country must pass a government security assessment.

GREAT FIREWALL OF CHINA

The world's largest population of internet users are contained within China's Great Firewall—the world's most sophisticated censorship ecosystem. China's internet is only connected to the worldwide web through a few servers, which are closely monitored by the state.

CONTENT MODERATION

Chinese tech companies employ thousands of human moderators to help censor content deemed undesirable by the government. Even private conversations within messaging apps are subject to review.

IDENTITY REGISTRATION

Internet companies and service providers are responsible for requesting and verifying real names from users when they register. While this prevents the negative issues anonymity can bring, it also makes it easier for the government to track and persecute Internet users.

CHINA'S "GREAT CANNON"

While this cyber warfare tool isn't overtly deployed often, it can have devastating effects on its target. The Great Cannon, which essentially unleashes a massive DDoS attack on its target, was used in 2019 against a popular Hong Kong pro-democracy forum.

Source: Huang, 2019

Countries listed as "Not Free" by Freedom House fared much worse in **OECD's Digital Trade Restrictiveness Index.**

○ Free ○ Not free

FREE

- Argentina
- Australia
- Canada
- Estonia
- France
- Germany
- Hungary
- Iceland
- Italy
- Japan
- South Africa
- United Kingdom
- United States

CHANGE IN SCORE 2014–2019
▼ 0.008

NOT FREE

- China
- Russia
- Saudi Arabia
- Turkey

CHANGE IN SCORE 2014–2019
▼ 0.115

Not free countries were far more likely to grow more restrictive in terms of trade.

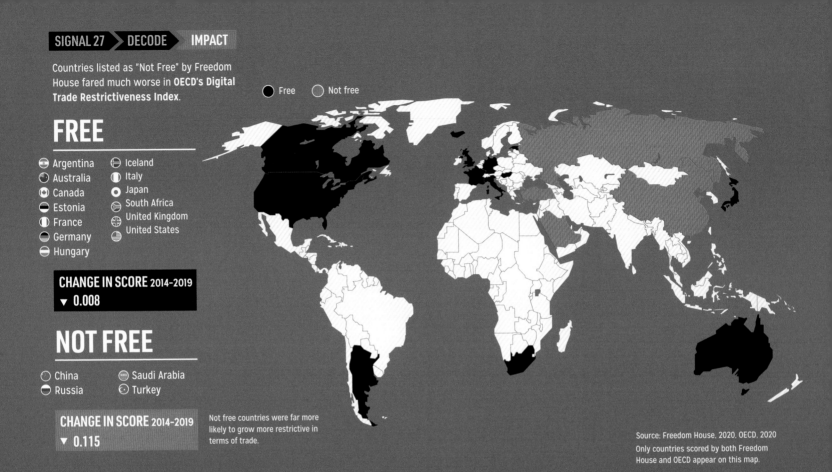

Source: Freedom House, 2020, OECD, 2020

Only countries scored by both Freedom House and OECD appear on this map.

As with any big shift, there will be winners and losers in a world with a more fragmented and convoluted internet.

WINNERS

BIG CLOUD VENDORS
Services like AWS and Azure have the scale to adapt to regional requirements and data sovereignty rules.

CHINESE TECH FIRMS
Companies like Huawei and CEIEC, which provide large-scale solutions to nations looking to control their country's internet.

FACEBOOK AND GOOGLE
As the internet becomes more complex, advertisers will trust that Google and Facebook are compliant to local regulations around

LOSERS

U.S. RETAIL AND DIGITAL SERVICES
Between a walled-off Chinese market, and Europe's strict GDPR rules, many U.S. companies face an uphill climb in serving

AD TECH NETWORKS
As different jurisdictions enact new privacy laws, operating ad networks based on cookies will become a losing battle.

FREE SPEECH
Ultimately, citizens living in countries with increased censorship and internet shutdowns will see their freedom of speech curtailed.

DISSONANCE

SPLINTERNET AND BIPOLAR WORLD

At its heart, the splinternet signal is a story about two competing versions of what the internet should be, each spearheaded by companies in the world's two superpowers:

🌐 China   🇺🇸 United States

"I think the most likely scenario now is not a splintering, but rather a bifurcation into a Chinese-led internet and a non-Chinese internet led by America."

—Eric Schmidt, former Google CEO

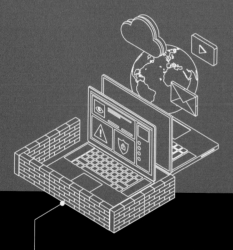

Companies that help facilitate the Chinese Firewall are able to find new markets for their technology.

"We should respect the right of individual countries to independently choose their own path of cyber development."

—Xi Jinping, president of China

UTOPIAN DREAMS FOR A FREE AND OPEN INTERNET SLIPPED AWAY LONG AGO.

As the growing movement toward stricter privacy laws indicates, even the "free and open" internet is far from perfect. Each society and government has a different idea of how an ideal version of the web should look. Until recently, much of the world was using an internet heavily influenced by the values of Silicon Valley technocrats.

As countries assert more control over their version of cyberspace, it remains to be seen whether the internet remains a global network, or whether national intranets become the norm.

THE SIGNALS
ARE YOURS

With the help of AI and machine learning, humans are now crunching data on all things imaginable.

As CNBC correspondent Eamon Javers put it, we can think of it as the Michael Lewis book and film *Moneyball*—except not just for baseball, but for everything.*

There's no doubt that mountains of data can lead to new insights, but until our brains and machines can talk directly, humans are still stuck trying to make sense of a complex world with very limited amounts of processing power.

The point of *Signals* is not to predict what will happen in the future. Instead, it is to help you create a mental model of the big picture—a conceptual but data-driven map of the broad forces that are shaping the future of business, investing, and the world at large.

By highlighting the stories behind multidecade shifts in demographics or the ripple effects of technological progress, we can start to see the forest for the trees.

And by using this framework the world will feel a lot less noisy, allowing you to better harness the power of the next insight you stumble upon.

JEFF DESJARDINS
Editor-in-chief, Visual Capitalist

*Source: Javers, E. (2014, February 12). Inside the wacky world of weird data: What's getting crunched. CNBC.

BIBLIOGRAPHY

AGING WORLD

ORIGIN STORY → United Nations, Department of Economic and Social Affairs, Population Division. (2019). World Urbanization Prospects: The 2018 Revision, Online Edition. *United Nations.* Retrieved September 8, 2020, from https://population.un.org/wpp/
- OECD. (2020). OECD Labour Force Statistics 2020. OECD Publishing, Paris. Retrieved September 8, 2020, from https://doi.org/10.1787/5842cc7f-en
- Farley, T. and Cohen, D. (2006, May 1). Prescription for a Healthy Nation: A New Approach to Improving Our Lives by Fixing Our Everyday World. Beacon Press.
- O'Neill, A. (June, 2019). Fertility Rate of the World and Continents 1950-2020. *Statista.* Retrieved September 8, 2020, from https://www.statista.com/statistics/1034075/fertility-rate-world-continents-1950-2020/

SIGNAL → United Nations, Department of Economic and Social Affairs, Population Division. (2019). 2019 Revision of World Population Prospects. United Nations. Retrieved September 8, 2020, from https://population.un.org/wpp/

DECODE → United Nations, Department of Economic and Social Affairs, Population Division. (2019). 2019 Revision of World Population Prospects. United Nations. Retrieved September 8, 2020, from https://population.un.org/wpp/
- United Nations, Department of Economic and Social Affairs, Population Division. (2018). World Population Ageing 2019. United Nations. Retrieved September 8, 2020, from https://www.un.org/en/development/desa/population/publications/pdf/ageing/WorldPopulationAgeing2019-Highlights.pdf

IMPACT → World Economic Forum. (2017, May). We'll Live to 100 - How Can We Afford It? *World Economic Forum.* Retrieved September 8, 2020, from http://www3.weforum.org/docs/WEF_White_Paper_We_Will_Live_to_100.pdf
- National Transfer Accounts. (2016). National Transfer Accounts: Data Sheet. National Transfer Accounts Project. Retrieved September 9, 2020, from https://www.ntaccounts.org/doc/repository/NTA%20Data%20Sheet%202016.pdf
- Lee, R. and Mason, A. (2017, March). Cost of Aging. International Monetary Fund. *Finance and Development, 54,* (1). Retrieved September 9, 2020, from https://www.imf.org/external/pubs/ft/fandd/2017/03/lee.htm

URBAN EVOLUTION

ORIGIN STORY → Florida, R. (2018, October 23). Wages Are Higher in Urban Areas, but Growing Faster in Rural Ones. Bloomberg CityLab. Retrieved September 9, 2020, from https://www.bloomberg.com/news/articles/2018-10-23/urban-wages-in-the-u-s-are-vhigher-rural-wages-are-growing-more
- World Bank via Our World in Data. (2018). Share of the Labor Force Employed in Agriculture, 1991 to 2017. Our World in Data. Retrieved September 12, 2020, from https://ourworldindata.org/grapher/share-of-the-labor-force-employed-in-agriculture?tab=chart&time=1991..2017&country=~OWID_WRL

SIGNAL → Ritchie, H. and Roser, M. (2018, September). Urbanization. Our World In Data. Retrieved September 9, 2020, from https://ourworldindata.org/urbanization
- World Bank. (2020, April 20). Urban Development Overview. The World Bank. Retrieved September 9, 2020, from https://www.worldbank.org/en/topic/urbandevelopment/overview
- Satterthwaite, D. (2020, January 16). The World's 100 Largest Cities from 1800 to 2020, and Beyond. International Institute for Environment and Development. Retrieved September 9, 2020, from https://www.iied.org/worlds-100-largest-cities-1800-2020-beyond

- Hoornweg, D. and Pope, K. (2014, January). Global Cities Institute Working Paper No. 04: Socioeconomic Pathways and Regional Distribution of the World's 101 Largest Cities. Global Cities Institute. Retrieved September 9, 2020, from https://docs.wixstatic.com/ugd/672989_62cfa13ec4ba47788f78ad660489a2fa.pdf

DECODE
- Lin, V. et al. (2017, March 20) Synergistic Development in the Beijing-Tianjin-Hebei Region: An International Comparative Perspective. Boston Consulting Group. Retrieved September 9, 2020,from https://www.bcg.com/en-ca/synetic-development-in-the-beijing-tianjin-hebei-region-an-international-comparative-perspective
- Ritchie, H. and Roser, M. (2018, September). Urbanization. Our World In Data. Retrieved September 9, 2020, from https://ourworldindata.org/urbanization

IMPACT
- Phys.org. (2019, August 16). Sinking City: Indonesia's Capital on Brink of Disaster. Phys.org. Retrieved September 9, 2020, from https://phys.org/news/2019-08-city-indonesia-capital-brink-disaster.html
- Geophysical Fluid Dynamics Laboratory, NOAA. (2020, June 12). Global Warming and Hurricanes. NOAA. Retrieved September 12, 2020, from https://www.gfdl.noaa.gov/global-warming-and-hurricanes/
- Hauer, M. (2017, April 17). Migration Induced by Sea-Level Rise Could Reshape the US Population Landscape. *Nature Climate Change*, 7, 321-325. Retrieved September 9, 2020, from https://doi.org/10.1038/nclimate3271
- Climate Impact Lab. (2019). Climate Change and Heat-Induced Mortality in India. Tata Center For Development at UChicago. Retrieved September 9, 2020, from https://epic.uchicago.edu/wp-content/uploads/2019/10/IndiaMortality_webv2.pdf
- CoreLogic. (2019). 2019 Wildfire Risk Report. CoreLogic, Inc. Retrieved September 9, 2020, from https://www.corelogic.com/downloadable-docs/wildfire-report_0919-01-screen.pdf

RISING MIDDLE CLASS

ORIGIN STORY
- OECD. (2019). Equity Market Review of Asia 2019. OECD Capital Market Series, Paris. Retrieved September 9, 2020, from http://www.oecd.org/daf/ca/oecd-equity-market-review-asia.htm
- Pramanik, A. K. (2017, February 24). The Technology That's Making a Difference in the Developing World. U.S. Global Leadership Coalition. Retrieved September 9, 2020, from https://www.usglc.org/blog/the-technology-thats-making-a-difference-in-the-developing-world/

SIGNAL
- Gapminder. (2020). Number of People by Income [online chart tool]. Gapminder Foundation. Retrieved September 9, 2020, from https://www.gapminder.org/tools/#$chart-type=mountain
- Hellebrandt, T. and Mauro, P. via Our World in Data. (2013). Global Income Inequality. Our World in Data. Retrieved September 9, 2020, from https://ourworldindata.org/global-economic-inequality
- Kharas, H. (2017, February 28). The Unprecedented Expansion of the Global Middle Class. The Brookings Institution. Retrieved September 9, 2020, from https://www.brookings.edu/research/the-unprecedented-expasion-of-the-global-middle-class-2/
- McNamara, C. L,. Labonte, R., Schram, A. et al. (2021). Glossary on Free Trade Agreements and Health Part 1: The Shift from Multilateralism and the Rise of 'WTO-Plus' Provisions. *Journal of Epidemiology and Community Health*, 75, 402-406

DECODE
- World Data Lab via The Brookings Institution. (2018, September 27). A Global Tipping Point: Half the World Is Now Middle Class or Wealthier. The Brookings Institution. Retrieved September 9, 2020, from https://www.brookings.edu/blog/future-development/2018/09/27/a-global-tipping-point-half-the-world-is-now-middle-class-or-wealthier/
- World Data Lab. (2019, April 17). Emerging Trends in the Global Middle Class: A Private Conversation with Dr. Homi Kharas. World Data Lab. Retrieved September 9, 2020, from https://worlddata.io/blog/emerging-trends-in-the-global-middle-class-a-private-conversation-with-dr-homi-kharas
- Canals, C.. (2019, September 16). The Emergence of the Middle Class: An Emerging-Country Phenomenon. Caixa Bank Research. Retrieved September 9, 2020, from https://www.caixabankresearch.com/en/economics-markets/labour-market-demographics/emergence-middle-class-emerging-country-phenomenon
- Kharas, H. (2017, February 28). The Unprecedented Expansion of the Global Middle Class. The Brookings Institution. Retrieved September 9, 2020, from https://www.brookings.edu/wp-content/uploads/2017/02/global_20170228_global-middle-class.pdf

IMPACT
- World Bank. (2019). GDP per Capita (current US$) [online chart tool]. World Bank Group. Retrieved May 2019, from https://data.worldbank.org/indicator/NY.GDP.PCAP.CD
- OECD. (2019). Meat Consumption [online chart tool]. OECD. Retrieved May 2019, from https://data.oecd.org/agroutput/meat-consumption.htm#indicator-chart
- Federal Reserve Bank of Cleveland. (2020, February 12). Is the Middle Class Worse Off Than It Used to Be? Federal Reserve Bank of Cleveland. Retrieved September 9, 2020, from https://www.clevelandfed.org/newsroom-and-events/publitions/economic-commentary/2020-economic-commentaries/ec-202003-is-middle-class-worse-off.aspx

- Keyu, K. J. (2015, November 12). What's Holding Back China's Consumers? World Economic Forum. Retrieved September 9, 2020. https://www.weforum.org/agenda/2015/11/whats-holding-back-chinas-consumers
- Lung, R. and Batbold, D. (2018). The Geography of the Global Middle Class: Where They Live, How They Spend. Visa and Oxford Economics. Retrieved September 9, 2020. https://usa.visa.com/dam/VCOM/global/partner-with-us/documents/middle-class-spending-whitepaper.pdf

DECENTRALIZATION OF MEDIA

ORIGIN STORY
- Kepios, We Are Social, and Hootsuite. (2021). Digital 2021 Global Overview Report. We Are Social and Hootsuite. Retrieved June 14, 2021, from https://wearesocial.com/digital-2021
- Edelman, via Salmon, F. (2021, January 21). Media Trust Hits New Low. Axios. Retrieved June 14, 2021 from https://www.axios.com/media-trust-crisis-2bf0ec1c-00c0-4901-9069-e26b21c283a9.html
- Hindman, D. B. and Wiegand, K. (2008, March). The Big Three's Prime-Time Decline: A Technological and Social Contact. Journal of Broadcasting & Electronic Media. Retrieved September 8, 2020, from https://robertoigarza.files.wordpress.com/2008/10/art-the-big-threes-prime-time-decline-hindman-2008.pdf
- Perrin, N. (2019, March 21). US Advertisers Still Eager to Target at Scale with Duopoly. eMarketer. Retrieved September 8, 2020, from https://www.emarketer.com/content/us-advertisers-still-eager-to-target-at-scale-with-duopoly
- Wasserman, T. (2013, August 9). This Is the World's First Banner Ad. Mashable. Retrieved September 12, 2020, from https://mashable.com/2013/08/09/first-banner-ad/

SIGNAL
- Watson, A. via Statista. (2020, February 21). Number of Commercial Radio Stations in the U.S. from 1952 to 2019. Statista. Retrieved September 8, 2020, from https://www.statista.com/statistics/252235/number-of-commercial-radio-stations-in-the-us/
- Watson, A. via Statista. (2019, November 21). Number of Commercial TV Stations in the U.S. 1950-2017. Statista. Retrieved September 8, 2020, from https://www.statista.com/statistics/189655/number-of-commercial-television-stations-in-the-us-since-1950/
- Watson, A. via Statista. (2020, March 3). Number of Daily Newspapers in the U.S. 1970-2018. Statista. Retrieved September 8, 2020, from https://www.statista.com/statistics/183408/number-of-us-daily-newspapers-since-1975/
- Kepios, We Are Social, and Hootsuite. (2021). Digital 2021 Global Overview Report. We Are Social and Hootsuite. Retrieved June 14, 2021, from https://wearesocial.com/digital-2021
- Internet Live Stats. (n.d.). Total Number of Websites. Internet Live Stats. Retrieved June 15, 2021, from https://www.internetlivestats.com/total-number-of-websites/
- Pew Research Center. (1996, May 13). TV News Viewership Declines. Pew Research Center. Retrieved September 11, 2020, from https://www.pewresearch.org/politics/1996/05/13/tv-news-viewership-declines/
- Pew Research Center via Suciu, P. for Forbes. (2019, October 11). More Americans Are Getting Their News From Social Media. Forbes. Retrieved September 11, 2020, from https://www.forbes.com/sites/petersuciu/2019/10/11/more-americans-are-getting-their-news-from-social-media/
- Domo. (2019). Data Never Sleeps 7.0. Domo. Retrieved September 9, 2020, from https://www.domo.com/learn/data-never-sleeps-7
- Wordpress. (2020). About Us [webpage]. Wordpress. Retrieved September 9, 2020, from https://wordpress.com/about/?aff=2718
- Clement, J. via Statista. (2020, August 25). Hours of Video Uploaded to YouTube Every Minute as of May 2019. Statista. Retrieved September 9, 2020, from https://www.statista.com/statistics/259477/hours-of-video-uploaded-to-youtube-every-minute/

DECODE
- Shampnois, B. (2019, May 23). Personalization & Customer Data: Why Context Is Critical to Optimize Your Customer Experience. Brooks Bell. Retrieved September 9, from https://www.brooksbell.com/resource/blog/personalization-customer-data-why-context-is-critical-to-optimize-your-customer-experience/
- PwC. (2020). IAB Internet Advertising Revenue Report. PricewaterhouseCoopers. Retrieved September 9, 2020, from https://www.iab.com/wp-content/uploads/2020/05/FY19-IAB-Internet-Ad-Revenue-Report_Final.pdf
- eMarketer. (2019, February 20). US Digital Ad Spending Will Surpass Traditional in 2019. eMarketer. Retrieved September 9, 2020, from https://www.emarketer.com/newsroom/index.php/us-digital-ad-spending-will-surpass-traditional-in-2019/
- Berg, M. (2020, December 18) The Highest-Paid YouTube Stars of 2020. Forbes. Retrieved June 14, 2021, from https://www.forbes.com/sites/maddieberg/2020/12/18/the-highest-paid-youtube-stars-of-2020/?sh=4b784f0d6e50

IMPACT
- Gallup. (2018). Indicators of News Media Trust. Gallup Foundation. Retrieved September 9, 2020, from https://kf-site-production.s3.amazonaws.com/media_elements/files/000/000/216/original/KnightFoundation_Panel4_Trust_Indicators_FINAL.pdf
- UNC Hussman School of Journalism and Media. (2020). News Deserts and Ghost Newspapers: Will Local News Survive? UNC Hussman School of Journalism and Media. Retrieved September 9, 2020, from https://www.usnewsdeserts.com/reports/news-deserts-and-ghost-newspapers-will-local-news-survive/the-news-landscape-in-2020-transformed-and-diminished/vanishing-newspapers/

- Newman, N. (2020). Journalism, Media, and Technology Trends and Predictions 2020. Reuters Institute for the Study of Journalism. Retrieved September 9, 2020, from http://www.digitalnewsreport.org/publications/2020/journalism-media-and-technology-trends-and-predictions-2020
- Pew Research Center. (2020, January 24). U.S. Media Polarization and the 2020 Election: A Nation Divided. Pew Research Center. Retrieved September 9, 2020, from https://www.journalism.org/2020/01/24/u-s-media-polarization-and-the-2020-election-a-nation-divided/

RISING WEALTH INEQUALITY

ORIGIN STORY
- U.S. Bureau of Labor Statistics. (2020). Databases, Tables & Calculators by Subject [online tool]. U.S. Bureau of Labor Statistics. Retrieved September 7, 2020, from https://www.bls.gov/data/
- U.S. Bureau of Labor Statistics. (2020). Consumer Price Index for All Urban Consumers: Medical Care in U.S. City Average [CPIMEDSL]. Federal Reserve Bank of St. Louis (FRED). Retrieved September 12, 2020, from https://fred.stlouisfed.org/series/CPIMEDSL
- Boyington, B., & Kerr, E. (2019, September 19). 20 Years of Tuition Growth at National Universities. *US News*. Retrieved September 7, 2020, from https://www.usnews.com/education/best-colleges/paying-for-college/articles/2017-09-20/see-20-years-of-tuition-growth-at-national-universities

SIGNAL
- Credit Suisse. (2019). Global Wealth Report 2019. Credit Suisse Research Institute. Retrieved September 7, 2020, from https://www.credit-suisse.com/media/assets/corporate/docs/about-us/research/publications/global-wealth-report-2019-en.pdf
- Roser, M. and Ortiz-Ospina, E. via Our World in Data. (2013, May 25). Global Extreme Poverty. Our World in Data. Retrieved September 7, 2020, from https://ourworldindata.org/extreme-poverty
- OECD. ((n.d.). GDP and Spending - Gross Domestic Product (GDP) - OECD Data. (n.d.). Retrieved September 7, 2020, from https://data.oecd.org/gdp/gross-domestic-product-gdp.htm
- *Forbes* 2019 Billionaire List. (n.d.). Retrieved September 7, 2020, from https://www.forbes.com/billionaires/

DECODE
- FRED Economic Data. (2019). Federal Reserve Bank of St. Louis. Retrieved September 7, 2020, from https://fred.stlouisfed.org/
- Distribution of Household Wealth in the U.S. since 1989 (2020). Federal Reserve. Retrieved September 7, 2020, from https://www.federalreserve.gov/releases/z1/dataviz/dfa/distribute/chart/
- Parker, K. and Fry, R. (2020, July 27). More than Half of U.S. Households Have Some Investment in the Stock Market. Pew Research Center. Retrieved September 7, 2020, from https://www.pewresearch.org/fact-tank/2020/03/25/more-than-half-of-u-s-households-have-some-investment-in-the-stock-market/
- Yahoo Finance - Stock Market Live, Quotes, Business & Finance News. (n.d.). Retrieved September 7, 2020, from https://ca.finance.yahoo.com/

IMPACT
- Mishel, L., & Kandra, J. (2020, August 18). CEO Compensation Surged 14% in 2019 to $21.3 Million. Economic Policy Institute. Retrieved September 7, 2020, from https://www.epi.org/publication/ceo-compensation-surged-14-in-2019-to-21-3-million-ceos-now-earn-320-times-as-much-as-a-typical-worker/
- Shierholz, H. (2019, August 27). Labor Day 2019: Working People Have Been Thwarted in Their Efforts to Bargain for Better Wages by Attacks on Unions. Economic Policy Institute. Retrieved September 7, 2020, from https://www.epi.org/publication/labor-day-2019-collective-bargaining/
- Trade Union - OECD Data. (n.d.). OECD.Stat. Retrieved September 07, 2020, from https://stats.oecd.org/Index.aspx?DataSetCode=TUD#
- Horowitz, J. M. et al. (2020, January 9). Views of U.S. Economic Inequality. Pew Research Center. Retrieved September 7, 2020, from https://www.pewsocialtrends.org/2020/01/09/views-of-economic-inequality/

CLIMATE PRESSURES

ORIGIN STORY → BP p.l.c. (2020). bp Statistical Review of World Energy 2020. BP p.l.c.. Retrieved September 8, 2020, from https://www.bp.com/content/dam/bp/business-sites/en/global/corporate/pdfs/energy-economics/statistical-review/bp-stats-review-2020-full-report.pdf
- NOAA/ESRL, via Our World in Data. (2018). Atmospheric Concentrations of CO2 Continue to Rise. Our World in Data. Retrieved August 10, 2020, from https://ourworldindata.org/co2-and-other-greenhouse-gas-emissions
- Earth System Research Laboratories Global Monitoring Laboratory. (2020, August). Trends in Atmospheric Carbon Dioxide. NOAA Oceanic and Atmospheric Research. Retrieved September 8, 2020, from https://www.esrl.noaa.gov/gmd/webdata/ccgg/trends/co2_data_mlo.pdf
- Food and Agriculture Organization of the United Nations. (2012). State of the World's Forests 2012. Food and Agriculture Organization of the United Nations. Retrieved September 8, 2020, from http://www.fao.org/3/a-i3010e.pdf
- Kharas, H. and Hamel, K. (2018, September 27). A Global Tipping Point: Half the World Is Now Middle Class or Wealthier. The Brookings Institute. Retrieved September 8, 2020, from https://www.brookings.edu/blog/future-development/2018/09/27/a-global-tipping-point-half-the-world-is-now-middle-class-or-wealthier/

SIGNAL → Jia, G. et al. via the Intergovernmental Panel on Climate Change. (2020, January). Climate Change and Land. Intergovernmental Panel on Climate Change. Retrieved September 8, 2020, from https://www.ipcc.ch/site/assets/uploads/sites/4/2020/08/05_Chapter-2-V3.pdf
- Lindsey, R. (2020, August 14). Climate Change: Atmospheric Carbon Dioxide. NOAA Climate.gov. Retrieved June 14, 2021, from https://www.climate.gov/news-features/understanding-climate/climate-change-atmospheric-carbon-dioxide
- Navigant. (2019). Total GHG Emissions Worldwide: 53.7 Gt CO eq (2017). Navigant, a Guidehouse Company. Retrieved September 11, 2020, from https://guidehouse.com/media/www/site/downloads/energy/2019/asn_navigant_emissionsflowchart.pdf

DECODE → Union of Concerned Scientists. (2008, July 16; revised 2020, August 12). Each Country's Share of CO2 Emissions. Union of Concerned Scientists. Retrieved September 8, 2020, from https://www.ucsusa.org/resources/each-countrys-share-co2-emissions
- Intergovernmental Panel on Climate Change. (2020, January). Climate Change and Land. Intergovernmental Panel on Climate Change. Retrieved September 8, 2020, from https://www.ipcc.ch/site/assets/uploads/sites/4/2020/02/SPM_Updated-Jan20.pdf
- Union of Concerned Scientists. (2018, Jun 4; revised 2018, June 6). The Science Connecting Extreme Weather to Climate Change. Union of Concerned Scientists. Retrieved September 8, 2020, from https://www.ucsusa.org/resources/science-connecting-extreme-weather-climate-change

IMPACT → Climate Action Tracker. (2021). Temperatures - Addressing Global Warming. Climate Action Tracker. Retrieved June 16, 2021, from https://climateactiontracker.org/global/temperatures/
- Economist Intelligence Unit. (2019, November 20). Global Economy Will Be 3 Percent Smaller by 2050 Due to Lack of Climate Resilience. The Economist Intelligence Unit. Retrieved September 8, 2020, from https://www.eiu.com/n/global-economy-will-be-3-percent-smaller-by-2050-due-to-lack-of-climate-resilience/
- Fagan, M. and Huang, C. (2020, October 16). Many Globally Are as Concerned about Climate Change as about the Spread of Infectious Diseases. Pew Research Center. Retrieved June 14, 2021, from https://www.pewresearch.org/fact-tank/2020/10/16/many-globally-are-as-concerned-about-climate-change-as-about-the-spread-of-infectious-diseases/

WATER CRISIS

ORIGIN STORY → Ritchie, H. and Roser, M. via Our World in Data. (2015; revised 2018, July). Water Use and Stress. Our World in Data. Retrieved September 11, 2020, from https://ourworldindata.org/water-use-stress

- World Health Organization. (2019, June 18). 1 in 3 People Globally Do Not Have Access to Safe Drinking Water – UNICEF, WHO. World Health Organization. Retrieved September 11, 2020, from https://www.who.int/news-room/detail/18-06-2019-1-in-3-people-globally-do-not-have-access-to-safe-drinking-water-unicef-who
- NASA. (2019; updated 2020, September 9). Arctic Sea Ice Minimum. NASA's Jet Propulsion Laboratory. Retrieved September 11, 2020, from https://climate.nasa.gov/vital-signs/arctic-sea-ice/

SIGNAL

- Luo, T. et al. via World Resources Institute. (2015, August). Aqueduct Projected Water Stress Country Rankings. World Resources Institute. Retrieved September 11, 2020, from https://www.wri.org/publication/aqueduct-projected-water-stress-country-rankings?utm_campaign=WRIAqueduct&utm_source=blogpostgraphic&utm_medium=image
- UN Water. (2020, March 21). World Water Development Report 2020: Water and Climate Change. United Nations. Retrieved September 11, 2020, from https://www.unwater.org/publications/world-water-development-report-2020/
- Perlman, H. et al. via U.S. Geological Survey. (2019). All of Earth's Water in a Single Sphere! United States Geological Survey. Retrieved September 11, 2020, from https://www.usgs.gov/media/images/all-earths-water-a-single-sphere

DECODE

- Otto, B. and Schleifer, L. via World Resources Institute. (2020, February 10). Domestic Water Use Grew 600% over the Past 50 Years. World Resources Institute. Retrieved September 11, 2020, from https://www.wri.org/blog/2020/02/growth-domestic-water-use
- World Bank Group. (2019). Urban Population (% of total population) [online chart tool]. Retrieved September 11, 2020, from https://data.worldbank.org/indicator/SP.URB.TOTL.IN.ZS
- UN Water. (2019, March 18). World Water Development Report 2019: Leaving No One Behind. United Nations. Retrieved September 11, 2020, from https://www.unwater.org/publications/world-water-development-report-2019/
- OECD/FAO. (2019). OECD-FAO Agricultural Outlook 2019–2028. OECD iLibrary. Retrieved September 11, 2020, from https://www.oecd-ilibrary.org/agriculture-and-food/oecd-fao-agricultural-outlook-2019-2028_agr_outlook-2019-en
- Roser, M. for Our World in Data. (2019). Pesticides. Our World in Data. Retrieved September 11, 2020, from https://ourworldindata.org/pesticides

IMPACT

- Strong, C. et al. via World Resources Institute. (2020, January). Achieving Abundance: Understanding the Cost of a Sustainable Water Future. World Resources Institute. Retrieved September 11, 2020, from https://files.wri.org/s3fs-public/achieving-abundance.pdf
- Global Commission on Adaptation (2019) and World Bank (2016) via World Resources Institute. (2020, January). Achieving Abundance: Understanding the Cost of a Sustainable Water Future. World Resources Institute Retrieved September 11, 2020, from https://files.wri.org/s3fs-public/achieving-abundance.pdf
- Gleick, P. et al. (2018) via World Resources Institute. (2020, September). Ending Conflicts over Water. World Resources Institute. Retrieved September 11, 2020, from https://www.wri.org/publication/ending-conflicts-over-water

ELECTRIFICATION OF EVERYTHING

ORIGIN STORY

- Goldenberg, C. et al. via Rocky Mountain Institute (RMI). (2018, February). Demand Flexibility: The Key to Enabling a Low-Cost, Low-Carbon Grid. Rocky Mountain Institute. Retrieved September 11, 2020, from https://rmi.org/wp-content/uploads/2018/02/Insight_Brief_Demand_Flexibility_2018.pdf
- Hutchins, P. via U.S. Energy Information Administration. (2019, July 10). U.S. Utility-Scale Battery Storage Power Capacity to Grow Substantially by 2023. U.S. Energy Information Administration. Retrieved September 11, 2020, from https://www.eia.gov/todayinenergy/detail.php?id=40072
- World Bank Group. (2019). Access to Electricity. (% of Population). Retrieved June 14, 2021, from https://data.worldbank.org/indicator/EG.ELC.ACCS.ZS?end=2018&start=1990&view=chart&year_high_desc=true
- Newzoo (2021). Global Mobile Market Report. Newzoo. Retrieved June 14, 2021, from https://newzoo.com/key-numbers/
- Gu, T. via Newzoo. (2019, September 17). Newzoo's Global Mobile Market Report: Insights into the World's 3.2 Billion Smartphone Users, the Devices They Use & the Mobile Games They Play. Newzoo. Retrieved September 11, 2020, from https://newzoo.com/insights/articles/newzoos-global-mzbile-market-report-insights-into-the-worlds-3-2-billion-smartphone-users-the-devices-they-use-the-mobile-games-they-play/

SIGNAL

- National Renewable Energy Laboratory. (2018, July 9). NREL Analysis Explores Demand-Side Impacts of a Highly Electrified Future. National Renewable Energy Laboratory. Retrieved September 11, 2020, from https://www.nrel.gov/news/program/2018/analysis-demand-side-electrification-futures.html
- IEA. (2019, November 21). Global Electricity Demand by Region in the Stated Policies Scenario, 2000–2040. International Energy Agency. Retrieved September 11, 2020, from https://www.iea.org/data-and-statistics/charts/global-electricity-demand-by-region-in-the-stated-policies-scenario-2000-2040
- Jadun, P. et al. via National Renewable Energy Laboratory. (2017). Electrification Futures Study: End-Use Electric Technology Cost and Performance Projections through 2050. National Renewable Energy Laboratory. Retrieved September 11, 2020, from https://www.nrel.gov/docs/fy18osti/70485.pdf
- IEA. (2019, November 21). Electricity Generation by Fuel and Scenario, 2018–2040. International Energy Agency. Retrieved September 11, 2020, from https://www.iea.org/data-and-statistics/charts/electricity-generation-by-fuel-and-scenario-2018-2040ta-are-giant-tech-companies-collecting-from-you.html

DECODE

- IEA. (2019, November 26). Electricity Demand Growth by End-Use and Scenarios in Advanced and Developing Economies, 2018–2040. International Energy Agency. Retrieved September 11, 2020, from https://www.iea.org/data-and-statistics/charts/electricity-demand-growth-by-end-use-and-scenarios-in-advanced-and-developing-economies-2018–2040
- Billimoria, S. et al. via Rocky Mountain Institute (RMI). (2018). The Economics of Electrifying Buildings. Rocky Mountain Institute. Retrieved September 11, 2020, from https://rmi.org/insight/the-economics-of-electrifying-buildings/
- Mosquet, X. et al. via Boston Consulting Group. (2020, January 2). Who Will Drive Electric Cars to the Tipping Point? Boston Consulting Group. Retrieved September 11, 2020, from https://www.bcg.com/en-us/publications/2020/drive-electric-cars-to-the-tipping-point
- IEA. (2020, Jan 29). Installed Power Generation Capacity by Source in the Stated Policies Scenario, 2000–2040. International Energy Agency. Retrieved September 11, 2020, from https://www.iea.org/data-and-statistics/charts/installed-power-generation-capacity-by-source-in-the-stated-policies-scenario-2000–2040
- Heiligtag, S. via McKinsey & Company. (2019, May 9). Fueling the Energy Transition: Opportunities for Financial Institutions. McKinsey & Company. Retrieved September 11, 2020, from https://www.mckinsey.com/industries/electric-power-and-natural-gas/our-insights/fueling-the-energy-transition-opportunities-for-financial-institutions

IMPACT

- Energy Insights by McKinsey. (2019, January). Global Energy Perspective 2019: Reference Case. McKinsey & Company. Retrieved September 11, 2020, from https://www.mckinsey.com/~/media/McKinsey/Industries/Oil%20and%20Gas/Our%20Insights/Global%20Energy%20Perspective%202019/McKinsey-Energy-Insights-Global-Energy-Perspective-2019_Reference-Case-Summary.ashx
- Benchmark Mineral Intelligence. (2019, July 30). Lithium's Price Paradox. Benchmark Mineral Intelligence. Retrieved September 12, 2020, from https://www.benchmarkminerals.com/lithiums-price-paradox/
- Mosquet, X. et al. via Boston Consulting Group. (2020, January 2). Who Will Drive Electric Cars to the Tipping Point? Boston Consulting Group. Retrieved September 11, 2020, from https://www.bcg.com/en-us/publications/2020/drive-electric-cars-to-the-tipping-point

INFORMATION OVERLOAD

ORIGIN STORY
- Jarich, P. et al. via GSMA Intelligence. (2019). Global Mobile Trends 2020 New Decade, New Industry? GSMA Intelligence. Retrieved September 11, 2020, from https://data.gsmaintelligence.com/api-web/v2/research-file-download?id=47743151&file=2863-071119-GMT-2019.pdf
- Reinsel, D. et al. via IDC. (2018, November). The Digitization of the World from Edge to Core. International Data Corporation (IDC). Retrieved September 8, 2020, from https://www.seagate.com/files/www-content/our-story/trends/files/idc-seagate-dataage-whitepaper.pdf
- Pielot, M. et al. (2018, September). Dismissed!: A Detailed Exploration of How Mobile Phone Users Handle Push Notifications. MobileHCI'18 Article No. 3, 1-11. Retrieved September 11, 2020, from https://dl.acm.org/doi/10.1145/3229434.3229445

SIGNAL
- Reinsel, D. et al. via IDC. (2018, November). The Digitization of the World from Edge to Core. International Data Corporation (IDC). Retrieved September 8, 2020, from https://www.seagate.com/files/www-content/our-story/trends/files/idc-seagate-dataage-whitepaper.pdf
- eMarketer via Bond Internet Trends. (2019). Daily Hours Spent with Digital Media per Adult User, USA. Bond Internet Trends. Retrieved September 11, 2020, from https://www.bondcap.com/report/itr19/#view/41
- Nielsen. (2020, August 13). The Nielsen Total Audience Report: August 2020. Nielsen. Retrieved September 11, 2020, from https://www.nielsen.com/us/en/insights/report/2020/the-nielsen-total-audience-report-august-2020/
- U.S. Bureau of Labor Statistics. (2020). Reading for Personal Interest: Average Hours Spent Reading per Day, U.S. Adults. U.S. Bureau of Labor Statistics. Retrieved September 11, 2020, from https://www.bls.gov/
- Watson, A. via Statista. (2019, December 9). Number of Podcast Listeners in the U.S. 2014–2023. Statista. Retrieved September 11, 2020, from https://www.statista.com/statistics/786826/podcast-listeners-in-the-us/
- StreamHatchet. (2020). COVID-19 Impact on Streaming Audiences. StreamHatchet. Retrieved September 11, 2020, from https://docs.google.com/presentation/d/11jqIT3R4tmTgqBzy0_Kt6EaIsISD30EkKAuAihmRrJ4/present?slide=id.p

DECODE
- Clinton, D. via Loup Ventures. (2018, June 12). Defining the Future of Human Information Consumption. Loup Ventures. Retrieved September 11, 2020, from https://loupventures.com/defining-the-future-of-human-information-consumption/

IMPACT
- Reinsel, D. et al. via IDC. (2018, November). The Digitization of the World from Edge to Core. International Data Corporation (IDC). Retrieved September 8, 2020, from https://www.seagate.com/files/www-content/our-story/trends/files/idc-seagate-dataage-whitepaper.pdf
- Wojcik, S. via Pew Research Center. (2018, April 9). 5 things to know about bots on Twitter. Pew Research Center. Retrieved September 11, 2020, from https://www.pewresearch.org/fact-tank/2018/04/09/5-things-to-know-about-bots-on-twitter/

DATA AS A MOAT

ORIGIN STORY
- Amazon. (n.d.). The Beginners Guide to Selling on Amazon. Amazon.com, Inc.. Retrieved September 9, 2020, from https://sell.amazon.com/beginners-guide.html
- Apple. (2020, January 28). Apple Reports First Quarter Results. Apple Inc. Retrieved September 9, 2020, from https://www.apple.com/newsroom/2020/01/apple-reports-record-first-quarter-results/

- Brandom, R. (2019, May 7). There Are Now 2.5 Billion Active Android Devices. The Verge. Retrieved September 12, 2020, from https://www.theverge.com/2019/5/7/18528297/google-io-2019-android-devices-play-store-total-number-statistic-keynote
- Clement, J. via Statista. (2020, August 10). Number of Monthly Active Facebook Users Worldwide as of 2nd Quarter 2020. Statista. Retrieved September 9, 2020, from https://www.statista.com/statistics/264810/number-of-monthly-active-facebook-users-worldwide/
- *The Economist*. (2019, September 12). Drastic Falls in Cost Are Powering Another Computer Revolution. *The Economist*. Retrieved July 2, 2021, from https://www.economist.com/technology-quarterly/2019/09/12/drastic-falls-in-cost-are-powering-another-computer-revolution
- IBM. (2018, September 6). Hu-manity.co Collaborates with IBM Blockchain on Consumer App to Manage Personal Data Property Rights. IBM Inc. Retrieved September 9, 2020, from https://newsroom.ibm.com/2018-09-06-Hu-manity-co-Collaborates-with-IBM-Blockchain-on-Consumer-App-to-Manage-Personal-Data-Property-Rights
- Elumalai, A. and Roberts, R. via McKinsey. (2019, August 26). Unlocking Business Acceleration in a Hybrid Cloud World. McKinsey Digital. Retrieved September 9, 2020, from https://www.mckinsey.com/business-functions/mckinsey-digital/our-insights/unlocking-business-acceleration-in-a-hybrid-cloud-world

SIGNAL

- Macrotrends. (2005–2019). Stock Comparisons: Revenue. Macrotrends. Retrieved September 9, 2020, from https://www.macrotrends.net/stocks/stock-comparison?s=revenue&axis=single&comp=AMZN:GOOGL:AAPL:FB:MSFT
- Clement, J. via Statista. (2020, August 10). Number of Monthly Active Facebook Users Worldwide as of 2nd Quarter 2020. Statista. Retrieved September 9, 2020, from https://www.statista.com/statistics/264810/number-of-monthly-active-facebook-users-worldwide/
- Valens Research. (2020, August 6). Do You Want Your Brand to Reach a Wider Audience? Use This Email Platform That Has 1.8 Billion Users. Valens Research. Retrieved September 10, 2020, from https://www.valens-research.com/dynamic-marketing-communique/do-you-want-your-brand-to-reach-a-wider-audience-use-this-email-platform-that-has-1-8-billion-users-every-thursday-fyo/
- Amazon. The Beginners Guide to Selling on Amazon. Amazon. Retrieved September 9, 2020, from https://sell.amazon.com/beginners-guide.html
- Apple. (2020, January). Apple Reports First Quarter Results. Apple. Retrieved September 9, 2020, from https://www.apple.com/newsroom/2020/01/apple-reports-record-first-quarter-results/
- CB Insights. (2019, September 17). The Race for AI: Here Are the Tech Giants Rushing to Snap Up Artificial Intelligence Startups. CB Insights. Retrieved September 9, 2020, from https://www.cbinsights.com/research/top-acquirers-ai-startups-ma-timeline/

DECODE

- Vigderman, A. and Turner, G. (2020, July). The Data Big Tech Companies Have on You. Security.org. Retrieved September 9, 2020, from https://www.security.org/resources/data-tech-companies-have/
- Digital Information World. (2020, August 12). The Information Major Tech Companies Collect from Their Users. Digital Information World. Retrieved September 9, 2020, from https://www.mckinsey.com/business-functions/mckinsey-digital/our-insights/unlocking-business-acceleration-in-a-hybrid-cloud-world
- Elumalai, A. and Roberts, R. via McKinsey. (2019, August 26). Unlocking Business Acceleration in a Hybrid Cloud World. McKinsey Digital. Retrieved September 9, 2020, from https://www.mckinsey.com/business-functions/mckinsey-digital/our-insights/unlocking-business-acceleration-in-a-hybrid-cloud-world
- Amazon. (2020, January 31). 10-K 2019. https://ir.aboutamazon.com/sec-filings/default.aspx
- Apple. (2019, October 31). 10-K 2019. https://investor.apple.com/sec-filings/sec-filings-details/default.aspx?FilingId=13709514
- Alphabet. (2020, February 4). 10-K 2019. https://abc.xyz/investor/static/pdf/20200204_alphabet_10K.pdf?cache=cdd6dbf
- Microsoft. (2020, July 31). 10-K 2019. https://microsoft.gcs-web.com/static-files/4e7064ed-bbf7-4140-a8cb-79aba77421b9
- Facebook. (2020, January 30). 10-K 2019. http://d18rn0p25nwr6d.cloudfront.net/CIK-0001326801/45290cc0-656d-4a88-a2f3-147c8de86506.pdf
- IDC. (2019, September 4). Worldwide Spending on Artificial Intelligence Systems Will Be Nearly $98 Billion in 2023, According to New IDC Spending Guide. International Data Corporation. Retrieved September 9, 2020, from https://www.idc.com/getdoc.jsp?containerId=prUS45481219#:~:text=According%20to%20the%20recently%20updated,will%20be%20spent%20in%202019
- IDC. (2020, August 25). Worldwide Spending on Artificial Intelligence Is Expected to Double in Four Years, Reaching $110 Billion in 2024, According to New IDC Spending Guide. International Data Corporation. Retrieved September 9, 2020, from https://www.businesswire.com/news/home/20200825005099/en/Worldwide-Spending-Artificial-Intelligence-Expected-Double-Years

IMPACT

- Grand View Research, via MarketResearch.com. (2020). Artificial Intelligence Market Size, Share & Trends Analysis Report by Solution (Hardware, Software, Services), by Technology (Deep Learning, Machine Learning), by End Use, by Region, and Segment Forecasts, 2020–2027. MarketResearch.com. Retrieved August 10, 2021, from https://www.marketresearch.com/Grand-View-Research-v4060/Artificial-Intelligence-Size-Share-Trends-13485050/
- PwC. (2017). Sizing the Prize What's the Real Value of AI for Your Business and How Can You Capitalise? PricewaterhouseCoopers. Retrieved September 7, 2020, from https://www.pwc.com/gx/en/issues/data-and-analytics/publications/artificial-intelligence-study.html

CYBER'S WILD WEST

ORIGIN STORY

- Bravo, T. (2020, January 15). Wild Wide Web. World Economic Forum. Retrieved September 8, 2020, from https://reports.weforum.org/global-risks-report-2020/wild-wide-web/

- ITU. (n.d.). Individuals Using the Internet 2005-2019*. ITU. Retrieved September 8, 2020, from https://www.itu.int/en/ITU-D/Statistics/Pages/stat/default.aspx
- Gomez, M. (2020, July 12). Dark Web Price Index 2020. Privacy Affairs. Retrieved September 8, 2020, from https://www.privacyaffairs.com/dark-web-price-index-2020/
- McGuire, M. (2018, April 20). Into the Web of Profit. Bromium.com. Retrieved September 7, 2020, from https://www.bromium.com/wp-content/uploads/2018/05/Into-the-Web-of-Profit_Bromium.pdf

SIGNAL
- ITRC. (2021, January 28). 2020 End-of-Year Data Breach Report. Identity Theft Resource Center. Retrieved June 11, 2021, from https://notified.idtheftcenter.org/s/
- Eoyang, M. et al. (2018, October 29). To Catch a Hacker: Toward a Comprehensive Strategy to Identify, Pursue, and Punish Malicious Cyber Actors. Third Way. Retrieved September 12, 2020, from https://www.thirdway.org/report/to-catch-a-hacker-toward-a-comprehensive-strategy-to-identify-pursue-and-punish-malicious-cyber-actors
- F-secure. (2019, July 31). Cyber Threat Landscape for the Finance Sector. F-Secure. Retrieved September 12, 2020, from https://blog-assets.f-secure.com/wp-content/uploads/2019/08/01125725/f-secure-cyber-threat-landscape-finance-sector.pdf
- IBM. (2020, July 29). Cost of a Data Breach Study. IBM. Retrieved September 8, 2020, from https://www.ibm.com/security/data-breach

DECODE
- IBM. (2020, July 29). Cost of a Data Breach Study. IBM. Retrieved September 8, 2020, from https://www.ibm.com/security/data-breach
- McCandless, D. et al. (2020, May 11). World's Biggest Data Breaches & Hacks. databreaches.net, IDTheftCentre and Media Reports. Information Is Beautiful. Retrieved September 8, 2020, from https://www.informationisbeautiful.net/visualizations/worlds-biggest-data-breaches-hacks/
- VPN Mentor. (2020, June 16). Report: Data Breach in Biometric Security Platform Affecting Millions of Users. VPN Mentor. Retrieved September 12, 2020, from https://www.vpnmentor.com/blog/report-biostar2-leak/
- Whittaker, Z. (2019, September 4). A Huge Database of Facebook Users' Phone Numbers Found Online. Techcrunch. Retrieved September 12, 2020, from https://techcrunch.com/2019/09/04/facebook-phone-numbers-exposed/?guccounter=1
- Sandler, R. (2019, July 29). Capital One Says Hacker Breached Accounts of 100 Million People; Ex-Amazon Employee Arrested. *Forbes*. Retrieved September 12, 2020, from https://www.forbes.com/sites/rachelsandler/2019/07/29/capital-one-says-hacker-breached-accounts-of-100-million-people-ex-amazon-employee-arrested/#27002a9541d2

IMPACT
- CBInsights. (2019, July 30). Cybersecurity Trends. CBInsights. Retrieved September 7, 2020, from https://www.cbinsights.com/reports/CB-Insights_Cybersecurity-Trends.pdf
- Deloitte. (2019, March 4). The Future of Cyber Survey 2019. Deloitte & Touche LLP. Retrieved September 7, 2020, from https://www2.deloitte.com/content/dam/Deloitte/us/Documents/finance/us-the-future-of-cyber-survey.pdf
- Australian Cyber Security Growth Network. (2019, December 19). Australia's Cyber Security Sector Competitiveness Plan 2019. Australian Cyber Security Growth Network. Retrieved September 7, 2020, from https://www.austcyber.com/resources/sector-competitiveness-plan/chapter1

04 TECHNOLOGICAL INNOVATION

ACCELERATING TECHNOLOGY

ORIGIN STORY

- Laws, D. (2018, April 02). 13 Sextillion & Counting: The Long & Winding Road to the Most Frequently Manufactured Human Artifact in History. Computer History Museum. Retrieved September 8, 2020, from https://computerhistory.org/blog/13-sextillion-counting-the-long-winding-road-to-the-most-frequently-manufactured-human-artifact-in-history/
- Reinsel, D. et al. via IDC. (2018, November). The Digitization of the World from Edge to Core. International Data Corporation (IDC). Retrieved September 8, 2020, from https://www.seagate.com/files/www-content/our-story/trends/files/idc-seagate-dataage-whitepaper.pdf
- International Telecommunication Union. (2019). Measuring Digital Development - Facts and Figures 2019. International Telecommunication Union. Retrieved September 8, 2020, from https://www.itu.int/en/ITU-D/Statistics/Documents/facts/FactsFigures2019.pdf
- Schrittweiser, J. et al. (2019, November 19). Mastering Atari, Go, Chess, and Shogi by Planning with a Learned Model. DeepMind. Retrieved September 8, 2020, from https://deepmind.com/research/publications/Mastering-Atari-Go-Chess-and-Shogi-by-Planning-with-a-Learned-Model
- Wetterstrand, K. A. (2020, August 25). DNA Sequencing Costs: Data from the NHGRI Genome Sequencing Program (GSP). National Human Genome Research Institute. Retrieved September 8, 2020, from https://www.genome.gov/about-genomics/fact-sheets/DNA-Sequencing-Costs-Data

SIGNAL

- Jurveston, S. (2016, December 10). Moore's Law over 120 Years. Flickr. Retrieved September 8, 2020, from https://www.flickr.com/photos/jurvetson/31409423572/
- Kurzweil, R. (2005, September 22). The Singularity Is Near. Page 67. Viking Press. Retrieved September 8, 2020, from http://www.singularity.com/charts/page67.html
- Experts Exchange. (2015) via Routley, N. (2017, November 4). Visualizing the Trillion-Fold Increase in Computing Power. Visual Capitalist. Retrieved September 8, 2020, from https://www.visualcapitalist.com/visualizing-trillion-fold-increase-computing-power/
- Ritchie, H. (2017). Technology Adoption. Our World in Data. Retrieved September 8, 2020, from https://ourworldindata.org/technology-adoption

DECODE

- Top500. (2020, June). Performance Development. Top500. Retrieved September 8, 2020, from https://www.top500.org/statistics/perfdevel/
- Cisco. (2020, March 9). Cisco Annual Internet Report (2018–2023) White Paper. Retrieved September 8, 2020, from https://www.cisco.com/c/en/us/solutions/collateral/executive-perspectives/annual-internet-report/white-paper-c11-741490.html
- Reinsel, D. (2018, November). The Digitization of the World from Edge to Core. International Data Corporation (IDC). Retrieved September 8, 2020, from https://www.seagate.com/files/www-content/our-story/trends/files/idc-seagate-dataage-whitepaper.pdf
- Taylor, B. (2018, April 10). 200 Years of the United States Stock Market in One Graph. Global Financial Data. Retrieved September 8, 2020, from http://www.globalfinancialdata.com/200-years-of-the-united-states-stock-market-in-one-graph/
- Unesco Institute for Statistics. (2020). How Much Does Your Country Invest in R&D? Unesco Institute for Statistics. Retrieved September 9, 2020, from http://uis.unesco.org/apps/visualisations/research-and-development-spending/
- Renaissance Capital. (2020, January 5). US IPO Market: 2020 Annual Review. Renaissance Capital. Retrieved June 1, 2021, from https://www.renaissancecapital.com/review/2020USReview_Public.pdf
- Behrmann, E. and Wilkes, W. (2021, May 6). BMW CEO Sees Semiconductor Investment Wave Easing Supply Crunch. BNN Bloomberg. Retrieved June 1, 2021, from https://www.bnnbloomberg.ca/bmw-ceo-sees-semiconductor-investment-wave-easing-supply-crunch-1.1600235

IMPACT

- World Economic Forum. (2016). The Global Risks Report 2016: 11th Edition. World Economic Forum. Retrieved September 9, 2020, from http://www3.weforum.org/docs/GRR/WEF_GRR16.pdf
- Renaissance Capital. (2019, December 23). US IPO Market: 2019 Annual Review. Renaissance Capital. Retrieved September 9, 2020, from https://www.renaissancecapital.com/review/2019_US_IPO_Review_Press.pdf
- International Data Corporation (IDC). (2020). IDC - Global ICT Spending: Forecast 2020–2023. International Data Corporation (IDC). Retrieved September 9, 2020, from https://www.idc.com/promo/global-ict-spending/forecast
- Coppola, G. et al. (2021, May 5). Chip Shortage Forces Carmakers to Leave Out Some High-End Features. Bloomberg. Retrieved July 2, 2021, from https://www.bloomberg.com/news/articles/2021-05-06/chip-shortage-forces-carmakers-to-strip-out-high-tech-features

THE 5G REVOLUTION

ORIGIN STORY → Fortune Business Insights. (2019, July). 5G Infrastructure Market Size, Share and Industry Analysis by Component (Fibers, Cables, Antenna, Transceiver, Wireless Backhaul, Modem, Router), by Communication Infrastructure (Small Cell, Macro Cell, Radio Access Network (RAN), Distributed Antenna System (DAS)), and Regional Forecast 2019–2026. Fortune Business Insights. Retrieved September 10, 2020, from https://www.fortunebusinessinsights.com/industry-reports/5g-infrastructure-market-100869
- Gartner. (2019, October 17). Gartner Predicts Outdoor Surveillance Cameras Will Be Largest Market for 5G Internet of Things Solutions over Next Three Years. Gartner, Inc. Retrieved September 10, 2020, from https://www.gartner.com/en/newsroom/press-releases/2019-10-17-gartner-predicts-outdoor-surveillance-cameras-will-be
- Statcounter. (2020). Desktop vs Mobile vs Tablet Market Share Worldwide. Statcounter GlobalStats. Retrieved September 10, 2020, from https://gs.statcounter.com/platform-market-share/desktop-mobile-tablet
- 3GPP. (2020). 3GPP: A Global Initiative. Retrieved September 10, 2020, from https://www.3gpp.org/

SIGNAL → McKinsey & Company. (2020, January). The 5G Era. McKinsey & Company. Retrieved September 10, 2020, from https://www.mckinsey.com/~/media/mckinsey/industries/advanced%20eletrics/our%20isights/the%205g%20era%20new%20horizons%20for%20advanced%20electronics%20and%20industrial%20companies/the-5g-era-new-horizons-for-advanced-electronics-and-industrial-companies.ashx
- GSMA. (2020). 5G Global Launches & Statistics. GSM Association. Retrieved September 10, 2020, from https://www.gsma.com/futurenetworks/ip_services/understanding-5g/5g-innovation/
- World Economic Forum & PWC. (2020, January). The Impact of 5G: Creating New Value across Industries and Society. World Economic Forum. Retrieved September 10, 2020, from http://www3.weforum.org/docs/WEF_The_Impact_of_5G_Report.pdf

DECODE → IHS Markit. (2019, November). The 5G Economy: How 5G Will Contribute to the Global Economy. IHS Markit. Retrieved September 10, 2020, from https://www.qualcomm.com/media/documents/files/ihs-5g-economic-impact-study-2019.pdf
- McKinsey & Company. (2020, January). The 5G Era. McKinsey & Company. Retrieved September 10, 2020, from https://www.mckinsey.com/~/media/mckinsey/industries/advanced%20electronics/our%20insights/the%205g%20era%20new%20horizons%20for%20advanced%20electronics%20and%20industrial%20companies/the-5g-era-new-horizons-for-advanced-electronics-and-industrial-companies.ashx

IMPACT → Kennedy, S. via Center for Strategic & International Studies. (2020, July 27). Washington's China Policy Has Lost Its Wei. Center for Strategic & International Studies. Retrieved September 10, 2020, from https://www.csis.org/analysis/washingtons-china-policy-has-lost-its-wei
- Business Performance Innovation Network. (2019, May). Opportunities and Challenges in a 5G Connected Economy. BPI Network. Retrieved September 10, 2020, from https://futurecio.tech/wp-content/uploads/2019/09/2019Report_SecuringFutureSmartWorld.pdf
- GSMA. (2020). 5G Global Launches & Statistics. GSM Association. Retrieved September 10, 2020, from https://www.gsma.com/futurenetworks/ip_services/understanding-5g/5g-innovation/

THE NEW SPACE RACE

ORIGIN STORY → Euroconsult. (2019). Satellites to Be Built and Launched by 2028. Euroconsult. Retrieved September 9, 2020, from https://www.euroconsult-ec.com/research/WS319_free_extract_2019.pdf
- Union of Concerned Scientists. (2005, December 8; Updated 2020, April 1). UCS Satellite Database. Union of Concerned Scientists. Retrieved September 9, 2020, from https://www.ucsusa.org/resources/satellite-database
- Markets and Markets. (2020, August 12). Small Satellite Market Worth $7.1 Billion by 2025. Markets and Markets. Retrieved September 9, 2020, from https://www.marketsandmarkets.com/Market-Reports/small-satellite-market-150947396.html
- Mosher, D. (2018, December 15). Elon Musk Beat a World Record for Rocket Launches in 2018. Here's Every History-Making SpaceX Mission of the Year. Business Insider. Retrieved September 9, 2020, from https://www.businessinsider.com/spacex-falcon-9-commercial-rocket-record-most-launches-2018-12

SIGNAL → Euroconsult. (2019). Satellites to Be Built and Launched by 2028. Euroconsult. Retrieved September 9, 2020, from https://www.euroconsult-ec.com/research/WS319_free_extract_2019.pdf
- Union of Concerned Scientists. (2005, December 8; Updated 2020, April 1). UCS Satellite Database. Union of Concerned Scientists. Retrieved September 9, 2020, from https://www.ucsusa.org/resources/satellite-database

DECODE → Johnson-Freese, J. (2018, December 19). China Launched More Rockets into Orbit in 2018 Than Any Other Country. *MIT Technology Review*. Retrieved September 9, 2020, from https://www.technologyreview.com/2018/12/19/66274/china-launched-more-rockets-into-orbit-in-2018-than-any-other-country/

- Euroconsult. (2019). Satellites to Be Built and Launched by 2028. Euroconsult. Retrieved September 9, 2020, from https://www.euroconsult-ec.com/research/WS319_free_extract_2019.pdf
- Union of Concerned Scientists. (2005, December 8; Updated 2020, April 1). UCS Satellite Database. Union of Concerned Scientists. Retrieved September 9, 2020, from https://www.ucsusa.org/resources/satellite-database

IMPACT
- Euroconsult. (2019). Satellites to Be Built and Launched by 2028. Euroconsult. Retrieved September 9, 2020, from https://www.euroconsult-ec.com/research/WS319_free_extract_2019.pdf
- Grijpink, F. et al. (2020, February). Connected World: An Evolution in Connectivity Beyond the 5G Revolution. McKinsey Global Institute. Retrieved September 9, 2020, from https://www.mckinsey.com/~/media/mckinsey/industries/technology%20media%20and%20telecommunications/telecommunications/our%20insights/connected%20world%20an%20evolution%20in%20connectivity%20beyond%20the%205g%20revolution/mgi_connected-world_discussion-paper_february-2020.pdf
- Federal Aviation Association, via Bloomberg. (2018). The New Rockets Racing to Make Space Affordable. Bloomberg. Retrieved September 12, 2020, from https://www.bloomberg.com/graphics/2018-rocket-cost/

CRISPR: GENE EDITING AT SCALE

ORIGIN STORY
- Zimmer, C. (2015, February 6). Breakthrough DNA Editor Born of Bacteria. *Quanta Magazine*. Retrieved September 9, 2020, from https://www.quantamagazine.org/crispr-natural-history-in-bacteria-20150206/
- Lewis, T. (2013, April 14). Human Genome Project Marks 10th Anniversary. Live Science. Retrieved September 9, 2020, from https://www.livescience.com/28708-human-genome-project-anniversary.html
- Weintraub, K. (2016, July 5). 20 Years after Dolly the Sheep Led the Way—Where Is Cloning Now? *Scientific American*. Retrieved September 9, 2020, from https://www.scientificamerican.com/article/20-years-after-dolly-the-sheep-led-the-way-where-is-cloning-now/

SIGNAL
- Wetterstrand, K. A. (2020, August 25). DNA Sequencing Costs: Data from the NHGRI Genome Sequencing Program (GSP). National Human Genome Research Institute. Retrieved September 9, 2020, from https://www.genome.gov/about-genomics/fact-sheets/DNA-Sequencing-Costs-Data
- *The Economist*. (2015, August 22). Genome Editing: The Age of the Red Pen. The Economist Group Limited. Retrieved September 9, 2020, from https://www.economist.com/briefing/2015/08/22/the-age-of-the-red-pen
- Hsu, P. et al. (2014, June 5). Development and Applications of CRISPR-Cas9 for Genome Engineering. *Cell*, 157(6). Pages 1262-1278. Retrieved September 9, 2020, from https://www.sciencedirect.com/science/article/pii/S0092867414006047

DECODE
- Bergan, B. (2017, August 07). 11 Incredible Things CRISPR Has Helped Us Achieve in 2017. Futurism. Retrieved September 9, 2020, from https://futurism.com/neoscope/11-incredible-things-crispr-has-helped-us-achieve-in-2017
- Plumer B., et al. (2018, December 27). A Simple Guide to CRISPR, One of the Biggest Science Stories of the Decade. Vox. Retrieved September 9, 2020, from https://www.vox.com/2018/7/23/17594864/crispr-cas9-gene-editing
- Veerasamy, K. (2018, November 21). CRISPR: Discovery and Potential Applications. Xeraya Capital. Retrieved September 9, 2020, from https://www.slideshare.net/kumaraguruveerasamy/crispr-discovery-potential-applications-123587963
- Schwartz, M. (2018). Target, Delete, Repair: CRISPR Is a Revolutionary Gene-Editing Tool, but It's Not without Risk. Stanford Medicine. Retrieved September 9, 2020, from https://stanmed.stanford.edu/2018winter/CRISPR-for-gene-editing-is-revolutionary-but-it-comes-with-risks.html
- Cohen, J. (2019, August 1). Did CRISPR Help—or Harm—the First-Ever Gene-Edited Babies? Science. Retrieved September 9, 2020, from https://www.sciencemag.org/news/2019/08/did-crispr-help-or-harm-first-ever-gene-edited-babies
- Brodwin, E. (2020, April 16). Scientists Tap CRISPR's Search-and-Detect Skills to Create a Rapid COVID-19 Test. STAT. Retrieved September 9, 2020, from https://www.statnews.com/2020/04/16/coronavirus-test-crispr-mammoth-biosciences/
- Zsögön, A. et al. (2018, October 1). De Novo Domestication of Wild Tomato Using Genome Editing. Nature Biotechnology. Retrieved September 9, 2020, from https://www.nature.com/articles/nbt.4272

IMPACT
- iPlytics. (2019, February 8). Recent Patent Trends in CRISPR. iPlytics. Retrieved September 9, 2020, from https://www.iplytics.com/report/recent-patent-trends-crispr
- Plumer B., et al. (2018, December 27). A Simple Guide to CRISPR, One of the Biggest Science Stories of the Decade. Vox. Retrieved September 9, 2020, from https://www.vox.com/2018/7/23/17594864/crispr-cas9-gene-editing
- Scheufele, D. et al. (2017, August 11). U.S. Attitudes on Human Genome Editing. *Science*. Retrieved September 9, 2020, from https://science.sciencemag.org/content/357/6351/553
- AP-NORC Center. (2018). Human Genetic Engineering: December 2018 Poll. The Associated Press and NORC. Retrieved September 12, 2020, from https://apnorc.org/projects/human-genetic-engineering/

INDEBTED WORLD

ORIGIN STORY → OECD. (2020b). Household Debt (indicator). OECD. Retrieved September 7, 2020, from https://data.oecd.org/hha/household-debt.htm
- Banerjee, R. and Hofmann, B. (2018). The Rise of Zombie Firms: Causes and Consequences. *BIS Quarterly Review*. Retrieved September 9, 2020, from https://www.bis.org/publ/qtrpdf/r_qt1809g.pdf
- OECD. (2020a). General Government Debt (indicator). OECD. Retrieved September 7, 2020, from https://data.oecd.org/gga/general-government-debt.htm

SIGNAL → Tiftik, E. et al. (2020, January 13). Global Debt Monitor - Sustainability Matters. Institute of International Finance. Retrieved September 7, 2020, from https://www.iif.com/Portals/0/Files/content/Global Debt Monitor_January2020_vf.pdf
- Tiftik, E. and Mahmood, K. (2020, April 6). Global Debt Monitor COVID-19 Lights a Fuse. International Institute of Finance. Retrieved September 7, 2020, from https://www.iif.com/Portals/0/Files/content/Research/Global Debt Monitor_April2020.pdf
- The Economist Intelligence Unit. (2012, September 3). The Global Debt Clock. *The Economist*. Retrieved September 7, 2020, from https://www.economist.com/content/global_debt_clock

DECODE → Gaspar, V., Lam, W., and Raissi, M. (2020, April 15). Fiscal Policies to Contain the Damage from COVID-19. IMFBlog. Retrieved September 7, 2020, from https://blogs.imf.org/2020/04/15/fiscal-policies-to-contain-the-damage-from-covid-19/
- Peter G. Peterson Foundation. (2020). Key Drivers of the National Debt. PGPF. Retrieved September 7, 2020, from https://www.pgpf.org/the-fiscal-and-economic-challenge/drivers
- International Monetary Fund, via Federal Reserve. (2020). Total Debt to Equity for United States [TOTDTEUSQ163N], Retrieved August 10, 2020, from https://fred.stlouisfed.org/series/TOTDTEUSQ163N
- International Monetary Fund. (2020, April). Global Financial Stability Report: Markets in the Time of COVID-19. International Monetary Fund. Retrieved September 7, 2020, from https://www.imf.org/en/Publications/GFSR/Issues/2020/04/14/global-financial-stability-report-april-2020

IMPACT → Tiftik, E., and Guardia, P. D. (2020, March 26). IIF Weekly Insight COVID-19 Exacerbates Household Debt Burdens. Institute of International Finance. Retrieved September 7, 2020, from https://www.iif.com/Portals/0/Files/content/200326Weekly Insight_vf.pdf
- Stolba, S. L. (2020, March 9). Debt Reaches New Highs in 2019, but Credit Scores Stay Strong. Experian. Retrieved September 7, 2020, from https://www.experian.com/blogs/ask-experian/research/consumer-debt-study/
- Tiftik, E. and Mahmood, K. (2020, April 6). Global Debt Monitor COVID-19 Lights a Fuse. International Institute of Finance. Retrieved September 7, 2020, from https://www.iif.com/Portals/0/Files/content/Research/Global Debt Monitor_April2020.pdf

FALLING INTEREST RATES

ORIGIN STORY → Roser, M. (2016). War and Peace. Our World in Data. Retrieved September 10, 2020, from https://ourworldindata.org/war-and-peace
- Benigno, G. and Fornaro, L. (2019, April 1). The Keynesian Growth Approach to Macroeconomic Policy and Productivity. Liberty Street Economics, Federal Reserve Bank of New York. Retrieved September 10, 2020, from https://libertystreeteconomics.newyorkfed.org/2019/04/the-keynesian-growth-approach-to-macroeconomic-policy-and-productivity.html

- Schmelzing, P. (2018, May 24). The 'Suprasecular' Stagnation. VoxEU. Retrieved September 10, 2020, from https://voxeu.org/article/suprasecular-stagnation
- Schmelzing, P. (2020, January). Eight Centuries of Global Real Interest Rates, R-G, and the 'Suprasecular' Decline, 1311–2018. Bank of England. Retrieved September 7, 2020, from https://www.bankofengland.co.uk/-/media/boe/files/working-paper/2020/eight-centuries-of-global-real-interest-rates-r-g-and-the-suprasecular-decline-1311-2018.pdf

SIGNAL
- Schmelzing, P. (2020, January 3). Eight Centuries of Global Real Interest Rates, R-G, and the 'Suprasecular' Decline, 1311–2018.
- Goldman Sachs Investment Research via Isabelnet. (2019, May 15). More than 200 Years of US Interest Rates in One Chart. Retrieved September 8, 2020, from https://www.isabelnet.com/more-than-200-years-of-us-interest-rates-in-one-chart/
- International Monetary Fund via World Bank. Real Interest Rate (%) - United States. [online chart tool] (n.d.). World Bank Group. Retrieved September 8, 2020, from https://data.worldbank.org/indicator/FR.INR.RINR?locations=US

DECODE
- OECD. (2021). Short term interest rates (indicator). OECD. Retrieved June 14, 2021, from https://data.oecd.org/interest/short-term-interest-rates.htm
- Freddie Mac. (2020, September 03). Mortgage Rates. Retrieved September 8, 2020, from http://www.freddiemac.com/pmms/
- Schmelzing, P. (2020, January 3). Eight Centuries of Global Real Interest Rates, R-G, and the 'Suprasecular' Decline, 1311–2018.
- Mee, K. (2019, September 04). Six Reasons Why It Can Make Sense to Buy a Bond with a Negative Yield. Schroders. Retrieved September 8, 2020, from https://www.schroders.com/en/uk/adviser/insights/markets/six-reasons-why-it-can-make-sense-to-buy-a-bond-with-a-negative-yield/

IMPACT
- Neely, C. J. (2020, February 28). Negative U.S. Interest Rates? Federal Reserve Bank of St. Louis. Retrieved September 8, 2020, from https://research.stlouisfed.org/publications/economic-synopses/2020/02/28/negative-u-s-interest-rates
- International Monetary Fund via World Bank. Deposit Interest Rate (%) [online chart tool]. (n.d.). World Bank Group. Retrieved September 8, 2020, from https://data.worldbank.org/indicator/FR.INR.DPST?end=2019
- Mercer. (2019, July 2). European Asset Allocation Survey 2019. Mercer. Retrieved September 7, 2020, from https://www.mercer.com/content/dam/mercer/attachments/private/ie-2019-mercer-european-asset-allocation-survey-2019-final.pdf

CENTRAL BANK IMPOTENCE

ORIGIN STORY
- World Bank Group. (2019). Population growth (annual %). Retrieved September 7, 2020, from https://data.worldbank.org/indicator/SP.POP.GROW?end=2019
- Rabouin, D. (2020, June 15). "Zombie" Companies May Soon Represent 20% of U.S. Firms. DB Global Research via Axios Visuals. Retrieved September 7, 2020, from https://www.axios.com/zombie-companies-us-e2c8be18-6786-484e-8fbe-4b56cf3800ac.html
- Federal Reserve Bank of St. Louis. (2019). FRED Economic Data. Retrieved September 7, 2020, from https://fred.stlouisfed.org/

SIGNAL
- Ovaska, M. (2020). Central Bank Balance Sheets. Reuters Graphics. Retrieved September 7, 2020, from https://graphics.reuters.com/GLOBAL-CENTRALBANKS/010041ZQ4B7/index.html
- Bank for International Settlements. (2020). Central Bank Policy Rates. Retrieved September 7, 2020, from https://www.bis.org/statistics/cbpol.htm
- Central Bank News. (2020). Inflation Targets. Central Bank News. Retrieved September 7, 2020, from http://www.centralbanknews.info/p/inflation-targets.html
- Federal Reserve Bank of Dallas. (2020). Trimmed Mean PCE Inflation Rate. Federal Reserve Bank of St. Louis. Retrieved September 10, 2020, from https://fred.stlouisfed.org/graph/?g=1ED0

DECODE
- World Bank, via Macrotrends. (2020). Japan Inflation Rate 1960–2020. Macrotrends. Retrieved September 7, 2020, from https://www.macrotrends.net/countries/JPN/japan/inflation-rate-cpi
- Japan Macro Advisors. (2020, August 4). Bank of Japan Balance Sheet. Japan Macro Advisors. Retrieved September 7, 2020, from https://www.japanmacroadvisors.com/page/category/bank-of-japan/boj-balance-sheet/
- Statista Research Department. (2020, June 8). Average Annual Real Wages in Japan from 2000 to 2018. Statista. Retrieved September 7, 2020, from https://www.statista.com/statistics/612513/average-annual-real-wages-japan/
- Federal Reserve Bank of St. Louis. (2019). FRED Economic Data. Retrieved September 7, 2020, from https://fred.stlouisfed.org/
- Yahoo Finance - Stock Market Live, Quotes, Business & Finance News. (2020). Retrieved September 7, 2020, from https://ca.finance.yahoo.com/

IMPACT
- Bank of America Research Investment Committee and Haver Analytics, via Zerohedge. (2020). Bank of America Research Investment Committee. Retrieved September 7, 2020, from https://www.zerohedge.com/markets/here-stunning-chart-blows-all-modern-central-banking
- Deutsche Bank, via Zerohedge. (2020). Bank of Japan Owns Almost 80% of All ETFs Domiciled in Japan. Deutsche Bank Global Research. Retrieved September 7, 2020, from https://www.zerohedge.com/s3/files/inline-images/BOJ%20owns%2080%25%20of%20ETFs.jpg?itok=-TPsSn4V
- CNBC. (2020). JP10Y-JP: Japan 10 Year Treasury - Stock Price, Quote and News. CNBC. Retrieved September 7, 2020, from https://www.cnbc.com/quotes/?symbol=JP10Y-JP

STOCK MARKET CONCENTRATION

ORIGIN STORY

- Kepios, We Are Social, and Hootsuite. (2020). Digital 2020 Global Overview Report. We Are Social and Hootsuite. Retrieved September 9, 2020, from https://wearesocial.com/digital-2020
- CB Insights. (2019, November 6). The Top 20 Reasons Startups Fail. CB Insights. Retrieved September 9, 2020, from https://www.cbinsights.com/research/startup-failure-reasons-top/
- Greenwich Associates. (2019). Investing in the Digital Age: Media's Role in the Institutional Investor Engagement Journey. Greenwich Associates [research commissioned by LinkedIn]. Retrieved September 9, 2020, from https://business.linkedin.com/content/dam/me/business/en-us/marketing-solutions/cx/2019/pdfs/investing-in-the-digital-age-research-by-greenwich-associates-2019.pdf

SIGNAL

- Hulbert, M. (2020, May 30). Why the Stock Market Right Now Is Stronger Than Even The Most Bullish Investors Believe. MarketWatch. Retrieved June 11, 2021, from https://www.marketwatch.com/story/why-the-stock-market-right-now-is-stronger-than-even-the-most-bullish-investors-believe-2020-05-29
- BMO Global Asset Management. (2020). FAAMG Stocks Contribution to S&P 500® Return. BMO Global Asset Management. Retrieved June 11, 2021, from https://www.bmogam.com/us-en/advisors/market-charts/faamg-stocks-contribution-to-sp-500-return/
- Sources for the Chart "Market Capitalization of Top 5 Firms as % of Total Market Capitalization":
- Euronext. (2020). Euronext Brussels. Euronext. Retrieved September 12, 2020, from https://www.euronext.com/en/markets/brussels
- Bolsa de Madrid. (2020). IBEX35. Bolsas y Mercados Españoles. Retrieved September 12, 2020, from https://www.bolsamadrid.es/docs/SBolsas/InformesSB/FS-Ibex35_ING.pdf
- Hang Send Indexes. (2020). Hang Seng Index. Hang Seng Indexes. Retrieved September 12, 2020, from https://www.hsi.com.hk/static/uploads/contents/en/dl_centre/factsheets/hsie.pdf
- NSE India. (2020). Nifty 50 Index. NSE India. Retrieved September 12, 2020, from https://www.nseindia.com/products-services/indices-nifty50-index
- MSCI. (2020). MSCI Australia Index. MSCI. Retrieved September 12, 2020, from https://www.msci.com/documents/10199/ec1e0308-fb1a-42b7-baa3-756cab1a9de1
- MSCI. (2020). MSCI France Index. MSCI. Retrieved September 12, 2020, from https://www.msci.com/documents/10199/a4197489-9d3d-4f46-8c87-c7ec1685c2fe
- MSCI. (2020). MSCI Canada Index. MSCI. Retrieved September 12, 2020, from https://www.msci.com/documents/10199/641d0cad-f861-4cb0-b9c5-7d37f0d33f55
- MSCI. (2020). MSCI China All Shares Index. MSCI. Retrieved September 12, 2020, from https://www.msci.com/msci-china-all-shares
- Nikkei Indexes. (2020). Nikkei 225 Index. Nikei Indexes. Retrieved September 12, 2020, from https://indexes.nikkei.co.jp/en/nkave/index/profile?idx=nk225
- FTSE Russell. (2020). FTSE 100. FTSE Russell. Retrieved September 12, 2020, from https://www.ftserussell.com/analytics/factsheets/home/constituentsweights
- S&P 500 via Slickcharts. (2020). S&P 500 Companies by Weight. Slickcharts. Retrieved September 12, 2020, from https://www.slickcharts.com/sp500
- MSCI. (2020). MSCI ACWI. MSCI. Retrieved September 12, 2020.

DECODE

- Carlson, B. (2017, July 20). The Biggest Stocks. A Wealth of Common Sense. Retrieved September 9, 2020, from https://awealthofcommonsense.com/2017/07/the-biggest-stocks/
- S&P 500 via Slickcharts. (2020). S&P 500 Companies by Weight. Slickcharts. Retrieved September 9, 2020, from https://www.slickcharts.com/sp500
- S&P Global via finbox. (2020). [online chart tool]. finbox. Retrieved September 9, 2020, from https://finbox.com/NASDAQGS:AAPL/charts
- Gurdus, L. (2019, November 9). ETF Assets Rise to Record $4 Trillion and Top Industry Expert Says It's Still 'Early Days'. CNBC. Retrieved September 9, 2020, from https://www.cnbc.com/2019/11/09/etf-assets-rise-to-a-record-4-trillion-and-its-still-early-days.html
- Aviva Investors. (2018, November 30). Beware the Risks of Equity Market Concentration. Aviva Investors. Retrieved September 12, 2020, from https://www.avivainvestors.com/en-ca/views/aiq-investment-thinking/2018/11/the-risks-of-equity-market-concentration/
- McDevitt, K. and Watson, N. (2020, January 29). The Decade in Fund Flows: A Recap in 5 Charts. Morningstar Research Services LLC. Retrieved September 9, 2020, from https://www.morningstar.com/insights/2020/01/29/fund-flows-recap
- Divine, J. (2019, November 14). Has Passive Investing Become Fraught With Risk? U.S. News. Retrieved September 9, 2020, from https://money.usnews.com/investing/funds/articles/do-index-funds-etfs-quietly-pose-a-systemic-risk-michael-burry-thinks-so

IMPACT

- Goldman Sachs Asset Management Connect. (2020, August 19). Concentrating on Market Concentration. Goldman Sachs. Retrieved September 9, 2020, from https://www.gsam.com/content/gsam/us/en/advisors/market-insights/gsam-connect/2020/Concentrating_on_Market_Concentration.html
- S&P Dow Jones Indices. (2020). S&P 500 Equal Weight Index. S&P Global. Retrieved September 9, 2020, from https://www.spglobal.com/spdji/en/indices/equity/sp-500-equal-weight-index/#overview
- Bae, K. et al. (2020, June 29). Why Is Stock Market Concentration Bad for the Economy? Journal of Financial Economics (JFE), Forthcoming. Retrieved September 12, 2020, from https://papers.ssrn.com/sol3/papers.cfm?abstract_id=3655312

DWINDLING CORPORATE LONGEVITY

ORIGIN STORY
- PitchBook. (2019, August 9). 2019 Unicorn Report. PitchBook. Retrieved September 9, 2020, from https://pitchbook.com/news/reports/2019-unicorn-report
- Bain & Company. (2020). Corporate M&A Report 2020. Bain & Company. Retrieved September 9, 2020, from https://www.bain.com/insights/topics/global-corporate-ma-report/
- Anthony, S. et al. (2018, February). 2018 Corporate Longevity Forecast: Creative Destruction Is Accelerating. Innosight. Retrieved September 9, 2020, from https://www.innosight.com/insight/creative-destruction/
- Kemp, S. (2019, January 31). Digital 2019: Global Digital Overview. Datareportal. Retrieved September 9, 2020, from https://datareportal.com/reports/digital-2019-global-digital-overview

SIGNAL
- Viguerie, S. et al. (2021). 2021 Corporate Longevity Forecast. Innosight. Retrieved June 11, 2021, from https://www.innosight.com/wp-content/uploads/2021/05/Innosight_2021-Corporate-Longevity-Forecast.pdf
- Anthony, S. et al. (2018, February). 2018 Corporate Longevity Forecast: Creative Destruction Is Accelerating. Innosight. Retrieved September 2, 2020, https://www.innosight.com/wp-content/uploads/2017/11/Innosight-Corporate-Longevity-2018.pdf
- S&P Dow Jones Indices. (2020). S&P 500. S&P Dow Jones Indices. Retrieved September 9, 2020, from https://www.spglobal.com/spdji/en/indices/equity/sp-500/#overview
- Mauboussin, M. et al. (2017, February 7). Corporate Longevity: Index Turnover and Corporate Performance. Credit Suisse. Retrieved September 9, 2020, from https://plus.credit-suisse.com/rpc4/ravDocView?docid=V6y0SB2AF-WErIce

DECODE
- PitchBook. (2021, April 13). PitchBook- NVCA Venture Monitor Q1 2021. Pitchbook. Retrieved June 11, 2021, from https://files.pitchbook.com/website/files/pdf/Q1_2021_PitchBook-NVCA_Venture_Monitor.pdf
- Mauboussin, M. et al. (2017, February 7). Corporate Longevity: Index Turnover and Corporate Performance. Credit Suisse. Retrieved September 9, 2020, from https://plus.credit-suisse.com/rpc4/ravDocView?docid=V6y0SB2AF-WErIce
- Ritchie, H. (2017). Technology Adoption. Our World in Data. Retrieved September 8, 2020, from https://ourworldindata.org/technology-adoption
- Anthony, S. (2016, July 15). Kodak's Downfall Wasn't about Technology. *Harvard Business Review.* Retrieved September 9, 2020, from https://hbr.org/2016/07/kodaks-downfall-wasnt-about-technology
- Satell, G. (2014, September 5). A Look Back at Why Blockbuster Really Failed and Why It Didn't Have To. *Forbes.* Retrieved September 9, 2020, from https://www.forbes.com/sites/gregsatell/2014/09/05/a-look-back-at-why-blockbuster-really-failed-and-why-it-didnt-have-to/#603cc3201d64
- Keyes, D. (2020, February 24). E-commerce Sales Surpassed 10% of Total Retail Sales in 2019 for the First Time. Business Insider. Retrieved September 9, 2020, from https://www.businessinsider.com/ecommerce-topped-10-percent-of-us-retail-in-2019-2020-2
- Droesch, B. (2021, February 1). How Will the Pandemic Affect US Ecommerce Sales in 2021? eMarketer. Retrieved June 14, 2021, from https://www.emarketer.com/content/how-will-pandemic-affect-us-ecommerce-sales-2021

IMPACT
- Govindarajan, V. et al. (2019, March 20). R&D Spending Has Dramatically Surpassed Advertising Spending. *Harvard Business Review.* Retrieved September 9, 2020, from https://hbr.org/2019/05/rd-spending-has-dramatically-surpassed-advertising-spending
- PWC. (2020). Talent Trends 2020 - Upskilling: Building Confidence in an Uncertain World. PWC. Retrieved September 9, 2020, from https://www.pwc.com/gx/en/ceo-survey/2020/trends/pwc-talent-trends-2020.pdf
- PWC. (2019). Talent Trends 2019: Upskilling for a Digital World. PWC. Retrieved September 9, 2020, from https://www.pwc.com/gx/en/ceo-survey/2019/Theme-assets/reports/talent-trends-report.pdf
- Garelli, S. (2016). Why You Will Probably Live Longer Than Most Big Companies. IMD. Retrieved September 12, 2020, from https://www.imd.org/research-knowledge/articles/why-you-will-probably-live-longer-than-most-big-companies
- Reeves, M. (2015, December 2). Die Another Day: What Leaders Can Do about the Shrinking Life Expectancy of Corporations. BCG. Retrieved September 12, 2020, from https://www.bcg.com/publications/2015/strategy-die-another-day-what-leaders-can-do-about-the-shrinking-life-expectancy-of-corporations

SUSTAINABLE INVESTING

ORIGIN STORY
- Hale, J. (2020, February 14). Sustainable Funds U.S. Landscape Report. Morningstar Research. Retrieved September 8, 2020, from https://www.morningstar.com/lp/sustainable-funds-landscape-report
- Global Carbon Atlas. (2018). Global CO2 Emissions. Global Carbon Atlas. Retrieved September 8, 2020, from http://www.globalcarbonatlas.org/en/CO2-emissions

- Sabin Center for Climate Change Law. (2020). Climate Change Litigation Databases. Sabin Center for Climate Change Law, Arnold & Porter. Retrieved September 8, 2020, from http://climatecasechart.com/

SIGNAL

- Deutsche Bank Research. (2019, September). Climate Change and Corporates: Past the Tipping Point with Customers and Stock Markets. Deutsche Bank Research. Retrieved September 8, 2020, from http://docs.publicnow.com/viewDoc.asp?filename=8046%5CEXT%5C3B53F66870B80187A7F1A1F8B85F2867372367F0 _2F12C25AD131FC5E85DBEE3CF39A6D339B1B9C10.PDF
- Collins. S, Sullivan, K. (2020, February, 20). Advancing Environmental, Social, and Governance Investing. Deloitte & Touche LLP. Retrieved September 8, 2020, from https://www2.deloitte.com/us/en/insights/industry/financial-services/esg-investing-performance.html
- Global Sustainable Investment Alliance. (2018). 2018 Global Sustainable Investment Review. Global Sustainable Investment Alliance. Retrieved September 8, 2020, from http://www.gsi-alliance.org/wp-content/uploads/2019/06/GSIR_Review2018F.pdf

DECODE

- Morgan Stanley Institute for Sustainable Investing. (2019). Sustainable Signals: Individual Investor Interest Driven by Impact, Conviction, and Choice. Morgan Stanley Institute for Sustainable Investing. Retrieved September 8, 2020, from https://www.morganstanley.com/pub/content/dam/msdotcom/infographics /sustainable-investing/Sustainable_Signals_Individual_Investor_White_Paper_Final.pdf
- Hamel, K. et al. (2018, April 30). How to Harness the Spending Power of Millennials: Move beyond the US. The Brookings Institution. Retrieved September 8, 2020, from https://www.brookings.edu/blog/future-development/2018/04/30/how-to-harness-the-spending-power-of-millennials-move-beyond-the-us/
- MSCI. (2021). MSCI ACWI ESG Leaders Index. MSCI. Retrieved June 14, 2021, from https://www.msci.com/documents/10199/9a760a3b-4dc0-4059-b33e-fe67eae92460
- Governance and Accountability Institute, Inc. (2019). 2020 S&P 500 Flash Report: 90% of S&P 500 Index® Companies Publish Sustainability / Responsibility Reports in 2019. Governance and Accountability Institute. Retrieved September 11, 2020, from https://www.ga-institute.com/research-reports/flash-reports/2020 -sp-500-flash-report.html

IMPACT

- Principles for Responsible Investment. (2021). PRI Update Q1 2021. Principles for Responsible Investment. Retrieved June 14, 2021, from https://www.unpri.org /download?ac=12423&adredir=1
- U.S. Energy Information Administration. (2019, October 2). EIA Projects That Renewables Will Provide Nearly Half of World Electricity by 2050. United States Energy Information Administration. Retrieved September 11, 2020, from https://www.eia.gov/todayinenergy/detail.php?id=41533#:~:text=EIA%20projects%20that%20renewables %20will%20provide%20nearly%20half%20of%20world%20electricity%20by%202050,-Source%3A%20U.S.%20Energy&text=In%202018%2C%2028%25%20of%20global ,%2C%20wind%2C%20and%20solar%20technologies.

06 CONSUMER BEHAVIOR

FRICTIONLESS RETAIL

ORIGIN STORY
- Hamel, K. and Kharas, H. (2018) A Global Tipping Point: Half the World Is Now Middle Class or Wealthier. Brookings. Retrieved August 10, 2021, from https://www.brookings.edu/blog/future-development/2018/09/27/a-global-tipping-point-half-the-world-is-now-middle-class-or-wealthier/
- European Commission. (n.d.). Knowledge for Policy: Growing Consumption. European Commission. Retrieved September 10, 2020, from https://ec.europa.eu/knowledge4policy/growing-consumerism_en
- Accenture Interactive. (2018). Pulse Check 2018. Accenture. Retrieved September 10, 2020, from https://www.accenture.com/_acnmedia/PDF-77/Accenture-Pulse-Survey.pdf
- Nolan, M. via Accenture Newsroom. (2020, June 16). A LICENSE FOR GROWTH Customer-Centric Supply Chains. Accenture. Retrieved September 10, 2020, from https://www.accenture.com/_acnmedia/PDF-127/Accenture-Customer-Centric-Supply-Chains-License-Growth.pdf
- Market Research Future. (2020, September). Global Omnichannel Retail Commerce Platform Market Research Report. Market Research Future. Retrieved September 10, 2020, from https://www.marketresearchfuture.com/reports/omnichannel-retail-commerce-platform-market-6956

SIGNAL
- CBInsights. (2020). State of Retail Tech: Ahead In 2020. CBInsights. Retrieved September 11, 2020, from https://www.cbinsights.com/reports/CB-Insights_Retail-Trends-2020.pdf
- Hadwick, A. via Eye For Transport. (2019). Dynamic Disruption Distribution: 2019 State of Retail Supply Chain Report. Eye for Transport. Retrieved September 11, 2020, from https://www.eft.com/publications?qt-reports_page=2#qt-reports_page
- Scriven, R. (2020). Warehouse Automation Market Off to a Strong Start in 2020. Interact Analysis. Retrieved September 12, 2020, from https://www.interactanalysis.com/warehouse-automation-market-off-to-a-strong-start-in-2020/

DECODE
- Ali, F. (2021, April 16). Amazon Prime Reaches 200 Million Members Worldwide. Digital Commerce 360. Retrieved June 15, 2021: https://www.digitalcommerce360.com/article/amazon-prime-membership/
- The E-Commerce Observer via Rakuten Intelligence. (2019, May 6). Rakuten Intelligence. Retrieved September 11, 2020, from https://www.rakutenintelligence.com/observer/marriott-tries-home-sharing-amazon-ups-the-ante-on-shipping-speeds
- Smith. S. (2017, October 10). Smart Store Technologies to Generate over $78 Billion in Annual Transaction Revenue by 2022. Juniper Research via Business Wire. https://www.businesswire.com/news/home/20171010005945/en/Juniper-Research-Smart-Store-Technologies-Generate-78
- Bridges, T. et al. via Capgemini Research Institute. (2020). Smart Stores: Rebooting the Retail Store through in-Store Automation. Capgemini. Retrieved September 10, 2020, from https://www.capgemini.com/wp-content/uploads/2020/01/Report-%E2%80%93-Smart-Stores-1.pdf
- PYMNTS. (2020, February) The Future of Unattended Retail. PYMNTS.com and USA Technologies. https://www.pymnts.com/wp-content/uploads/2020/02/The-Future-Of-Unattended-Retail-Report_February-2020.pdf
- Cook, A. V. et al. via Deloitte Insights. (2020, January 10). Augmented Shopping: The Quiet Revolution. Deloitte & Touche LLP. Retrieved September 11, 2020, from https://www2.deloitte.com/us/en/insights/topics/emerging-technologies/augmented-shopping-3d-technology-retail.html

IMPACT
- McKinsey & Company. (2020, January). Future of Retail Operations: Winning in a Digital Era. McKinsey & Company. Retrieved September 11, 2020, from https://www.mckinsey.com/~/media/McKinsey/Industries/Retail/Our%20Insights/Future%20of%20retail%20operations%20Winning%20in%20a%20digital%20era/McK_Retail-Ops-2020_FullIssue-RGB-hyperlinks-011620.pdf
- Wellener, P. et al. via Deloitte Insights. (2018, August 23). Distinctive Traits of Digital Frontrunners in Manufacturing: Embracing the Fourth Industrial Revolution. Deloitte & Touche LLP. Retrieved September 11, 2020, from https://www2.deloitte.com/us/en/insights/focus/industry-4-0/digital-leaders-in-manufacturing-fourth-industrial-revolution.html
- U.S. Bureau of Labor Statistics. (2020). Employment Projections Data: Employment by Detailed Occupation. U.S. Bureau of Labor Statistics. Retrieved September 11, 2020, from https://www.bls.gov/emp/tables/emp-by-detailed-occupation.htm
- Frey, C. B. and Osborne, M. (2013). The Future of Employment: How Susceptible Are Jobs to Computerization? Oxford Martin School & University of Oxford. Retrieved June 15, 2021, from https://www.oxfordmartin.ox.ac.uk/publications/the-future-of-employment/

THE RISE OF MEATLESS MEAT

ORIGIN STORY
- Ritchie, H. via Our World in Data. (2020, February 04). Less Meat is Nearly Always Better Than Sustainable Meat, to Reduce Your Carbon Footprint. Our World in Data. Retrieved September 11, 2020, from https://ourworldindata.org/less-meat-or-sustainable-meat
- BBC News. (2019, May 2). Beyond Meat: Shares in Vegan Burger Company Sizzle 160%. BBC. Retrieved September 11, 2020, from https://www.bbc.com/news/business-48141428
- United Nations - Department of Economic and Social Affairs. (2019, June 17). World Population Prospects 2019: Highlights. United Nations. Retrieved September 11, 2020, from https://www.un.org/development/desa/publications/world-population-prospects-2019-highlights.html
- Allen, M. et al. (2018, September 8). The Dirt on Clean Eating: A Cross Sectional Analysis of Dietary Intake, Restrained Eating and Opinions about Clean Eating among Women. *Nutrients*, 10(9), 1266. Retrieved September 11, 2020, from https://www.mdpi.com/2072-6643/10/9/1266

SIGNAL
- Gerhardt, C. et al. via Kearney. (2020). When Consumers Go Vegan, How Much Meat Will Be Left on the Table for Agribusiness? Kearney. Retrieved September 11, 2020, from https://www.kearney.com/consumer-retail/article?/a/when-consumers-go-vegan-how-much-meat-will-be-left-on-the-table-for-agribusiness
- The Good Food Institute. (2020). Plant-based Market Overview. The Good Food Institute. Retrieved September 11, 2020, from https://www.gfi.org/marketresearch
- Bashi, Z. et al. for McKinsey & Company. (2019, August 16). Alternative Proteins: The Race for Market Share Is On. Google Trends. McKinsey & Company. Retrieved September 11, 2020, from https://www.mckinsey.com/industries/agriculture/our-insights/alternative-proteins-the-race-for-market-share-is-on

DECODE
- Springmann, M. et al. (2019, November 12). Multiple Health and Environmental Impacts of Foods. *PNAS*, 116(46) 23357-23362. Retrieved September 11, 2020, from https://www.pnas.org/content/116/46/23357
- UN FAO, 2020, via Our World in Data. (2020). Number of Animals Slaughtered for Meat, World, 1961 to 2018 [chart]. Our World in Data. Retrieved September 12, 2020, from https://ourworldindata.org/grapher/animals-slaughtered-for-meat
- Merrill, D. et al. (2018, July 31). Here's How America Uses Its Land. Bloomberg. https://www.bloomberg.com/graphics/2018-us-land-use/

IMPACT
- CBInsights via Monigroup. (2019). Our Meatless Future: How The $90B Global Meat Market Gets Disrupted. Monigroup. Retrieved September 11, 2020, from https://www.monigroup.com/article/our-meatless-future-how-90b-global-meat-market-gets-disrupted
- Markets and Markets. (2020, June 26). Dairy Alternatives Market Worth $36.7 billion by 2025. Markets and Markets. Retrieved September 11, 2020, from https://www.marketsandmarkets.com/PressReleases/dairy-alternative-plant-milk-beverages.asp
- Bashi, Z. et al. via McKinsey & Company. (2019, August 16). Alternative Proteins: The Race for Market Share Is On. McKinsey & Company. Retrieved September 11, 2020, from https://www.mckinsey.com/industries/agriculture/our-insights/alternative-proteins-the-race-for-market-share-is-on
- Gerhardt, C. et al. via Kearney. (2020). When Consumers Go Vegan, How Much Meat Will Be Left on the Table for Agribusiness? Kearney. Retrieved September 11, 2020, from kearney.com/consumer-retail/article?/a/when-consumers-go-vegan-how-much-meat-will-be-left-on-the-table-for-agribusiness-

CONNECTED HEALTH

ORIGIN STORY
- United Nations. (2019). Global Issues: Ageing. United Nations. Retrieved September 11, 2020, from https://www.un.org/en/sections/issues-depth/ageing
- Roser, M. et al. via Our World in Data. (2015). Internet. Our World in Data. Retrieved September 11, 2020, from https://ourworldindata.org/internet
- Jones, G. L. et al. via McKinsey & Company. (2019, June 20). Promoting an Overdue Digital Transformation in Healthcare. McKinsey & Company. Retrieved September 11, 2020, from https://www.mckinsey.com/industries/healthcare-systems-and-services/our-insights/promoting-an-overdue-digital-transformation-in-healthcare
- Plant Based Foods Association (PBFA). (2019, June 12). U.S. Plant-Based Retail Market Worth $4.5 Billion, Growing at 5X Total Food Sales. Plant Based Foods Association. Retrieved September 11, 2020, from https://plantbasedfoods.org/2019-data-plant-based-market/

SIGNAL
- Rock Health and Stanford Center for Digital Health. (2019). Digital Health Consumer Adoption Report 2019. Rock Health. Retrieved September 11, 2020, from https://rockhealth.com/reports/digital-health-consumer-adoption-report-2019/
- Cordina, J. et al. via McKinsey & Company. (2019, April). Healthcare Consumerism Today: Accelerating the Consumer Experience. McKinsey & Company. Retrieved September 11, 2020, from https://www.mckinsey.com/~/media/McKinsey/Industries/Healthcare%20Systems%20and%20Services/Our%20Insights/Healthcare%20consumerism%20today%20Accelerating%20the%20consumer%20experience/Healthcare-consumerism-today-Accelerating-the-consumer-experience.pdf
- Accenture - Health. (2019, February 12). Today's Consumers Reveal the Future of Healthcare. Accenture. Retrieved September 11, 2020, from https://www.accenture.com/us-en/insights/health/todays-consumers-reveal-future-healthcare
- Ciampa, D. via Deloitte Perspectives. (2018, December 19). The Fight for Device Relevance: Could the Practicality of Wearables Be a Boon for Future Sales? Deloitte & Touche LLP. Retrieved September 11, 2020, from https://www2.deloitte.com/us/en/pages/technology-media-and-telecommunications/articles/wearable-device-usage-versus-penetration.html

DECODE
- VMware via YouTube. (2017, July 5). Connected Healthcare: Improving Health and Saving lives. VMware via YouTube.com. Retrieved September 11, 2020, from https://www.youtube.com/watch?v=6SrkIL6x-DA&ab_channel=VMware
- Remes, J. et al. (2020, July 8). Prioritizing Health: A Prescription for Prosperity. McKinsey. Retrieved February 14, 2020. https://www.mckinsey.com/industries/health-care-systems-and-services/our-insights/prioritizing-health-a-prescription-for-prosperity#
- Drobac et al. (2014, June 20). Connected Care Is Key to Accountable Care: The Case for Supporting Telehealth in ACOs. AJMC. Retrieved September 12, 2020, from https://www.ajmc.com/view/connected-care-is-key-to-accountable-care-the-case-for-supporting-telehealth-in-acos
- Fera, B. et al. via Deloitte Insights. (2020, April 30). The Future of Virtual Health: Executives See Industrywide Investments on the Horizon. Deloitte & Touche LLP. Retrieved September 11, 2020, from https://www2.deloitte.com/us/en/insights/industry/health-care/future-of-virtual-health.html
- Iqvia Institute. (2017, November). The Growing Value of Digital Health: Evidence and Impact on Human Health and the Healthcare System. Iqvia Institute. Retrieved September 11, 2020, from https://www.iqvia.com/-/media/iqvia/pdfs/institute-reports/the-growing-value-of-digital-health.pdf?&_=1599844314147
- CBInsights. (2019, September 13). Where Tech Giants Are Betting on Digital Health. CBInsights. Retrieved September 11, 2020, from https://www.cbinsights.com/research/tech-giants-digital-healthcare-investments/

IMPACT
- Global Wellness Institute. (2018, October). Global Wellness Economy Monitor. Global Wellness Institute. Retrieved September 11, 2020, from https://globalwellnessinstitute.org/wp-content/uploads/2019/04/GWIWellnessEconomyMonitor2018_042019.pdf
- Goldman Sachs via Seeking Alpha. (2015, December 3). Goldman Sachs Predicts Digital Healthcare Will Revolutionize the Industry. Seeking Alpha. Retrieved September 11, 2020, from https://seekingalpha.com/instablog/1240561-ray-dirks/4602236-goldman-sachs-predicts-digital-healthcare-will-revolutionize-industry
- Micca, P. et al. for Deloitte Insights. (2020, March 12). Health Tech Investment Trends: How Are Investors Positioning for the Future of Health? Rock Health. Deloitte & Touche LLP. Retrieved September 11, 2020, from https://www2.deloitte.com/us/en/insights/industry/health-care/health-tech-investment-trends.html
- Global Web Index. (2020). Digital Healthcare: Understanding the Evolution and Digitization of Healthcare. Global Web Index. Retrieved September 11, 2020, from https://www.globalwebindex.com/hubfs/Downloads/Digital%20Healthcare%20Report.pdf

BIPOLAR WORLD

ORIGIN STORY
- World Bank. (2019). GNI per capita, PPP (current international $) - China. Retrieved September 7, 2020, from https://data.worldbank.org/indicator /NY.GNP.PCAP.PP.CD?locations=CN
- FRED - Federal Reserve Bank of St. Louis. (2020, September 1). Federal Debt: Total Public Debt. Retrieved September 8, 2020, from https://fred.stlouisfed.org /series/GFDEBTN
- Bush, R. C. and Rigger, S. (2019, January 16). The Taiwan Issue and the Normalization of US-China Relations. The Brookings Institution. Retrieved September 8, 2020, from https://www.brookings.edu/research/the-taiwan-issue-and-the-normalization-of-us-china-relations/

SIGNAL
- Morrison, W. M. (2019, June 25). China's Economic Rise: History, Trends, Challenges, and Implications for the United States. Congressional Research Service. Retrieved September 7, 2020, from https://fas.org/sgp/crs/row/RL33534.pdf
- Leng, A. and Rajah, R. (2019, December 18). Chart of the Week: Global Trade through a US-China Lens. Lowy Institute. Retrieved September 8, 2020, from https://www.lowyinstitute.org/the-interpreter/chart-week-global-trade-through-us-china-lens
- CEIC. (2020, July 10) China: Cross-border RMB Settlement: Accumulation: Trade: Economic Indicators. Retrieved September 8, 2020, from https://www.ceicdata.com/en/china/crossborder-rmb-settlement/crossborder-rmb-settlement-accumulation-trade

DECODE
- Ding, Y. and Xiao, A. (2020, June 15). China's Belt and Road Initiative in a Post-Pandemic World. Invesco Limited. Retrieved September 8, 2020, from https://www.invesco.com/invest-china/en/institutional/insights/chinas-belt-and-road-initiative-in-a-post-pandemic-world.html
- Steil, B. and Della Rocca, B. (2019, May 8). Belt and Road Tracker. Greenberg Center for Geoeconomic Studies. Retrieved September 8, 2020, from https://www.cfr.org/article/belt-and-road-tracker
- Dreher, A. et al. (2017, September 15). Aid, China, and Growth: Evidence from a New Global Development Finance Dataset. College of William & Mary. Retrieved September 7, 2020, from https://wmpeople.wm.edu/asset/index/mjtier/aidchinaandgrowth

IMPACT
- Nor, T. M. and Mora, C. T. (2018, January 24). Reserve Currency Blocs: A Changing International Monetary System? International Monetary Fund. Retrieved September 8, 2020, from https://www.imf.org/en/Publications/WP/Issues/2018/01/25/Reserve-Currency-Blocs-A-Changing-International-Monetary-System-45586
- Gourinchas, P. (2019, May 16). The Dollar Hegemon? Evidence and Implications for Policy Makers. Paris School of Economics. Retrieved September 7, 2020, from https://www.parisschoolofeconomics.eu/IMG/pdf/chaire-bdf-sept-2019-speaker-gourinchas.pdf
- Carney, M. (2019, August 23). The Growing Challenges for Monetary Policy in the Current International Monetary and Financial System. Bank of England. Retrieved September 7, 2020, from https://www.bankofengland.co.uk/-/media/boe/files/speech/2019/the-growing-challenges-for-monetary-policy-speech-by-mark-carney.pdf
- SWIFT. (2020). RMB Tracker. Retrieved September 12, 2020, from https://www.swift.com/our-solutions/compliance-and-shared-services/business-intelligence /renminbi/rmb-tracker/rmb-tracker-document-centre

PEAK GLOBALIZATION

ORIGIN STORY
- UNCTAD. (January 2020a). Global Investment Trends Monitor No. 33. United Nations. Retrieved September 11, 2020, from https://unctad.org/en/PublicationsLibrary /diaeiainf2020d1_en.pdf

- UNCTAD. (2020b). World Investment Report 2020: International Production beyond the Pandemic. United Nations. Retrieved September 11, 2020, from https://unctad.org/en/PublicationsLibrary/wir2020_en.pdf
- Lund, S. et al. via McKinsey Global Institute. (2019, January 16). Globalization in Transition: The Future of Trade and Value Chains. McKinsey & Company. Retrieved September 11, 2020, from https://www.mckinsey.com/featured-insights/innovation-and-growth/globalization-in-transition-the-future-of-trade-and-value-chains

SIGNAL

- Kuznetsov, A. (2019). Disintegration of the World Trade System: Reasons and Consequences. *Finance: Theory and Practice*, 23, 50-61. 10.26794/2587-5671-2019-23-5-50-61.
- Evenett, S. J. and Fritz, J. (2021, June 2). Advancing Sustainable Development with FDI: Why Policy Must Be Reset. Global Trade Alert. Retrieved August 10, 2021, from https://www.globaltradealert.org/reports/75
- Credit Suisse. (2020). Untangling the Trade War. Credit Suisse. Retrieved September 12, 2020, from https://www.credit-suisse.com/microsites/private-banking/investment-outlook/en/global-economy/trade-war.html
- Evenett, S. J. and Fritz, J.. (2020, January 23). How Has Global Trade Policy Shifted Over the Past 3 years? Brookings Institute. Retrieved September 12, 2020, from https://www.brookings.edu/blog/future-development/2020/01/23/how-has-global-trade-policy-shifted-over-the-past-3-years/

DECODE

- Fitch Solutions. (2016, October 29). Three Scenarios for Globalisation: 2017-2030. Fitch Solutions. Retrieved September 12, 2020, from https://www.fitchsolutions.com/country-risk-sovereigns/economics/three-scenarios-globalisation-2017-2030-29-10-2016
- Altman, S. A. (2020, May 20). Will Covid-19 Have a Lasting Impact on Globalization? *Harvard Business Review*. Retrieved September 12, 2020, from https://hbr.org/2020/05/will-covid-19-have-a-lasting-impact-on-globalization
- World Trade Organization. (2019, October 1). WTO Lowers Trade Forecast as Tensions Unsettle Global Economy. World Trade Organization. Retrieved September 11, 2020, from https://www.wto.org/english/news_e/pres19_e/pr840_e.htm
- Baldwin, R. E. and Evenett, S. J. (2020, April 29). COVID-19 and Trade Policy: Why Turning Inward Won't Work. VoxEU.org. Retrieved September 12, 2020, from https://voxeu.org/content/covid-19-and-trade-policy-why-turning-inward-won-t-work
- Lund, S. et al. (2019, January 16). Globalization in Transition: The Future of Trade and Value Chains. McKinsey & Company. Retrieved September 12, 2020, from https://www.mckinsey.com/featured-insights/innovation-and-growth/globalization-in-transition-the-future-of-trade-and-value-chains

IMPACT

- Altman, S. A. and Bastian, P. (2020). DHL Global Connectedness Index. DHL. Retrieved June 1, 2021, from https://www.dhl.com/content/dam/dhl/global/dhl-spotlight/documents/pdf/spotlight-g04-global-connectedness-index-2020.pdf
- Lund, S. et al. (2019, January 16). Globalization in Transition: The Future of Trade and Value Chains. McKinsey & Company.

SPLINTERNET

ORIGIN STORY

- Cornell Law School. (2020). U.S. Constitution Communications Decency Act, 47 U.S.C. §230. Cornell Law School: Legal Information Institute. Retrieved September 11, 2020, from https://www.law.cornell.edu/uscode/text/47/230
- Schultz, C. (2013, August 28). See How Fast ARPANET Spread in Just Eight Years. *Smithsonian Magazine*. Retrieved September 9, 2020, from https://www.smithsonianmag.com/smart-news/see-how-fast-arpanet-spread-in-just-eight-years-2341268/
- Reuters, via *LA Times*. (1988, December 13). IN BRIEF: New Transatlantic Cable Ready. *LA Times*. Retrieved September 9, 2020, from https://www.latimes.com/archives/la-xpm-1988-12-13-mn-382-story.html

SIGNAL

- Freedom House. (2019, November). Freedom on the Internet: The Crisis of Social Media. Freedom House. Retrieved September 9, 2020, from https://freedomhouse.org/sites/default/files/2019-11/11042019_Report_FH_FOTN_2019_final_Public_Download.pdf
- Taye, B. (2020, February). Targeted, Cut Off, and Left in the Dark. Access Now. Retrieved September 9, 2020, from https://www.accessnow.org/cms/assets/uploads/2020/02/KeepItOn-2019-report-1.pdf
- Haynes, S. (2019, March 28). This African Country Has Had a Yearlong Ban on Social Media. Here's What's behind the Blackout. *Time*. Retrieved September 9, 2020, from https://time.com/5559491/chad-social-media-internet-ban-censorship/

DECODE

- Taye, B. (2020, February). Targeted, Cut Off, and Left in the Dark. Access Now.
- Tidy, J. and Dale, B. (2020, February 25). What Happens When the Internet Vanishes? BBC. Retrieved September 9, 2020, from https://www.bbc.com/news/technology-51620158
- Volodzko, D. (2019, February 25). Is South Korea Sliding toward Digital Dictatorship? *Forbes*. Retrieved September 9, 2020, from https://www.bbc.com/news/technology-51620158
- AfricaNews. (2019, August 1). Ethiopia Will Cut Internet as and When, 'It's Neither Water Nor Air' - PM Abiy. *AfricaNews*. Retrieved September 9, 2020, from https://www.africanews.com/2019/08/02/ethiopia-will-cut-internet-asand-when-it-s-neither-water-nor-air-pm-abiy/

- Huang, Z. (2019, April 18). 8 Ways China Controls the Internet. Inkstone News. Retrieved September 9, 2020, from https://www.inkstonenews.com/tech/what-china-can-teach-world-about-controlling-internet/article/3006687
- Freedom House. (2020). Freedom on the Internet: The Pandemic's Digital Shadow. Freedom House. Retrieved June 11, 2021, from https://freedomhouse.org/sites/default/files/2020-10/10122020_FOTN2020_Complete_Report_FINAL.pdf

IMPACT

- Tech Native. (2019, May 29). Winners and Losers in the Age of the 'Splinternet'. Tech Native. Retrieved September 9, 2020, from https://www.technative.io/winners-and-losers-in-the-age-of-the-splinternet/
- OECD. (2020). Digital Services Trade Restrictiveness Index [online dataset]. OECD. Retrieved September 9, 2020, from https://stats.oecd.org/Index.aspx?DataSetCode=STRI_DIGITAL